EAST EUROPEAN DISSENT

Volume 2
1965-70

EAST
EUROPEAN
DISSENT

Volume 2
1965-70

Edited by Vojtech Mastny

Assitant Professor of History
Columbia University (New York)

FACTS ON FILE, INC.   NEW YORK

EAST
EUROPEAN
DISSENT
Volume 2
1965-70

Library of Congress Catalog Card Number: 72-148185

ISBN 0-87196-197-0

9 8 7 6 5 4 3 2 1

PRINTED IN THE UNITED STATES OF AMERICA

CONTENTS

FOREWORD

THIS IS THE 2D VOLUME IN THE INTERIM HISTORY record of east European dissent. The first covered the years 1953-64—from Stalin's death to Khrushchev's overthrow. This volume resumes with 1965 and carries the record forward through 1970.

An analysis of the function and meaning of dissent in the Communist countries of eastern Europe has been presented in the introduction to the first volume. The material in this book is based almost completely on data published by FACTS ON FILE publications covering the period.

1965

The new Soviet leadership of Leonid I. Brezhnev and Aleksei N. Kosygin faced an upsurge of nationalism and internal dissent throughout eastern Europe in 1965. The Bucharest regime, at the behest of Nicolae Ceausescu, inaugurated as party leader in March, changed the country's constitution to emphasize Rumanian national individuality. It took the initiative to increase commercial and diplomatic links with the West. At the same time, Rumania advocated the loosening of the supranational organizations of the Soviet bloc, particularly the Warsaw military alliance and Comecon.

In June, a group of Bulgarian military officers, apparently intent on following the Rumanian example and asserting greater independence for their own country, attempted an abortive coup d'etat. Poland responded cautiously to the new "opening to the East" by France and Great Britain. The renewed anti-Soviet attacks by the pro-Chinese Albanians indicated that the Brezhnev-Kosygin leadership had failed to soothe the Moscow-Peking conflict. The unsuccessful Russian attempts to restore the solidarity of the Soviet bloc by means of multilateral talks with foreign Communist leaders only accentuated the extent of their discord.

Controversies about the lack of artistic freedom increased. In the Soviet Union, the official intimidation of dissenters culminated in the arrest of the writers Andrei D. Sinyavsky and Yuli M. Daniel, who were accused of publishing anti-Socialist slander abroad. The publicity of their case, however, enhanced rather than discouraged unrest. Polish intellectuals assailed their government, criticizing restrictions of freedom of expression. Uneasiness about the extent of permissible dissent was evident both in relatively liberal Yugoslavia—where the writer Mihajlo Mihajlov was tried for his anti-Soviet writings—and in regimented East Germany. The Ulbricht

*regime expelled high party officials who favored greater
independence from the Soviet model in economic policies.*

NATIONALIST TRENDS

Ceausescu's Program

Nicolae Ceausescu became first secretary of the Rumanian
Workers' (Communist) Party after the death of his predecessor,
Gheorghe Gheorghiu-Dej, in March. Rumania's increasingly
independent position within the Communist bloc was
highlighted by developments at the Rumanian Communist
Party Congress, held in Bucharest July 19-24.

During the Congress, attended by Soviet Communist Party
First Secy. Leonid I. Brezhnev and by General Secy. Teng
Hsiao-ping of the Central Committee of the Chinese party, the
Rumanian party Central Committee members adopted a new
party statute and approved a new state constitution; both
documents stressed Rumanian autonomy. Party members at the
Congress also approved a new 5-year plan emphasizing
industrial development; the purpose of the plan, said Ceausescu
in his opening address July 19, was to insure "national
independence and sovereignty in actual fact."

Ceausescu stressed Rumania's strict neutrality in the Sino-
Soviet dispute. He said that the "fundamental differences"
within the Communist world should be "discussed directly from
party to party, from leadership to leadership" in a "sincere and
comradely way." Rumanian neutrality was emphasized
throughout the week by the scrupulously equal treatment
accorded to the Soviet and Chinese delegations in matters of
protocol and press coverage. Brezhnev and Teng were greeted
at the airport July 17 by Ceausescu, Chief of State Chivu Stoica
and Premier Ion Gheorghe Maurer. In their July 20 addresses,
both Brezhnev and Teng praised the work of the Congress but
differed on the Vietnam issue. Brezhnev urged "unity and
solidarity of all revolutionary forces in the world" as the best
way to cope with the "imperialists." Teng proposed a
"revolutionary fight" and a "patriotic anti-imperialist struggle
of all countries and peoples." The "main danger in the

international Communist movement," he declared, was "modern revisionism."

Ceausescu, in his July 19 address, confirmed that under the new party statute, the name of the Rumanian Workers' Party would be changed to the Rumanian Communist Party. (The plan to change the party's name had been disclosed June 3.) Ceausescu said that since there had been 5 congresses held by the Rumanian Communist Party before World War II, the current congress would be renamed the 9th Congress of the Rumanian Communist Party, not the 4th Congress of the Rumanian Workers' Party. The purpose of the change, he said, was to establish a continuity with Rumania's Socialist movement and the long history and traditions of the Rumanian Communist Party. (The Rumanian Workers' Party had been established in May 1948 under Soviet occupation.)

Ceausescu, who had been named June 18 as chairman of a commission to draw up the new state constitution, declared July 19 that the new constitution would insure the "enhancement of the role of the Socialist state as the organizer of the whole activity of the Socialist system." (The Central Committee of the Rumanian Workers' Party had announced June 2 that Rumania was "completing Socialist construction" and was getting closer to the goal of "constructing communism.") The draft constitution, approved by the Congress July 24 for submission to Rumania's National Assembly, omitted all the 1952 Constitution's acknowledgement of the role of the USSR as Rumania's World War II "liberator." It also omitted the previous charter's declaration that Rumania's foreign policy was based on "friendship" with the USSR. Instead, "fraternal collaboration" with Communist states and "collaboration" with "other sociopolitical systems" were called the basis of foreign policy. He asserted that Rumania "takes a resolute stand for the abolition of all military blocs." (Ceausescu announced in his July 19 speech that Rumania would form economic ties "with all states irrespective of their social systems on the basis of mutual advantage." He praised Rumania's improved relations with Western Europe, which had "restored the old traditional ties.")* The new party statute omitted the previous one's praise

---

* The Congress was covered by Western journalists, who were admitted for the first time since the war. Leading Western newspapers went on sale in Bucharest July 17, also for the first time since the war; among them were the *N.Y. Times,* the *N.Y. Herald Tribune,* 2 French papers—*Le Monde* and *Le Figaro*—and the Swiss *Neue Zuercher Zeitung.*

of the Soviet Communist Party for its "experience" as the founder of the Soviet state. Removed also was a reference to Russia's "great Socialist October Revolution." (Polish, Czechoslovak, Hungarian and Bulgarian parties' statutes still paid respect to the Soviet CP's "experience.")

The 5-year plan for industrial expansion, approved July 24 by the Congress for submission to the National Assembly, called for an increase in gross national product (GNP) of 40% by 1970. Industrial growth was scheduled at 10.5% a year and agricultural growth at 3.5%. The Rumanian GNP was currently estimated at $9 billion and growing at a 6%-7% rate. Rumania's industrial growth rate, 14.4%, was the highest in Europe.

The Grand National Assembly (parliament) Aug. 21 unanimously adopted a new constitution, which contained the explicit statement that Rumanian foreign policy was to be based on the principles of national independence, equal rights of nations and nonintervention in other states' internal affairs.

(Hsinhua, the Communist Chinese news agency, reported Aug. 22 in Peking that Mao Tse-tung and other Chinese Communist Party leaders had sent a message to the Rumanian party praising Rumania's "new and magnificent program for Socialist construction." From Moscow, Brezhnev, Pres. Anastas Mikoyan and Premier Aleksei N. Kosygin sent a telegram hailing the constitution as an "important stage in the successful building of socialism.")

Abortive Coup in Bulgaria

In a communique published by the Bulgarian Telegraph Agency (BTA), it was disclosed June 19 that 5 senior army officers and 4 civilians had been convicted and sentenced to prison terms ranging from 3 to 15 years by a military court for conspiracy. (An abortive coup d'etat against the government of Premier Todor Zhivkov had been reported Apr. 15.)

The BTA announcement described the conspirators as "despicable power-seekers who, isolated from the people and spurred on by adventurist and careerist motives, committed offenses against the law." All 9 had "pleaded guilty to all charges brought against them and condemned their own criminal activities."

The 2 most prominent accused conspirators were Maj. Gen. Svetko Anev (also spelled Tsvetko Yanev), 50, commandant of the Sofia Military District, who received a 12-year sentence, and Tsolo Krustev, ex-ambassador to North Korea and a specialist on African-Asian affairs in the Foreign Ministry, who was sentenced to 15 years. Other army officers (no ranks given) sentenced included: Ivan Dimitrov Velchev, 15 years; Micho Ermenov Michev, 10 years; Lyuben Georgiev Dinov, 8 years; Blagoe Georgiev Mavrodimov, 5 years. The civilians sentenced included Boris Mihailov Temkov, journalist, 10 years; Avram Maginov Chernev, teacher, 3 years; Radojko Milanovic, cooperative employe, 3 years.

(Mikhail A. Suslov, member of the USSR Presidium, arrived in Sofia May 26 for a 10-day visit. During his stay, he made repeated declarations of Soviet support for the Zhivkov government. It had been reported Apr. 20 that the plot had been led by "liberals" seeking to increase Bulgaria's independence from the USSR.)

Zhikov, first secretary of the Bulgarian Communist Party, asserted in a July 16 interview in Vienna that the 9 convicted plotters were "pro-Chinese elements."

Albania Continues Denunciations

The Albanian Labor (Communist) Party newspaper *Zeri i Popullit* charged in an editorial Jan. 6 that the new Soviet leaders were attempting to give a public image of being more moderate than ex-Premier Nikita Khrushchev but actually were "following with tenacity the old Khrushchev line." The editorial asserted that a struggle already had begun in the USSR for the overthrow of the new leaders, whom it labelled "Khrushchevian revisionists."

The Albanian press agency (ATA) Feb. 3 broadcast the texts of (a) a Polish invitation to attend the January meeting of the Warsaw Pact nations, (b) Albania's letter rejecting the invitation and (c) a lengthy Albanian letter denouncing the USSR.

The 3d letter accused the Soviet government of breaking relations with Albania of ignoring agreements for the USSR to equip the Albanian army, of canceling credits and of withdrawing specialists. The letter said Albania would agree to participate in the Warsaw Pact again only after: (a) Condemnation by the member nations of the USSR's "illegal and hostile" acts against Albania, (b) restoration of Albania's "legitimate rights" in the organization, (c) Soviet return of Albanian military equipment, (d) Soviet compensation to Albania to cover defense costs and damage to the Albanian economy caused by the halting of Soviet aid, (e) Soviet admission of its "errors," (f) an end to Soviet arms shipments to Yugoslavia and India, (g) the prompt signing of a peace treaty with East Germany, (h) renunciation of the partial nuclear test ban treaty, (i) a Warsaw Pact warning that U.S. provision of nuclear weapons to West Germany would mean Soviet provision of such arms to the other Communist states.

In *Zeri i Popullit* Feb. 19 appeared a full-page condemnation of the "Khrushchevist troika" (Soviet Premier Aleksei N. Kosygin, Communist Party First Secy. Leonid I. Brezhnev and Pres. Anastas J. Mikoyan). It charged them with trying to reassert Soviet "hegemony" over all Communist states, of seeking leadership of all "revisionists" and of trying to create regional groups of Communist parties.

Estonia Bars Russian Immigrants

The *N.Y. Times* reported July 20 that the Estonian regime was attempting to curb a continuing flow of Russian immigrants into Estonia. According to the *Times,* the Estonian Communist Party had established new residence rules that forbade Russians to settle in Estonia's 3 principle cities (Tallinn, Narva and Kohtla-Jaerve) unless they had jobs officially assigned to them. Russians reportedly comprised about 40% of Tallinn's more than 300,000 residents, and Narva had been largely resettled by Russians after its World War II destruction.

Expansion of Western Ties

Polish Premier Jozef Cyrankiewicz conferred with French Pres. Charles de Gaulle in Paris Sept. 10, 11 and 15. The talks took place during an official visit to France made Sept. 10-16 by Cyrankiewicz and 2 Polish deputy ministers—Marian Naszkowski (foreign affairs) and Franciszek Modrzewski (foreign trade). In a communique of the Cyrankiewicz-de Gaulle meetings, released Sept. 15, the 2 leaders called for a "normalization of East-West relations ... with a view to progressively create an atmosphere of detente." A 5-year commercial agreement between Poland and France, drafted in June, would be signed in Warsaw, it was reported in the communique.

The 2 sides made no mention of the Oder-Neisse frontier of Germany and Poland. But Cyrankiewicz was reported to have said after his Sept. 10 meeting with de Gaulle that Poland was grateful for France's position on the Oder-Neisse frontier issue. He told reporters Sept. 15: "The people and government of Poland strongly appreciate the attitude of Gen. de Gaulle and the French government, which considers the postwar frontiers of Germany as definitive and impossible to modify...."

British Foreign Secy. Michael Stewart visited Poland Sept. 17-21. He conferred Sept. 18 with Premier Cyrankiewicz and met Foreign Min. Adam Rapacki Sept. 17 and 21. The visit was the first of a British foreign secretary to Poland since Ernest Bevin's in 1947. A communique on the Stewart-Rapacki talks, issued Sept. 21 in Warsaw, contained no mention of the problem of Germany but said both sides "had presented their positions on the way to guarantee the security of Europe." They agreed that "a European conference on the question of European security would be profitable."

The White House announced Sept. 13 that U.S. Pres. Lyndon B. Johnson had assigned to a newly appointed 7-man trade mission the task of visiting Poland and Rumania and seeking ways to increase U.S. sales to civilian industries in the 2 countries.

West German Foreign Min. Gerhard Schroeder, in an article published Sept. 16 in the U.S. quarterly *Foreign Affairs,* said that objections to establishing diplomatic relations with east European countries were no longer valid because these nations followed policies of national independence despite Soviet opposition. Schroeder said on West German TV Sept. 26 that diplomatic relations with eastern Europe were desirable as long as West Germany's "right to represent Germany as a whole is not undermined."

French Finance Min. Valery Giscard d'Estaing in Warsaw Oct. 25 signed a 5-year Franco-Polish agreement under which trade between the 2 nations was to be increased 50% by 1969. Poland would primarily buy machinery, and France would increase its purchases of Polish coal and finished industrial products. Giscard d'Estaing said Poland currently provided only .4% of France's imports.

Failure of Attempts to Restore Bloc Unity

19 pro-USSR Communist parties held a consultative conference in deep secrecy at a suburban villa near Moscow Mar. 1-5. Originally, the Soviet Union had billed the conference as a meeting of 26 Communist parties to draft preparations for a major unity conference of the world's 81 Communist parties. This idea apparently had to be abandoned when Communist China, pro-Peking Communist parties from Albania, North Vietnam, North Korea, Indonesia and Japan, and nonaligned Rumania refused to attend.

Those attending were delegates of the Soviet Communist Party and 17 pro-Soviet Communist parties—from Australia, Argentina, Bulgaria, Brazil, Britain, Czechoslovakia, Cuba, Hungary, Finland, France, East Germany, West Germany, India, Italy, Mongolia, Poland and Syria. A 19th delegation— from the U.S. Communist party—also attended but only in an observer's capacity.

A 5-page communique, signed by delegates of all 19 parties, was issued in Moscow Mar. 10. In it the signatories called for Communist unity against "colonialism" and "imperialism." They warned that internal divisions were weakening the international Communist movement in its support of "national liberation movements." They said that the delegates had agreed on a plan to hold a world Communist conference only after (a) a lengthy period of preparation, lasting perhaps several years and consisting of bilateral and multilateral talks between the main parties, then (b) a preliminary meeting of the world's 81 parties, including those of Peking and its allies. They failed to respond to the attacks of the Chinese Communists, who had denounced the USSR publicly throughout the conference and had charged the Soviet Union with ideological heresy, appeasement of the U.S. over Vietnam and police brutality against Asian students demonstrating in Moscow. The communique's subscribers appealed for an end to the bitterness between the USSR and Communist China.

The communique seemed to indicate that unity efforts had proved futile and that the Soviet Union had been unable to reassert its supremacy in the Communist world. Reliable Moscow sources reported that one group, led by the Indians and Australians, had insisted on a more militant attitude toward Peking, whereas another group, led by the Italians and British, had sought a more peaceful course.

The Soviet bloc's Council for Mutual Economic Assistance (Comecon) * was reported to be gradually pulling away from the influence of the Soviet Union. Polish Deputy Premier Piotr Jaroszewicz urged the Comecon Council (at a meeting in Prague) to speed its "inadequate" economic integration. In his speech, published in Warsaw Jan. 31, Jaroszewicz assailed Comecon's failure to coordinate national plans and industrial specialization.

INTELLECTUAL DISSENTERS

Soviet Writers

Leonid S. Sobolev, chairman of the Writers Union of the Russian Republic, told 400 members Mar. 3, at a conference of the Russian Republic's Writers Congress in Moscow, that "absolute freedom of speech" was a "false concept" that they should guard against. He said Soviet writers had to have a political viewpoint in whatever they wrote.

The Soviet Communist Party newspaper *Pravda* had indicated Jan. 14 that freer discussion of Communist Party matters might be permitted in the future by publishing an

---

* Comecon members: the USSR, Poland, Czechoslovakia, Hungary, Rumania, Bulgaria, East Germany, Albania and Mongolia.

anonymous letter from a party member charging unfair practices in party affairs and rigged discussions at party meetings. *Pravda* added in an editorial note that letters complaining about party "bossism" had increased sharply since Khrushchev was ousted.

Pravda in a 5,000-word article Sept. 9, accused *Izvestia,* the government paper, of attempting to restrict literary expression. The article, read in full over Radio Moscow the same day, was signed by chief *Pravda* editor Aleksei M. Rumyantsev.

Rumyantsev, 60, charged *Izvestia* and *Selskaya Zhizn (Rural Life*—the Communist Party's farm newspaper) with a "preconceived one-sided attitude" in denouncing authors who revealed the negative aspects of Soviet life. He said that Soviet conditions could be improved if authors exposed shortcomings; that "it is the hushing up or tendentious inflating of shortcomings, not exposure aimed at eliminating them, that breeds nihilism especially among the young people"; that *Izvestia's* attitude "would make it impossible for a literary medium such as satire to exist"; that the party's policy was to "defend the artists' freedom to choose theme and subject, style and manner of execution."

Izvestia, Selskaya Zhizn and *Pravda,* too, had been attacking 2 Soviet literary journals, *Novy Mir* and *Yunost (Youth),* and a number of authors, including Alexander Solzhenitsyn, Andrei Voznesensky, Vladimir F. Tendryakov, 42, Vasily Aksyonov, 33, and Alexei N. Arbuzov. In an Aug. 29 *Pravda* article, First Secy. Sergei P. Pavlov of Komsomol (Young Communist League) had criticized Soviet authors for "petty faultfinding" and for scepticism of "all that is fine and progressive." He said that the party must "tactfully correct those who deviate from the correct path and, flushed by success, begin to produce petty, false works."

Deputy Foreign Min. Mikhail V. Zimyanin replaced Rumyantsev Sept. 21 as chief editor of *Pravda.* Rumyantsev was reported to have suffered a heart attack and had resigned 2 weeks earlier to take a position in the Academy of Sciences.

Izvestia reported Oct. 10 that Lev N. Tolkunov, a deputy chief of the east European relations section of the Communist Party Central Committee, had been appointed editor-in-chief of *Izvestia.*

It was reported Oct. 21 from Moscow that 2 Soviet writers had confessed to charges of smuggling anti-Soviet literature out of the USSR for publication in the West. The 2 authors, Andrei D. Sinyavsky and Yuli M. Daniel (Daniello), had been arrested several weeks earlier and were reportedly in Lubyanka Prison in Moscow. Sinyavsky was reportedly the author of 5 anti-Soviet books published in Western Europe and the U.S. under the pseudonym Abram Tertz; Daniel allegedly had used the name Nikolai Arzhak for the one book he had published in the West.

The connection between Sinyavsky and Daniel and the publications issued in the West under the names Tertz and Arzhak was confirmed Nov. 10 in Paris by Jerzy Giedroyc, editor of the Polish language literary magazine *Kultura* and owner of a publishing house with worldwide rights to the works of Tertz and Arzhak. (Giedroyc Oct. 22 had denied any connection between Sinyavsky and Daniel and Tertz and Arzhak.)

The *N.Y. Times* reported Oct. 23 that Sinyavsky's arrest had been disclosed Oct. 9 in Rome at a conference of the European Community of Writers, an organization that included west and east European members. The announcement of the arrest was reportedly made by the Italian secretary general of the association, Giancarlo Vigorelli. Present at the meeting were Aleksandr Tvardovsky, editor of *Novy Mir,* which had published many articles by Sinyavsky, and Vasily Aksyonov, a short-story writer who had been criticized by *Izvestia* Aug. 13 for an allegedly unfavorable portrayal of Soviet taxicab drivers.

Izvestia's criticism of Aksyonov was ridiculed by *Yunost* in its September issue (published Sept. 25). *Novy Mir* Oct. 21 (in its September issue, which was sent to subscribers 3 weeks late) rebuffed the charges that Aksyonov's work had not portrayed a sufficiently attractive picture of Soviet life. It said: "The optimism and confidence ... of our life ... find support not in a picture of an illusory ... reality ... but in a sober understanding of life as it is."

Yevgeny Yevtushenko Oct. 3 read a new poem criticizing Soviet youth leaders for "try[ing] to knead our souls" in their "own image." In his poem, entitled *Letter to Yesenin* (in honor of poet Sergei Yesenin, who had committed suicide in 1925 at the age of 30), Yevtushenko said:

"... When a rosy-cheeked Komsomol chief

"Bangs his fist at us, poets,

"And wants to knead our souls like wax

"And wants to fashion them in his own image,

"His words, Yesenin, do not terrify us,

"Although it is also hard to be happy...."

The *N.Y. Times* reported Oct. 20 that the Soviet author Valery Tarsis "was seen at liberty and in apparent good health in Moscow last weekend after reports abroad that he had been arrested." It had been reported that Tarsis and Aleksandr Yesenin-Volpin, both of whom had published works abroad under their own names, had been locked up in mental wards.

The British Reuters news agency reported Dec. 11 that 200 students from the Gorky Institute of World Literature in Moscow had gathered Dec. 5 in Pushkin Square to demonstrate against the arrest of Sinyavsky, a former lecturer at the institute, and Daniel. The demonstrating students were reported to have demanded that a public trial for Sinyavsky and Daniel be held at the Gorky Institute. Several student leaders were detained by Soviet security agents but were later released.

Soviet writer Mikhail Sholokhov, the 1965 Nobel laureate for literature, was in Stockholm to receive his award and was reported Dec. 9 to have rebuffed attempts by British publisher Mark Bonham Carter to speak to him on behalf of Sinyavsky and Daniel. Carter, of the Collins publishing house, which published works by Abram Tertz (the pseudonym that Sinyavsky was said to have used), told newsmen that he had telephoned Sholokov 4 times and had gone to his room but had failed to contact Sholokov.

Mihajlov Case

A 3-judge court in Zadar, Croatia Apr. 30 convicted Mihajlo Mihajlov, 30, and sentenced him to 9 months in prison for writing articles ("Moscow Summer, 1964") containing alleged insulting references to the USSR and for mailing the articles to a foreign country (to an Italian publisher). The court initially sentenced him to 5 months in jail for each charge but later reduced the term to 9 months because Yugoslav law required one sentence for 2 criminal offenses. Mihajlov had been dismissed Apr. 28, the day his trial started, as a lecturing assistant at the Zadar branch of Zagreb University.

The Supreme Court of Croatia June 23 reversed the 9-month prison sentence given to Mihajlov by the Zadar District Court and replaced it with a 5-month suspended sentence. The appeals court upheld the 2d charge (of sending an insulting article to a foreign country) but voided the first one (of insulting the Soviet Union) because the article did not contain "elements of a criminal offense."

East German Critics of Government

Deputy Premier Erich Apel, 48, committed suicide in his East Berlin office Dec. 3 by shooting himself. The East German news agency ADN said Apel had taken his life "following a nervous breakdown." Apel, who was chief of East Germany's Planning Commission, had lived in the USSR during World War II as an emigrant from Nazi Germany. He had been responsible for introducing profit-inducement reforms into the East German economy.

The West German government press office asserted Dec. 10 that Apel had killed himself in protest against a trade agreement signed by the USSR with East Germany Dec. 3. According to Bonn, Apel opposed the pact because it exploited the East German economy for the benefit of the USSR. Bonn said Apel had argued about the matter Dec. 3 with the chairman of East Germany's Economic Council, Alfred Neumann, who signed the trade agreement only hours after Apel's death. (West Berlin Mayor Willy Brandt said Dec. 7 that Apel had forewarned contacts in the West of his intended action.)

(The 1966-70 trade pact reportedly bound East Germany to sell $12-15 billion worth of industrial goods, including 300-350 merchant ships, at prices up to 30% below world market levels. In return, the USSR would sell East Germany oil and grain at prices about $1/3$ above world prices. The pact was to cover approximately half of East Germany's exports during the 5-year period.)

The dismissal of Robert Havemann, 55, a prominent chemist, from the East German Academy of Science was announced Dec. 24. Havemann had published an article in the West German news weekly *Der Spiegel* advocating the "establishment of opposition parties in East Germany" as well as legalization of the West German Communist Party.

Poland

The Polish Foreign Ministry Dec. 27 revoked the accreditation of David Halberstam, 31, Warsaw correspondent of the *N.Y. Times,* and ordered him to leave the country for writing "slanderous articles about Poland."

Halberstam had reported in the *Times* Dec. 25 on a book, highly critical of the Polish regime, by Adam Schaff, a Marxist philosopher and member of the Polish United Workers' (Communist) Party (PUWP) Central Committee. The book, *Marxism and the Individual,* which had sold 20,000 copies, said that anti-Semitism, a highly privileged government elite, nationalism and increasing alienation were all problems that Poland had not solved.

Schaff's book was reviewed in *Nowe drogi (New Roads,* the party's ideological organ) by 15 writers, some of them Central Committee members. Zenon Kliszko, a Central Committee member and ideological adviser to PUWP First Secy. Wladyslaw Gomulka, said Schaff had neglected the Polish party and "writes about the party only when he says it does not fight adequately against anti-Semitism, which does not exist in Poland." Schaff replied in the same issue of *Nowe drogi:* "Lenin always taught us that self-criticism is the greatest force in the Communist Party and we must not be afraid to recognize our faults."

DEFECTIONS

Escapes from East Germany

23,000 East Germans had escaped into West Germany and West Berlin in the 4-year period since the Berlin Wall was built

Aug. 13, 1961, according to figures released in West Berlin Aug. 12. (About 3,500 of the escapes were to West Berlin.) The report listed 127 known deaths of East Germans attempting to flee to the West during the period—61 at the wall, 4 on the West Berlin-East German border and 62 along the frontier between East and West Germany. The West German government reported that 2,844,430 persons (including 23,000 soldiers or policemen) had fled from East Germany or East Berlin to West Germany between 1949 and the end of 1964.

During a 3-week engagement of East Berlin's Berliner Ensemble theater troupe in London, wardrobe assistant Rolf Prieser, 30, defected Aug. 26 and actor Christian Weisbrodd defected Aug. 29. Both went to West Germany. The troupe flew back to East Berlin Aug. 29.

Among escapes to the West reported in 1965:

May 7—2 East Germans seized a border guard's gun and fled to the U.S. sector of Berlin.

May 18—2 East German border guards fled to the U.S. sector of Berlin.

June 9—Gregor Neumann, 22, was seriously wounded by gunfire East German guards but escaped to West Berlin by swimming across the Spree River.

June 21—6 East Germans on the East German cruise ship *Fritz Heckert,* sailing 15 miles off the West German island of Fehmarn in the Baltic Sea, dove overboard and swam to nearby West German patrol boats.

July 5—Jochen Langmann, 24, was reported to have escaped to West Germany in June by crossing Bavarian-East German border at a point about 30 miles from Bayreuth. He was one of 30 East Germans reported to have escaped in 1965 at this 45-mile section of heavily forested border.

Aug. 29—2 East German women with a 4-month-old baby and 4 other children under 14 were reported to have crossed unnoticed into West Germany at Brunswick to join their husbands, who had escaped earlier.

Sept. 4—The Bavarian Interior Ministry reported that 5 East Germans had crossed a mine field Sept. 2-3 and had escaped into Bavaria.

Sept. 6—A 20-year-old East German drafted as a border guard fled to West Berlin.

Dec. 23—A 19-year-old East German escaped to the West by slipping past border guards, crossing a cleared and illuminated 300-yard "death strip" and swimming across a stream.

Dec. 28—U.S. officials in Berlin confirmed that an East German couple had successfully escaped to the West Dec. 19 by stealing U.S. Army uniforms and driving in an auto bearing U.S. Army license plates. The officials criticized the theft and condemned the West Berlin newspaper, *B. Z.*, which had reported the incident.

Horst Streit, 36, who had escaped Apr. 16 into West Berlin, was sentenced to 3 years in prison by a West Berlin court June 1 for fraudulently taking a wall-crossing pass from Dieter Mahrhold, a West Berlin business man, during the latter's Easter visit to East Berlin. Streit confessed to having posed as an East German secret police agent Apr. 16 in order to obtain Mahrhold's pass and identity papers. Mahrhold was arrested by the East German police when he reported that his papers had been taken. He and a friend, Juergen Rehbein, were held by the East Germans on charges of aiding Streit's escape. Judge Wilhelm Weinecke of the West Berlin court appealed June 1 to the East Germans to release Mahrhold and Rehbein. The East German authorities said Streit would have to be extradited before the 2 would be released.

Franz Lange, 23, a former East German border guard, was reported by the Lower Saxony (West German) Justice Ministry Aug. 29 to have fled back to East Germany to avoid prosecution by West German authorities for having forced 2 East Germans attempting to escape to the West to return at gunpoint when he was an East Berlin border guard. Lange had defected to the West in June 1964.

Heinz Schoeneberger, 27, was killed at about 1 a.m. Dec. 26 when he pulled his car out of a line of cars returning to West Berlin and attempted to crash through a barricade in an unsuccessful attempt to help 2 East Germans escape to the West. Schoeneberger, fatally wounded by East German border guards, managed to get out of his car and stagger across the border, but he died a few minutes later. An East Berlin court in Potsdam Dec. 30 sentenced Horst Schoeneberger, brother of the dead Heinz, to 12 years imprisonment for attempting to aid the escape of 2 East German girls.

Hungarian Economist Defects

The U.S. State Department disclosed Oct. 19 that Laszlo Szabo, 42, a Hungarian economist who had been working with the Hungarian embassy in London, had requested U.S. asylum. The Hungarian Foreign Ministry said Oct. 20 that it had protested to the U.S. and Great Britain over Szabo's defection. It said that Szabo's wife and daughter had returned to Budapest Oct. 20.

1966

Nicolae Ceausescu's speech of May 7 reiterated in strong terms Rumania's determination to assert national independence. After Brezhnev's unsuccessful intervention during a visit to Bucharest May 10-13, the Soviet Union tried to elicit joint criticism of Rumania from other east European countries. The Rumanians resisted by seeking diplomatic support from both the West and China. Later in May Rumania expressed the desire to establish diplomatic relations with West Germany. In mid-June, Chinese Premier Chou En-lai visited Rumania for a week before continuing to Albania.

The Moscow trial of the writers Sinyavsky and Daniel received great publicity, and their sentencing in February to long prison terms aroused international indignation. Yet the formal court procedures used against the defendants suggested that the Brezhnev-Kosygin regime hesitated to revert to the Stalinist methods of repression. Incidents of dissent among Soviet intellectuals proliferated.

In the 2 predominantly Catholic nations of eastern Europe, Hungary and Poland, religious opposition increased. In Hungary, alleged conspirators linked to the Catholic Church were tried and sentenced. In Poland, the celebrations of the 1,000th anniversary of statehood and Christianity were the focus for an ecclesiastical gesture of reconciliation with Germany that exacerbated the persistent conflict between the state and the church. Stefan Cardinal Wyszynski and other church officials invoked the right to religious freedom and resisted harassment of Catholic institutions and verbal attacks by Communist Party First Secy. Wladyslav Gomulka. The repressive policies of the government against dissent were criticized by the Marxist philosopher Leszek Kolakowski, and this act of temerity led to his expulsion from the Communist Party.

Incidents of dissent in Yugoslavia were illustrative more of the amount of freedom enjoyed than of the extent of its denial. On the one hand, the Yugoslav government tried and imprisoned the writer Mihajlo Mihajlov because he had attempted to test the constitutional liberties by publishing an opposition journal. On the other hand, if released from prison the prominent critic of the regime Milovan Djilas. Furthermore, the provincial cabinet in Slovenia demonstrated a degree of ministerial responsibility unprecedented in a Communist country when it resigned after a government-sponsored bill had been defeated in the Legislature.

CATHOLIC OPPOSITION

Church-State Conflict in Poland

The Polish government Jan. 8 withdrew the passport of Stefan Cardinal Wyszynski just before his scheduled departure Jan. 9 for Rome to attend the celebration of the 1,000th anniversary of Christianity in Poland.

A government communique published in Warsaw papers Jan. 9 charged that Wyszynski had "used his last trip to Rome [during the Ecumenical Council in Dec. 1965] ... for political activities damaging from the point of view of the interests of the Polish People's Republic." Wyszynski was specifically charged with allowing Polish bishops, during the Ecumenical Council meeting, to write a letter inviting West German bishops to Poland in May to attend a celebration of Christianity's 1,000 years in Poland. This invitation was intended as an initial step toward German-Polish reconciliation. Wyszynski was also accused of planning to share a platform in Rome with Prof. Oscar Halecki. Halecki, a former history teacher at Fordham University in New York, was described by the Polish government communique as an "anti-Communist refugee."

Wyszynski said Jan. 9 in a sermon to 2,000 persons at Warsaw's Church of St. Carlo Boromeus: "They charge me with the gravest, most harmful wrong." "They charge me, who have served the people for 20 years. I need not and shall not answer them." "You have known me well.... If you can bring yourself to, have confidence that I did not do the slightest harm to my fatherland." (U.S. Amb. John A. Gronouski, his wife and 2 daughters attended the service and heard the sermon.)

The Associated Press reported from Rome Jan. 8 that a Vatican spokesman had said: The Polish government action was "the 2d half of something that started when the Polish and West German bishops exchanged messages on questions regarding territorial claims by the Germans on Polish soil. Polish government officials had hinted that someone must pay for this error. We can see now who is paying for it." (The *N.Y. Times* reported Jan. 9 that in Dec. 1965 the German bishops had written to the Polish bishops a letter expressing regret for World War II Nazi war crimes.)

Halecki said in White Plains, N.Y. Jan. 10 that "my main reason for accepting [the invitation to Rome] was that the cardinal was going to be there; he wrote me twice last fall asking me to go."

Cardinal Wyszynski was cheered by 40,000-50,000 persons Apr. 17 as he arrived in front of the cathedral of Poznan for an outdoor mass concluding the first week of ceremonies marking the millennium of Christianity in Poland. In a competing ceremony, held at Poznan's main square at approximately the same time, First Secy. Wladyslaw Gomulka of the United Workers (Communist) Party, addressed a crowd of 200,000 and severely criticized Wyszynski. Gomulka's speech was part of the government's commemoration of the 1,000th anniversary of Poland's emergence as a nation. Gomulka charged that Wyszynski "fights against People's Poland [and] dares to say that he would not bow to the vital interests of the state." The church, he declared, "intends to play a political role" and contains "the same persons who in 1939 sounded the victory bells over Poland."

About 300,000 Roman Catholics took part in Czestochowa May 3 in rites marking Christianity's millennium in Poland. Wyszynski celebrated mass on the ramparts of the 14th century Jasna Gora Monastery after leading a procession of 68 bishops carrying the portrait of the Black Madonna of Czestochowa.

Referring to the government's refusal to allow Pope Paul VI to come to Czestochowa (Katowice Province), Wyszynski told the crowd: "The Holy Father wanted to come here to take part in the celebrations of the Polish church. Unfortunately, it was not God's will." (The pope had appointed Wyszynski Apr. 30 to represent him as pontifical legate during the ceremonies.)

Gomulka acknowledged the church celebration in a May Day speech May 1 by saying that the 1,000th anniversary of the Polish state May 3 "is strongly linked with the introduction of Christianity into the country." (The Czestochowa rites coincided with a government celebration at Katowice, 50 miles away, of the 45th anniversary of the 3d Upper Silesia uprising against Germany. 700,000 persons reportedly attended the government rally.)

In another celebration of the Christian millennium, Wyszynski celebrated high mass in Cracow May 8 and led a procession carrying a copy of the Black Madonna through the city. About 100,000 persons attended the mass, and most of the city's 500,000 inhabitants watched or marched in the procession, despite a last-minute order by city officials altering its route. In a sermon delivered May 22 to at least 200,000 pilgrims at the Shrine of Our Lady of Piekary at Piekary Slaskie, Wyszynski pleaded for a mutual respecting of rights between the Polish government and the Catholic church. (The Black Madonna, which was touring the country, had been brought to Piekary after it had been refused entry into nearby Katowice May 18.) Wyszynski warned the government that "after 10 centuries of Catholicism, we have a right to be a Catholic nation, and we do not resign that right."

A 3,500-word article in the government newspaper *Zycie Warszawy (Warsaw Life)* June 8 included the assertion that Wyszynski was "hostile to socialism and to the people's state" and thus was "unable to bring about a normalization of relations between the church and state." The article called on the Catholic clergy to support churchmen who favored church-state coexistence. It made favorable mention of Archbishop Boleslaw Kominek of Wroclaw, regarded as 2d in the hierarchy of the Polish church. Wyszynski and the episcopate were charged with using the millennial celebrations to further "reactionary political ambitions." Kominek disclosed June 19 that he had written a reply to the June 8 article and had asked

Zycie Warszawy to publish it. His reply, sent June 13, was that the article was "contrary to reality, has harmed the primate of Poland [Wyszynski] and also myself and also the good of the country."

A clash between police and a crowd of about 2,000 persons took place in Brzeg, Opole Province May 26 as local authorities evicted 5 priests from a house that was to be made into a dispensary. An earlier attempt to carry out the eviction May 25 had ended after a brief melee. Police May 26 dispersed the protesting crowd with tear gas and night sticks and made several arrests. Another outbreak occurred in Gdansk May 29, after a sermon by Wyszynski, when several hundred persons tore down and burned a government anti-church poster. Riot police dispersed the crowd and arrested several persons.

A millennial celebration in Lublin in southeastern Poland June 5 included a sermon by Wyszynski to an estimated crowd of 100,000 and a procession through the center of the city accompanying the Black Madonna. It was reported by Reuters that a government letter delivered to the episcopate in Lublin June 4 had warned that it would be a violation of the law for large crowds to collect around the Madonna in public places and that there was risk of public disturbances resulting from Wyszynski's addresses. At a ceremony in Olsztyn in northeastern Poland June 18, Wyszynski disclosed that police had seized the touring portrait of the Black Madonna the previous week and diverted it to the Warsaw Cathedral. He told worshippers June 19 at Frombork, a fishing port on the Vistula Lagoon where he had driven from Olsztyn with 42 bishops, that in their seizure of the Madonna the Polish authorities were acting "like children playing."

In a message made public in Munich June 17, Wyszynski told Julius Cardinal Dopfner of Munich of his hope that a "gigantic bridge" would link Poland and Germany "over everything which separated us in the past." He noted "the Christian sympathy in our celebrations shown by the most venerable German episcopate and our German brethren in faith."

During millennial celebrations in Czestochowa Aug. 28, Wyszynski expressed his distress at "all these forms of violence, of limiting freedom, of discriminations, of dividing us [as] a nation into those who believe [in Catholicism] and are 2d-class citizens with inferior rights and those who don't believe and have all rights." Wyszynski reminded the regime that "more than 90% [of the Polish people] are believers, and no one else but these believers have built the Nowa Huta foundry [5 miles east of Cracow] and all other steel mills and all factories and all industrial complexes."

The Education Ministry demanded Nov. 26 that the leaders of the Polish Catholic Church remove the rectors of 6 seminaries on the ground that they had barred government inspection of their instruction and administration. The 6 seminaries were located in Warsaw, Cracow, Gniezno (Poznan Province), Przemysl (Rzeszow Province), Zdunska Wola (Lodz Province) and Drohiczyn (Bialystok Province). The government announced Dec. 7 that it would close 4 of the seminaries (all but the Gniezno and Przemysl institutions).

In a letter drawn up at an emergency meeting of church bishops Dec. 13 and read from every pulpit Dec. 18, the church hierarchy warned that the government crackdown was "the beginning of a more extensive campaign that would soon deprive the church in Poland of young priests." The letter asked all of the church's 48 seminaries to send student-faculty delegations to the Shrine of the Black Madonna of Czestochowa for 30 days to pray for the survival of the seminaries.

Cardinal Wyszynski said at a Christmas gathering in Warsaw Cathedral Dec. 25 that only priests could train future priests, "not the Ministry of Education, officials of the Office for Religious Affairs, security services or even the police." The regime stated editorially Dec. 27 in *Trybuna Ludu,* The Communist Party organ, that government inspection of the seminaries was necessary because "views harmful to the interests of the community were often expressed during lectures on secular subjects."

Conspiracy in Hungary

Nepszabadsag, the Hungarian Communist Party newspaper, announced Feb. 19 that an undisclosed number of persons had been arrested for "conspiring" against the regime. No indication was given about when the arrests had taken place. The paper said those arrested belonged to a "conspiratorial group" that had taken part in the 1956 revolt and had been released in 1963 under a general amnesty. It said that they had worked with Western contacts to build an opposition movement that "would take over power at a suitable time and change the social system."

Several of those arrested were identified as members of Regnum Marianum, a Catholic institute in Budapest. Named in this group were 3 priests, Laszlo Emodyi, Istvan Keglevich and Laszlo Roszavolgyi, who were "sentenced again" to 4 to 5 years in prison. Emodyi had been associated with Jozsef Cardinal Mindszenty, 74, Hungarian church primate who had been in asylum since 1956 in the U.S. legation in Budapest. Other alleged plotters arrested included Miklos Vasarhelyi, Gyula Szonyi, Zsombor Kasanszly, Jozsef Kos and Jeno Soltesz. Kos, a journalist, and Soltesz were described by the London *Times* Feb. 21 as active backers of the late Imre Nagy, premier of the short-lived 1956 rebel government.

Jozsef Prantner, president of the State Office for Church Affairs, denied in an interview Mar. 3 that the arrest of the 3 priests meant that the government was cracking down on the Roman Catholic church. Prantner declined comment on the status of Mindszenty. (Franziskus Cardinal Koenig of Austria conferred with Mindszenty at the U.S. legation Mar. 6. It was reported that Koenig had attempted to persuade Mindszenty to leave Hungary.)

Bela Fabian, chairman of the Federation of Hungarian Former Political Prisoners, declared in New York Feb. 19 that the arrests had occurred 2 weeks after workers' riots protesting recent price increases. Fabian reported that 250 rioters had been arrested at a Csepel Works branch in Pecs. He said that all members of the 1956 rebel leadership who had remained in Hungary currently were back in prison.

GROWING DIVERSITY

Ceausescu Asserts Sovereignty

Rumanian Communist Party General Secy. Nicolae Ceausescu May 7 vigorously defended Rumania's policy of independence and national sovereignty. In a speech delivered in Bucharest on the 45th anniversary of the founding of the Rumanian Communist Party, Ceausescu held that the liquidation of military alliances would lead to a detente. Ceausescu defended Rumania's policy of improving relations with Western European nations and "with all countries regardless of social system." Ceausescu, reviewing the history of the Rumanian Communist Party, sharply criticized the domination of the Rumanian party by the Soviet-sponsored Comintern (Communist International) in the period between the 2 world wars; the Comintern, he said, "promoted the dismemberment" of Rumania "and the breaking up of the Rumanian people."

(The USSR had seized Rumanian Bessarabia and Bucovina in 1940 and had incorporated them into the Moldavian Soviet Socialist Republic of the Soviet Union. The southern half of Bucovina was returned to Rumania in 1945, but the remaining territory seized in 1940 was retained by the USSR.)

According to Ceausescu, in the 1920s, the formative years of the Rumanian Communist Party, the Moscow-directed Comintern disregarded the national peculiarities of Rumania. "Leadership cadres of the party, including the general secretaries, . . . [were appointed] from among people who did not know the Rumanian people's life or preoccupations," he said. The Comintern instructed the Rumanian Communist Party to "fight for the breaking away from Rumania of certain territories inhabited by an overwhelming majority of Rumanians. . . . [This] promoted the dismemberment of the national state and the breaking up of the Rumanian people."

As a result of Comintern domination of the Rumanian Communist Party, Ceausescu said, the Rumanians were unable to oppose Nazi Germany's aggression and were forced to accept the consequences of the 1939 Nazi-Soviet pact. "When the Germans were attacking [Poland and Czechoslovakia in 1939-40], the 1940 directives of the Comintern addressed to the Rumanian Communist Party, instead of appreciating the justice of the fight against the Hitlerite war . . . , criticized the Rumanian Communists for activity directed against the German aggression and for their position of defending the national independence of the fatherland," Ceausescu maintained. As a result of Comintern policy, Rumania was abandoned in 1940 "by all the powers of Europe" and "was left at the mercy of Germany." "As is known, the Dictate of Vienna was imposed on Rumania in Aug. 1940; under this, the northern part of Transylvania was stolen and delivered to Fascist Hungary."

(Under the Dictate of Vienna, Germany and Italy forced Rumania to cede northern Transylvania to Hungary. The territory, returned to Rumania in 1945, currently had a Hungarian population of more than one million persons and was reported to be a growing source of tension between Rumania and Hungary. Hungarian Central Committee Secy. Zoltan Komocsin, in a speech in Budapest Mar. 23, had criticized Communist nations that stressed "nationalism" at the expense of "proletarian internationalism." Without mentioning Rumania by name, Komocsin attacked the Bucharest policy of independence from the USSR. He declared that "the touchstone of proletarian internationalism ... [was] solidarity with the Soviet Union.")

Ceausescu asserted that a "number of theoreticians have been trying to lend credence to the [incorrect] idea that nations are an outdated social category, surpassed by history." But "history shows ... that the appearance of the nation as a form of human community and the development of the national life of the peoples is ... a necessary and obligatory stage in the evolution of all peoples," he said. "The victory of our country is an eloquent example in this respect. The Rumanian land— Moldavia [much of it currently part of the USSR], Transylvania [ceded back to Rumania by Hungary in 1945]— has been under foreign domination for many centuries.... Nonetheless, foreign domination did not succeed in smothering the people's desire for freedom and in changing its strong wish for unity."

"The steady strengthening of each Socialist nation not only does not conflict with the interests of socialist internationalism but, on the contrary, corresponds fully to the interests of the cause of the workers' class ... and of the general fight for the victory of socialism and peace in the world," Ceausescu argued. "The construction of socialism and communism is an expression of the will of each people," he held.

"It is in this that the invincibility of the new order lies, as well as its force and granite durability. There is no national communism and international communism. Communism is at the same time national and international. Socialism is not an abstract notion: It has become reality in 16 countries * and other peoples are going toward socialism.... Of decisive importance for the restoration and strengthening of the unity of the Communist and workers' movement is consistent respect for the basic norms of relations among parties, for the principle of independence, equality in rights, noninterference in internal affairs, and for proletarian internationalism."

The Rumanian party leader commented on the success of French Pres. de Gaulle's policy toward the North Atlantic Treaty Organization, whose troops he had given a year to leave France. In Ceausescu's opinion, too, military blocs were an obstacle to national sovereignty: "Life shows that in the contemporary world the only basis on which international relations among states can be established is respect for sovereignty and national independence, equality in rights, noninterference in internal affairs, and mutual advantage. The military blocs and the existence of military bases and of troops on the territory of other states is one of the barriers in the path of collaboration among the peoples. The existence of blocs as well as the sending of troops to other countries is an anachronism incompatible with the independence and national sovereignty of the peoples and normal relations among states. Increasingly wide circles of public opinion and an increasing number of states show the tendency—which has recently gained more and more ground—to liquidate military blocs, to liquidate foreign bases, and to withdraw the troops from the territory of other states. The achievement of this ardent wish of the peoples would be of outstanding importance and give a strong impetus to the development of trust among the peoples, to the *detente* of the international situation and to the consolidation of peace in the world."

Ceausescu said that "Rumania is developing relations of collaboration with all countries regardless of social system." "Deeming that this is one of the ways of strengthening confidence and collaboration among peoples," he continued,

---

* Ceausescu apparently implied that the Ukraine and Byelorussia, which had separate seats in the UN, were separate states.

Rumania "is developing economic, cultural and scientific relations with France, Italy, England, Austria, and other countries. I would like to stress particularly the possibilities existing for the development of economic, cultural and scientific relations between Rumania and France, which are bound by old traditions of friendship and collaboration."

Soviet Communist Party General Secy. Leonid I. Brezhnev visited Bucharest May 10-13 for talks with Ceausescu. Brezhnev's visit to Bucharest had not been announced in advance and received little coverage in the Soviet or Rumanian press. On Brezhnev's return to Moscow May 13, the Soviet news agency Tass reported that Brezhnev and Ceausescu had "exchanged opinions" but did not say what subjects had been discussed. Tass described the visit as "unofficial." A communique issued in Bucharest May 13 described the meeting as "an exchange of opinions on matters relating to the steady development of cooperation" between the 2 nations and parties "as well as other matters of mutual interest." The communique was the first official confirmation by either side that Brezhnev had been in Bucharest. It was reported that Brezhnev's trip had been precipitated by Ceausescu's May 7 speech.

An official in the Rumanian Foreign Ministry refused May 16 to confirm or deny a report, which had originated in Moscow, that Bucharest had circulated to the Warsaw Pact nations a note saying that the presence of Soviet troops on the territory of member nations was no longer justified. (Soviet troops had left Rumania in 1958 but were still based in East Germany, Hungary and Poland.) The official said: "Some elements of this are based on our well-known position on the presence of foreign troops." In language similar to Ceausescu's in his May 7 speech the official said: "The existence of ... blocs, as well as the dispatching of troops to other countries, represents an anachronism that is incompatible with the national independence and sovereignty of the peoples, with normal interstate relations."

The *N.Y. Times* reported May 17 from Moscow that Rumania was pressing for a revision of Warsaw Pact nuclear strategy that would permit pact nations to have a veto over the use of nuclear weapons stationed on their territory. Under the Rumanian plan, both Soviet approval and the approval of the nations where the weapons were stationed would be required before the weapons could be used. The *Times* quoted a Rumanian official in Moscow to say: "We want to avoid a situation like the Cuban crisis of 1962 in which foreign missiles could be fired from our territory without our consent." The *Times* reported that the proposal had been circulated among Warsaw Pact nations in preparation for the organization's expected summit meeting in July.

A Rumanian Foreign Ministry official declared in Bucharest May 18 that the Warsaw Pact was "sufficiently strong to meet present needs." Efforts to strengthen the pact, he said, could "contribute only to an equilibrium of terror." As long as NATO existed, there would be a need for the Warsaw Pact, he said. He denied that Rumania had circulated to the Warsaw Pact countries a note suggesting that Soviet troops be withdrawn. Rumania, he said, does "not interfere in the affairs of another country, and others do not interfere in ours."

Rumanian Foreign Trade Min. Gheorghe Cioara met West German Chancellor Ludwig Erhard in Bonn May 26 at the conclusion of a 9-day visit to West Germany. During his stay, Cioara had called for diplomatic relations between the 2 countries.

Rumania & Repercussions of the Sino-Soviet Rift

Rumanian First Deputy Premier Emil Bodnaras conferred in Peking May 13 with Communist Chinese Premier Chou En-lai. Bodnaras had gone to Peking from Hanoi, where he had met with North Vietnamese Premier Pham Van Dong. A communique on Bodnaras' talks with Dong, published May 13 in Bucharest, said that they had affirmed the principles of "sovereignty, independence, equality and non-interference in the interior affairs" of any nation.

The foreign ministers of 7 pro-Soviet east European nations met in Moscow June 6-17 in preparation for a July 4-6 Bucharest summit meeting. The Moscow meeting, originally scheduled to end June 9, was extended apparently because of a rift between Rumania and the other 6 nations. The *N.Y. Times* reported June 15 from Belgrade that a personal meeting June 11 between Rumanian Foreign Min. Corneliu Manescu and Soviet CP Gen. Secy. Leonid Brezhnev had been precipitated by a sharp disagreement between Manescu and East German

Foreign Min. Otto Winzer at the foreign ministers' meeting. According to the *Times,* which based its account on reports by "Eastern European diplomats" in Belgrade, Manescu had refused to indorse a declaration condemning West Germany as the chief "troublemaker" in Europe. Winzer, supported by Hungarian Foreign Min. Janos Peter, was reported to have denounced Manescu's refusal as "treason to the Communist cause" and a "stab in the back."

(At his June 11 meeting with Brezhnev, Manescu was reported to have insisted that future meetings between Warsaw Pact and North Atlantic Treaty nations be conducted bilaterally.)

Tass reported June 17 that the foreign ministers' meeting had been completed that day and that the Warsaw Treaty's Political Consultative Committee would meet in Bucharest in early July. (Tass June 11 had reported the conclusion of a 5-day meeting on economic planning; the deputy premiers of the 7 nations and Mongolia attended.)

Premier Chou En-lai visited Rumania June 16-24 and Albania June 24-28.

In Bucharest Chou conferred with Ceausescu, Premier Ion G. Maurer and Bodnaras. The highest ranking Chinese official accompanying Chou, Chao Yimin, candidate member of the Communist Party Central Committee, praised Rumania's independent policy in a speech delivered June 20 in Craiova. The Rumanian people, he declared, had been successful "in their fight against external control."

In what was reported to have been the most significant development of Chou's visit, he and Ceausescu appeared 2 hours late at a June 23 Chinese-Rumanian friendship rally in Bucharest. Both leaders had been scheduled to make lengthy speeches, but instead made brief impromptu statements devoid of political content. It was reported that Chou had planned to make a strong anti-Soviet speech at the rally and that Ceausescu had objected because it would have compromised Rumania's neutrality in the Sino-Soviet dispute.

No joint communique was issued at the end of Chou's visit. The Chinese news agency Hsinhua praised the Rumanian people June 24 for giving Chou a "grand and enthusiastic welcome" but made no mention of the Rumanian party leaders or government.

During the summit meeting of the 7 Warsaw Pact nations in Bucharest July 4-6, the leaders of the east European nations apparently failed in efforts to tighten the Warsaw Pact's military organization. The Russian delegation reportedly pressed for such measures but were opposed by Ceausescu, who also met alone with the Soviet leaders July 4 and 8.

Bulgarian Communist Party First Secy. and Premier Todor Zhivkov, 55, called Nov. 14 for the convening of a conference of the world Communist movement to deal with the problem of Communist China. The call came during the opening session of the Bulgarian Communist Party's 9th quadrennial congress, held in Sofia Nov. 14-19.

Soviet Premier Brezhnev, addressing the congress Nov. 15, gave only cautious endorsement to Zhivkov's call for a conference: "It is not accidental," he said, "that a number of fraternal parties have recently expressed the opinion that conditions are ripening for ... a new international conference." (In the version of Zhivkov's speech printed in the Bulgarian Communist Party daily *Rabotnichesko Delo* Nov. 15, the phrase "conditions are ripe" was changed to read "conditions are becoming ripe." Zhivkov used the latter language in his closing speech Nov. 19.)

Other speakers expressed varying degrees of enthusiasm for a conference. Among the East European countries, the East German and Hungarian delegates took strong anti-Chinese stands, but only the Czechoslovak representative explicitly supported the Bulgarian proposal. The Yugoslav delegate ignored the issue, and the Polish representative stressed the need for unity. Ceausescu, speaking immediately after Brezhnev, said Rumania "centers its foreign policy on friendship with all the Socialist countries." "In the present circumstances," he declared, "it is necessary that nothing should be done to deepen the divergencies and increase the threat of a split, that everything possible should be undertaken ... to reestablish a climate favoring the setting up of normal relations between parties."

OTHER DEVELOPMENTS

Hungarian Diplomatic Initiatives

Hungary joined others in the Soviet bloc late in 1966 in urging an international conference of Communist parties on the Sino-Soviet controversy. It also moved tentatively toward a rapprochement with West Germany from economic motives. At the same time, it made substantive progress toward rapprochement with the U.S.

Hungarian Socialist Workers' Party First Secy. Janos Kadar declared Nov. 28 that all Communist parties that considered "the time ripe" for a discussion of the problems posed by Communist China should proceed with plans to convene a conference for that purpose. The renewed call for such a conference, made by Bulgarian Communist Party First Secy. Zhivkov Nov. 14, came during the opening session of the Hungarian Communist Party's 9th Congress, held in Budapest Nov. 28-Dec. 2. Representatives of 32 foreign Communist parties attended the congress.

After declaring that "conditions for a major conference of the Communist and Workers' parties are ripening," Kadar said: "We must work so that the representatives of all those parties of the international working class movement that consider the time ripe for making a Marxist-Leninist analysis of the situation [posed by Communist China] meet and consult in a comradely manner and draw conclusions on the joint tasks to be carried out...." Although Kadar accused Communist China of "aspirations for hegemony, anti-Sovietism and splitting activities," he insisted that "there is no need for any kind of excommunication." "We wish to consult and unite ... with every revolutionary party and with all progressive forces," he said, "and thus also naturally with the Chinese Communist Party and the Albanian Labor Party."

Hungarian Premier Gyula Kallai said Nov. 30 that his country and the U.S. had agreed to raise their diplomatic missions to the ambassadorial level.

In a congress speech Dec. 1, Hungarian Foreign Min. Janos Peter called for closer ties between West Germany and eastern Europe's Communist states. He urged the new West German regime to abandon the policy of refusing to have diplomatic relations with countries that had diplomatic ties with East Germany.

Albanian Dissidence

The Polish government Feb. 23 demanded the recall of Albanian Amb.-to-Poland Koco Prifti on the grounds that the Albanian embassy had smuggled a discredited former Polish government official, Kazimierz Mijal, out of the country with an "Albanian diplomatic passport." Mijal, 55, had been communal economy minister but was removed from the government by Pres. Jozef Cyrankiewicz in 1957. He had been under investigation for circulating pro-Chinese Communist pamphlets in Warsaw. Albania denounced the Polish charge as false and demanded the recall of Polish Amb.-to-Albania Stanislaw Rogulsky, who had been appointed in January and was the first Polish ambassador to Albania in 5 years.

Communist Chinese Premier Chou En-lai arrived June 24 in Tirana, Albania, where he was greeted by Premier Mehmet Shehu with a speech assailing Rumania's "neutrality." Albania, Shehu declared, would not be misled by "acrobatic politicians" who were attempting to work with "the Khrushchev revisionists." Chou conferred June 25 with Labor (Communist) Party First Secy. Enver Hoxha and left June 28 for Pakistan for talks with Pres. Mohammad Ayub Khan. He returned to Peking July 1.

The Albanian Communist Party's 5th quinquennial congress, held in Tirana Nov. 1-5, was attended by representatives of Communist China and 29 other parties and groups.

In a speech delivered Nov. 4, Hoxha urged the pro-Chinese faction of the world Communist movement to make a definite and irrevocable break with the "revisionist" camp of the Soviet Union and its allies. The Rumanian and North Vietnamese delegates had indicated earlier in the congress that their countries would not adopt such a policy. The Rumanians urged respect for the right of every Communist country or party to develop relations as it saw fit. North Vietnamese Pres. Ho Chi Minh said in a message read to the congress Nov. 1 that the North Vietnamese were "extremely grateful to China and to the Soviet Union for their present support and sincere assistance in our fight against American aggression."

SOVIET UNION

Sinyavsky-Daniel Case

The Soviet government newspaper *Izvestia* Jan. 12 published the first official word on the cases of 2 writers, Andrei D. Sinyavsky and Yuli M. Daniel (Daniyel), both 40, reportedly under arrest for smuggling anti-Soviet works out of the USSR for publication in the West under the pseudonyms Abram Tertz and Nikolai Arzhak. The article, written by Secy. Gen. Dmitri I. Yeremin of the Moscow Writers Union, charged that the books published abroad under the names Tertz and Arzhak had in fact been written by Sinyavsky and Daniel. It accused the 2 writers of "high treason," "crimes against the Soviet regime," and of acting as "tools to fan psychological warfare against the Soviet Union." Sinyavsky, Yeremin said, deliberately had chosen a Jewish pseudonym (Tertz) to imply that anti-Semitism was prevalent in the USSR. Yeremin concluded that the works of the 2 authors were "bullets shot in the back of a people struggling for peace and universal happiness. Their activity is hostile to their country."

Sinyavsky and Daniel were convicted and sentenced in Moscow Feb. 14 by the Supreme Court of the Russian Republic. Both men received prison terms at hard labor: Sinyavsky 7 years, Daniel 5 years. The 2 writers were convicted under Article 70 of the Russian Republic's Criminal Code, which provided a maximum term of 7 years for "agitation or propaganda conducted for the purpose of undermining and weakening Soviet power ... [and] the dissemination with the same intent of slanderous material besmirching the Soviet state and social system."

The verdict, read by Lev N. Smirnov, chairman of the 3-man Soviet tribunal, said the defendants had intentionally written malicious material about the USSR. The "presence of such [malicious] intent was determined," declared Smirnov, "by the content of the work sent abroad." The work of the 2 authors "attracted the attention of bourgeois propaganda organs by their anti-Soviet content and were exploited in the ideological struggle against the Soviet Union." Tass, the official Soviet news agency, reported that no appeal could be made from the verdict but that the 2 writers would be eligible for parole after they had served ½ their sentences.

Western newsmen, excluded from the trial, received their accounts from Tass and from the Soviet press. According to Tass, the "open" trial was attended by about 70 Soviet journalists and literary figures, including Aleksandr Tvardovsky, editor of the literary journal *Novy Mir,* which had published some of Sinyavsky's reviews; Konstantin Fedin, first secretary of the USSR Writers' Union; Leonid Sobolev, chairman of the Russian Republic's Writers Union, and Aleksandr Chakovsky, editor of the literary newspaper *Literaturnaya Gazeta.* Throughout the 3-day trial (Feb. 10-12), held in a courthouse in western Moscow, 50-75 Soviet students sympathetic to the defendants gathered outside. The students, were mainly from the Gorky Institute of World Literature, where Sinyavsky and Daniel had taught. Komsomol (Communist Youth League) youths were also on the scene and berated Western newsmen; they dragged 2 French reporters to a police station Feb. 14 on charges of "sensational and slanderous" reporting, but the newsmen were released.

In a development that Western observers considered unusual in a Soviet political trial, both authors denied their guilt Feb. 10, the opening day of the trial. After hearing Judge Smirnov read an 18-page indictment, they answered affirmatively when asked if they understood the charge. They then replied to the judge's question: "Do you plead guilty?" Sinyavsky said: "Not at all." Daniel said: "No, neither in part nor in full."

Izvestia reported Feb. 10 that both writers had admitted during the investigation following their arrest that they were the authors of the Tertz and Arzhak books published in the West. Tass reported Feb. 10 that Daniel, compelled to admit under cross-examination that his writings had been used for anti-Soviet purposes, had said he "regretted it." Tass reported Feb. 11 that both writers insisted on the nonpolitical nature of their writings. Sinyavsky declared "the right of an artist to self-expression." When Prosecutor Oleg Temushkin read commentaries on Daniel's works by Western critics to demonstrate that Daniel's works had been interpreted as anti-Soviet, Daniel replied: "A man must remain a man in whatever conditions, under whatever circumstances."

In his final summation Feb. 12, Temushkin described the 2 authors' books as "a mockery of everything that is dear and sacred to a Soviet person: the motherland, the Communist ideal, the Soviet way of life, the morality of the people."

(It was reported in Paris Feb. 14 that the daughter of a former French naval attache in Moscow, Mrs. Helene Zamoyska-Pelletier, had admitted assisting Sinyavsky to smuggle his manuscripts to the West. Agence France-Presse reported that Mrs. Zamoyska-Pelletier had admitted "entire and exclusive responsibility" for aiding "my friend" and for making "Soviet literary works full of originality and talent known abroad." The Soviet indictment Feb. 10 had named Mrs. Zamoyska-Pelletier, a scholar of Russian languages at the University of Toulouse, as the person who brought the Sinyavsky and Daniel manuscripts to the West.)

The sentencing of Sinyavsky and Daniel provoked a chorus of criticism in Western literary circles. William Styron said in New York that the sentence "reveals that there is still a dreadful totalitarian atmosphere" in the USSR. Hannah Arendt said the trial was "an ugly reminder of something one had hoped had passed into history." The PEN Club, a London literary club, sent Premier Aleksei N. Kosygin a telegram deploring the "savage and inhuman" court decision. 49 authors from 5 nations (France, Italy, West Germany, the U.S. and Britain), in a Jan. 31 letter in the London *Times,* had called for the writers' release on the ground that their works were not propaganda and should be judged "solely on its literary and artistic merits." Among those signing the letter were Francois Mauriac, Guenter Grass, Alberto Moravia, Ignazio Silone, Hannah Arendt, W. H. Auden, Saul Bellow, Michael Harrington, Alfred Kazin, Mary McCarthy, Dwight Macdonald, Arthur Miller, Philip Rahv, Philip Roth, William Styron, Graham Greene, Julian Huxley, Philip Toynbee and Rebecca West.

2 U.S. experts on the Soviet Union, ex-Amb.-to-USSR George F. Kennan and Harold J. Berman, said Feb. 15 that the Sinyavsky-Daniel trial marked an improvement in Soviet judicial treatment of individuals accused of political crimes. Kennan said: "We must not forget that less than 20 years ago there would have been no trial at all and they would have rotted in concentration camps for offenses less than this." Berman, a specialist on Soviet law currently teaching at Harvard Law School, said: "At least the trial was genuine." Both Kennan and Berman criticized the trial and sentences, however, as excessively severe and detrimental to freedom of thought and expression.

The *N.Y. Times* reported Nov. 19 that 63 Moscow writers had petitioned the Soviet government and Communist Party in March to let them "stand surety" for Sinyavsky and Daniel. (The petition was one of a dozen documents relating to the Sinyavsky-Daniel affair that the publishing house of Harper & Row had received through undisclosed channels. None of the documents, consisting of protests addressed to Soviet authorities and newspapers, had been published in the Soviet Union.)

The petitioners said that, although they did not approve of the means by which the 2 authors had published their works abroad, "we cannot accept the view that their motives were in any way anti-Soviet." They added that "the condemnation of writers for the writing of satirical works creates an extremely dangerous precedent and threatens to hold up the progress of Soviet culture." "In our complex situation today," the petitioners declared, "we need more freedom for artistic experiment and certainly not its condemnation." Among the signers of the petition: Pavel G. Antokolsky, poet and translator; Kornei I. Chukovsky, 84, writer and translator; Lidiya K. Chukovskaya, critic and Chukovsky's daughter; Yefim Y. Dorosh, essayist; Ilya G. Ehrenburg, journalist and writer; Veniamin A. Kaverin, writer; Viktor B. Shklovsky, writer and critic; Lev I. Slavin, writer.

(The *N.Y. Times* had reported Jan. 13 that 3 writers had been arrested prior to a Dec. 5, 1965 protest at which Moscow students had demanded a public trial for Sinyavsky and Daniel. The 3 writers, Vladimir Bykovsky, Leonid Gubanov and Yulia

Vishnevskaya, 16, reportedly were confined to a Moscow
mental home.)

Tarsis Incident

Valery Tarsis, 59, a Russian writer who had written anti-
Soviet works under his own name, told Western newsmen in
Moscow Feb. 6 that he had received permission from Soviet
authorities to accept an invitation from the University of
Leicester (England) to lecture for 2 months. *Ward 7,* Tarsis'
journal of life in a Soviet mental hospital, had been published in
Britain and in the U.S. in 1965 under Tarsis' name.

Tarsis said Feb. 6 that he had been declared insane by
Soviet authorities and had been confined for 8 months in 1962-
63 to the Kashchenko Mental Hospital near Moscow, not for
mental illness but as an alternative to jailing him for anti-
Soviet writing. Since he was declared insane, he explained, he
was not held legally responsible by the Soviet authorities for his
actions. Referring to Sinyavsky and Daniel, who then were
about to go on trial, he described them as "cowards, hypocrites
and liars" who "posed as loyal Marxists while they wrote
exactly the opposite and hid behind assumed names."

Tarsis arrived in London Feb. 8 and held a press
conference Feb. 10 at the offices of his British publisher, Collins
& Harvill Press. He retracted his remarks on Sinyavsky and
Daniel as a "tactless mistake." He added: "While I am now in
this wonderful free city of London, Sinyavsky and Daniel are
in jail.... They belong in the same camp I belong to. They
struggle against the common enemy, and I wish them all the
best." Tarsis also said: "I am not a traitor to my country, I love
my country, by which I mean its whole people, not the
government that betrayed the national cause." Communism
was, in his experience of it, "police-fascism." Among the
reasons he cited for his permission to leave the USSR was the
fact that British philosopher Bertrand Russell had written to
Premier Aleksei N. Kosygin on his behalf. "More than half of
the Soviet Writers Union [members] are anti-Semites."

Pravda reported Feb. 21 that Tarsis had been deprived of
his Soviet citizenship "for actions discrediting to a citizen of
the USSR." Tarsis applied for Greek citizenship June 28. Greek

Interior Min. Phokion Zaimis announced July 23 that the request had been granted.

Liberal Writers Criticized

The London *Times* had reported Mar. 16 that 25 Soviet intellectuals had written to warn Communist Party First Secy. Brezhnev against the risks of rehabilitating Stalin, included were atomic scientists Petr L. Kapitsa, Igor Y. Tamm, Lev A. Artsimovich, Andrei D. Sakharov and Mikhail A. Leontovich; authors Konstantin G. Paustovsky and Viktor P. Nekrasov; Maya Plisetskaya, first ballerina of the Bolshoi Ballet; Mikhail A. Komm, a movie director, and Ivan M. Maisky, an academician and Stalin's wartime ambassador to Britain. Several speakers at the 23d Congress of the Soviet Communist Party, held in Moscow Mar. 29-Apr. 8, assailed Russian writers who criticized the Soviet Union. The keynote was set in the opening address by First Secy. Brezhnev. Brezhnev said: The "party is against ... arbitrary decisions on problems of art and literature." But, "unfortunately, there are hack artists who ... specialize in smearing our system and slandering our heroic people.... [These] renegades do not care for the interests of our socialist homeland ... sacred to every Soviet man. It is quite clear that the Soviet people cannot ignore the disgraceful activity of such people."

Moscow Communist Party First Secy. Nikolai G. Yegorychev Mar. 30 criticized "various journals ... movie screens ... the stage ... [that] give a one-sided and erroneous picture of our past and present and contain petty grumblings about temporary difficulties." He said some writers were more interested in their overseas reputations than in their "debt to their people." Byelorussian Communist Party First Secy. Pyotr M. Masherov Mar. 31 also scored "certain literary figures" who criticized the Soviet people.

Nobel Prize-winning author Mikhail A. Sholokhov Apr. 1 singled out for criticism the 2 Soviet authors sentenced in February for publishing anti-Soviet works abroad, Sinyavsky and Daniel. Sholokhov said: "Had these rascals with black consciences been caught in the memorable 1920s, when judgment was not by strictly defined articles of the criminal code but was guided by a 'revolutionary sense of justice,' the punishment meted out to these turncoats would have been quite different.... We paid too dear a price for what we have gained; we prize the Soviet power too highly to allow people to slander and vilify it with impunity."

Aleksandr Tvardovsky, 56, editor of *Novy Mir,* was not present at the congress. He had been a delegate at the preceding 2 party congresses and had addressed both of them. Party elections disclosed Apr. 8 indicated that Tvardovsky had lost his candidate-membership in the Central Committee.

Tvardovsky declared in the issue of *Novy Mir* that went on sale Apr. 13 that writing that presented a true picture of reality was in the interest of communism. Such writing, he said, sees "reality as it is, in all its complexity, in its real contradictions and movements." "When this reality is simplified or schematized, then art ceases to be art," he declared. In a 2d article Tvardovsky paid tribute to Anna Akhmatova, a poet who had died Mar. 5 and had been severely censured by Stalinist authorities. "The growth in ... [her] circle of readers," Tvardovsky wrote, "could not be impeded by the extremely unjust and crude attacks against her...."

Novy Mir marked its 500th issue Sept. 3-4 by publishing a 40-page article by the literary critic V. Lakshin on the need for artistic freedom. He wrote that, rather than being told "strictly where to look and what to see," the artist had the right "to look everywhere and see everything that affects him and troubles him on the wide path of life."

OTHER EVENTS

Kolakowski Expelled

Leszek Kolakowski, 39, a professor at the University of Warsaw and one of Poland's leading philosophers, was reported Oct. 31 to have been expelled from the United Workers (Communist) Party for an antiregime speech he had made Oct. 21. The speech, delivered at a university meeting during which a number of students reportedly criticized the regime, was said to have compared unfavorably existing realities with the

expectations following the anti-Stalinist revolution of Oct.
1956.

It was reported Dec. 7 that 21 Polish authors, all United
Workers Party members, had signed a letter to high party
officials in which they echoed Kolakowski's criticism of the
party's attitude towards artists and intellectuals. *Kultura,* a
Polish-language exile magazine published in Paris, reported
Dec. 9 that 13 of the letter's 21 signers had been expelled from
the party and that 5 students who had participated in the Oct.
21 meeting at the university had been suspended from classes.

Opposition in Yugoslavia

The Zadar District Court in Croatia Sept. 23 convicted
writer Mihajlo Mihajlov, 32, and sentenced him to one year in
prison on charges of "spreading false information aimed at
inciting displeasure and provoking dissatisfaction in the
population." The charges related to 3 antiregime articles that
Mihajlov, a former lecturer on the Zadar Philosophy Faculty,
had published abroad. He had been arrested Aug. 8 in
connection with his plans to found an opposition magazine
called *Free Voice.* (It was reported Nov. 22 that the entire
editorial board of *Free Voice,* consisting of 5 of Mihajlov's
followers, had been arrested.)

Ex-Vice Pres. Milovan Djilas was freed from prison Dec.
31 under an amnesty granted by Pres. Tito. Djilas, 55, had
served 4 years and 8 months of an 8-year 8-month sentence. He
had been convicted in 1962 on charges of divulging state secrets
in his book *Conversations with Stalin.*

Legislators in the Slovenian Republic, meanwhile, allowed
to differ, had asserted their constitutional prerogative—with
unexpected results. Slovenian Premier Janko Smole and his
cabinet resigned Dec. 7 after one of the parliamentary
chambers rejected a government-sponsored bill. This was
reportedly the first time in the history of Communist
Yugoslavia that a republican government had resigned over a
parliamentary defeat.

1967

Disintegration within the Soviet bloc was approaching a critical stage in 1967. Rumania Jan. 31 established diplomatic relations with West Germany, exercising a privilege hitherto reserved only to the USSR. Despite the renewal of bilateral "friendship" treaties with other countries of eastern Europe, Moscow failed in its repeated attempts—all of them opposed by the Yugoslavs—to enhance Soviet authority and to restore unity to the Communist world. Discord was especially evident at the Karlovy Vary meeting of the party leaders Apr. 24-26.

The 4th congress of Czechoslovak writers, held in Prague June 27-29, became a forum of opposition against the Novotny regime. The authorities at first reacted by persecuting individual writers, but this policy further encouraged unrest. The stagnation of the Czechoslovak economy gave additional impetus to criticism that spread within the Czechoslovak Communist Party.

Although reported incidents of dissent in the USSR increased dramatically, its containment was more successful than in Czechoslovakia. Additional intellectuals were tried and imprisoned. At the 4th writers' congress in Moscow May 22-27, opposition currents appeared, but on a much smaller scale than in Czechoslovakia.

The escape of Stalin's daughter, Svetlana Alliluyeva, to the West became the most celebrated case of defection from the Soviet Union. Apart from her personal motives, the incident demonstrated that even the most privileged members of the ruling class shared profound misgivings about the quality of life under communism.

COPING WITH DISUNITY

Yugoslavia Vs. Convening World Communist Conference

The Central Committee of the Yugoslav League of Communists Jan. 10 went on record in opposition to proposals for an international conference of Communist parties. The Yugoslav committee Jan. 10 adopted a resolution stating that "any management of the international workers' movement from one center, or obligatory keeping to formally taken, joint general documents, was outlived." The resolution favored bilateral and multilateral discussions between parties.

Yugoslav Pres. Tito paid an "unofficial" visit to the Soviet Union Jan. 28-31 at the invitation of Soviet Communist Party General Secy. Leonid I. Brezhnev. It was reported in a communique Jan. 31 that Soviet-Yugoslav relations and international problems had been discussed. The absence of any reference to the proposed conference on Communist China suggested disagreement on this point.

Rumania's Pact with West Germany

Bonn's "peace offensive" toward Communist eastern Europe achieved its first tangible success Jan. 31 when West Germany and Rumania agreed to establish full diplomatic relations at the ambassadorial level. West German Chancellor Kurt-Georg Kiesinger had stated in a major policy speech Dec. 31, 1966 that it was the intention of his government to normalize relations with eastern Europe.

The agreement was concluded in Bonn by West German Foreign Min. Willy Brandt and Rumanian Foreign Min. Corneliu Manescu. The groundwork had been laid Jan. 7-18 when a delegation headed by Hans Helmuth Rute, a senior official in the West German foreign ministry, conferred with Rumanian officials in Bucharest. The West German government announced officially Jan. 25 that Manescu would arrive in Bonn Jan. 30 for final talks on normalizing relations. After concluding the agreement Jan. 31, Manescu visited Cologne, Duesseldorf and Munich before returning home Feb. 3.

In a joint communique issued Jan. 31, the 2 sides declared that the establishment of relations "contributes to mutual understanding, ... [which will] serve the peace, the security, the long-term understanding and the peaceful coexistence of the peoples of Europe, as well as the reduction of international tensions."

Following the agreement between Bonn and Bucharest Jan. 31, the Soviet-West German controversy spilled over into other countries of the Communist bloc. *Neues Deutschland,* the East German Socialist Unity (Communist) Party daily, charged Feb. 3 that it was "deplorable" that Rumania had not demanded West German recognition of East Germany as a precondition for the establishment of relations. *Scinteia,* the Rumanian Communist Party daily, countered Feb. 4 by asserting that "the foreign policy of a Socialist country is set by the party and government of the respective country, and the party and government are responsible solely and only to their own people." It accused East Germany of violating the principles governing the relations between individual Socialist states by its "tactless and impermissible interference ... in the foreign policy moves of the Socialist Republic of Rumania."

(The Bucharest Declaration, adopted by the members of the Warsaw Pact in July 1966, had stipulated that the Socialist countries would establish diplomatic relations with West Germany only after West Germany had met these preconditions: [a] recognition of East Germany, [b] acceptance of the inviolability of Poland's western frontier [the Oder-Neisse line] and [c] renunciation of the use or possession of nuclear arms.)

Apparently in an effort to obtain assurances from the other east European nations that they would not follow the Rumanian example in establishing unconditional relations with West Germany, the Warsaw Pact nations held a hastily-called meeting in Warsaw Feb. 8-10. They had originally been scheduled to meet in East Berlin Feb. 7, but the meeting was moved to Warsaw at the last moment after Rumania had indicated that it would not attend a meeting in East Berlin because of the East German attack on its foreign policy.

Since Rumanian Foreign Min. Corneliu Manescu was on an official visit to Belgium Feb. 6-9, Rumania was represented at the talks by its deputy foreign minister, Mircea Malita. The other Warsaw Pact members were represented by their foreign ministers—Andrei Gromyko of the Soviet Union, Adam Rapacki of Poland, Otto Winzer of East Germany, Vaclav David of Czechoslovakia, Janos Peter of Hungary and Ivan Bashev of Bulgaria. (Although Albania was technically a member of the Warsaw Pact, it had not participated in the alliance's meetings since siding with Peking in the Sino-Soviet ideological dispute.)

On the opening day of the meeting Feb. 8, Polish United Workers' (Communist) Party First Secy. Wladyslaw Gomulka adumbrated the attitude of at least the Polish, East German and Czechoslovak side of the talks when he declared in a speech at Katowice in southern Poland that the establishment of diplomatic relations between West Germany and Socialist countries would not contribute to a detente in Europe "unless the West German government gives up its claims against the vital interests of the Socialist states."

In the communique issued at the conclusion of the meeting Feb. 10 the Soviet-bloc foreign ministers limited themselves to stating that "the development of the situation on the European continent since the Bucharest Declaration of July 1966" had been reviewed and that "a friendly exchange of views" had been held on "efforts of the Socialist countries to lessen international tensions and strengthen peace, security and cooperation in Europe."

In an indication that unanimity may not have been achieved at the Warsaw meeting, *Pravda,* the Soviet Communist Party daily, charged Feb. 24 that the major aim of West German foreign policy was to "undermine the united front of the Socialist countries in their struggle for security in Europe, to isolate the German Democratic Republic and to complicate the execution of the agreed policy of the Warsaw Treaty Countries." The *Pravda* article was followed by reports Feb. 25 that Hungarian Socialist Workers' (Communist) Party First Secy. Janos Kadar and Polish Defense Min. Marian Spychalski had arrived in Moscow that day for undisclosed talks with Soviet leaders. (Spychalski returned to Warsaw Feb. 27; Kadar returned to Budapest Mar. 1.) Czechoslovak Foreign Min. David ended an official 10-day visit to the Soviet Union Feb. 25 after having reached what was described as "full identity on all questions under discussion" with Soviet Foreign Min. Gromyko.

(Costantin Oancea, 38, was named Rumanian ambassador to West Germany July 10. He became Rumania's first envoy to West Germany since the 2 countries established full diplomatic relations Jan. 31.)

Bilateral Treaties

20-year treaties of friendship, cooperation and mutual assistance were signed in the Spring of 1967 by the USSR and a number of east European Communist governments. The first of these bilateral pacts, a renewal of the Czechoslovak-Polish treaty, was signed Mar. 1. The treaties, renewals of pacts originally concluded in the late 1940s, were viewed in part as a response to West Germany's drive for better relations with Communist eastern Europe.

An East German-Polish treaty was signed in Warsaw at the conclusion of talks Mar. 14-15 between East German Socialist Unity Party First Secy. Walter Ulbricht and Polish United Workers' Party First Secy. Wladyslaw Gomulka. Following the talks in Warsaw, Ulbricht went to Prague to sign a similar treaty after talks Mar. 16-17 with Czechoslovak Pres. Antonin Novotny. The Prague treaty, however, was notably different from the one signed in Warsaw in that it contained no article reaffirming the parties' guarantees of East Germany's "territorial integrity" and the "inviolability" of its borders with West Germany.

Ulbricht declared Mar. 17 that the new pacts had made it necessary for Bonn to seek "normal relations" with East Germany before making further progress in its campaign for diplomatic relations with other East European countries. Novotny, however, stressed that the Czechoslovak-East German treaty was "aimed at no other states."

Poland and Bulgaria renewed their current treaty of friendship, cooperation and mutual aid for a further 20 years Apr. 6. The new treaty was signed in Sofia after talks Apr. 3-6 between Gomulka and Bulgarian Communist Party First Secy. Todor Zhivkov. Commenting on the fact that the treaty had been renewed 2 years earlier than necessary, Sofia radio stressed that Bulgaria backed the "inviolability of the Oder-

Neisse border and, like Poland, sees a threat in the policy of the Bonn government, [which is] striving for the revisions of the results created in Europe by World War II."

Soviet Communist Party General Secy. Leonid Brezhnev conferred with Todor Zhivkov in Sofia May 10-16. The talks culminated in renewal of the Soviet-Bulgarian treaty of friendship, cooperation and mutual aid signed in 1948. The new treaty differed from the old one in its stress on close bilateral cooperation between the 2 countries.

The last in the series of east European bilateral treaties, an East German-Hungarian pact, was signed by Ulbricht and Hungarian Pres. Pal Losonczy in Budapest May 18. Speaking of the treaty May 18, a Budapest radio commentator confirmed that the timing of the treaty was closely related to West Germany's drive to establish diplomatic relations with Hungary.

Karlovy Vary Meeting

Leaders of 24 European Communist parties met for a conference on European security and Communist unity at Karlovy Vary, Czechoslovakia Apr. 24-26. The meeting was the first joint conference held for more than half a century by the Communist parties of eastern and western Europe.

The talks ended with the signing of a joint communique and a Declaration for Peace & Security in Europe Apr. 26. The declaration proposed the abolition of both the North Atlantic and the Warsaw Treaty organizations and their replacement with a joint European security system.

The invited parties that did not attend the Karlovy Vary meeting were the Dutch, Norwegian and Icelandic Communist parties of western Europe and the Rumanian, Yugoslav and Albanian parties of eastern Europe. The Swedish Communist Party was represented only by an observer, and it did not sign the declaration. (The Chinese party, in an article published in Peking's *Jenmin Jih Pao,* the official party newspaper, denounced the conference May 4 as a "meeting of counter-revolutionary gangsters.")

The conference was opened at the Czech spa's Imperial Hotel by Czechoslovak Pres. and Communist Party First Secy. Antonin Novotny. Among other leaders present: Soviet

Communist Party General Secy. Brezhnev, Polish Party First Secy. Gomulka, Bulgarian Party First Secy. Zhivkov, Hungarian Party First Secy. Kadar, East German Party First Secy. Ulbricht, French Communist Party Secy. Gen. Waldeck Rochet and Italian Communist Party Secy. Gen. Luigi Longo.

Gomulka, rejecting West Germany's recent attempts at diplomatic penetration of eastern Europe, proposed Apr. 25 that all the nations of Europe sign a treaty in which they would renounce force and pledge noninterference in one another's affairs. Kadar, however, held out the possibility of diplomatic relations with West Germany based on the "principles of peaceful coexistence."

Observers, including some Communists, agreed that in view of the Rumanian and Yugoslav boycott, the conference's major accomplishment was that it had been held at all. The wording of the declaration was viewed as vague and intended to allow different interpretations of its meaning. Communist sources confirmed that behind-the-scene talks had gone on at Karlovy Vary on world Communist unity but that a clear agreement on the question could not be reached.

Preparatory talks on the convening of the conference had been held in Warsaw Feb. 22-26. These talks, during which several European Communist parties set the agenda and drew up draft proposals for the April meeting, were boycotted by the Netherlands, Norwegian, Icelandic, Swedish, Rumanian, Yugoslav and Albanian parties. Luigi Longo of Italy was credited with having kept the Chinese question from both agendas.

East German Party Congress

First Secy. Walter Ulbricht opened the East Germany's 7th Socialist Unity (Communist) Party Congress in East Berlin Apr. 17 and proposed that the heads of government in East and West Germany meet and "negotiate an understanding between the 2 German states." His move followed initiatives Apr. 12 by Chancellor Kurt-Georg Kiesinger and Foreign Min. Willy Brandt of West Germany, together with Brandt's Social Democratic Party, for expanded social and economic cooperation with East Germany.

(2 months before the congress, the East German
Volkskammer Feb. 20 had unanimously passed a bill creating a
new and separate East German "nationality." Under the new
law, all persons residing on East German territory Oct. 17,
1949, when the regime took formal shape, "are citizens of the
G[erman] D[emocratic] R[epublic], no matter where they reside
at present." The law thus conferred East German citizenship on
millons of persons who had fled to West Germany since then.
Lt. Col. Friedrich Dickel, East German interior minister, said
when introducing the legislation that it was aimed at the
"revenge-seeking" West German government and would serve
to blunt Bonn's efforts to liquidate East Germany by the
Federal Republic's pan-German citizenship law.)

At the congress' closing session Apr. 22, party members
reelected Ulbricht to a new term as first secretary of the party
Central Committee and also reelected 2d Secy. Erich Honecker
and all other members of the party Politburo. The scientist
Klaus Fuchs, who had spent 9 years in a British prison for
espionage, was elected to the Central Committee.

The party members also approved this declaration on
German reunification: "The government of the GDR is and
will in future be ready to seek for ways toward a detente,
toward disarmament and toward the normalization of relations
between the 2 German states in factual negotiations, on a basis
of equality, with the government of the West German Federal
Republic."

Soviet Communist Party General Secy. Brezhnev,
addressing the congress Apr. 18, expressed skepticism
regarding Bonn's overtures for closer ties with eastern Europe.
He charged Bonn with harboring "the bacilli of the brown
plague" of Nazism, but he declared that "we Communists in no
way hold the opinion that ... [West Germany] is forever to be
branded with the mark of Cain."

Brezhnev also called for Communist unity and the
convening of a world conference of Communist parties to
assure such unity. Although he said that it was "now time to
consider concrete questions of preparation of this conference,"
he did not suggest a deadline or site for the meeting and spoke
only in general terms of the proposed conference's agenda.

(The proposed meeting was known to be opposed by the Chinese, Rumanian, Yugoslav, Albanian and Cuban Communist parties. Rejecting Brezhnev's appeal for unity talks, the Chinese Communist Party newspaper *Jenmin Jih Pao* editorialized Apr. 30: "Let us tell the Moscow gentlemen sternly: Under no circumstances will we take 'united action' with you who are a pack of rank traitors.")

Bolshevik Revolution Commemorated, World Meeting Planned

Moscow celebrations Nov. 3-7 of the 50th anniversary of the Bolshevik Revolution served as a forum for informal talks on world Communist unity among representatives of attending Communist parties.

A major purpose of the discussions was to set a date in 1968 for a "preparatory" meeting paving the way to a full-scale world Communist conference. Communist sources pointed out, however, that opposition from several ruling parties had blocked agreement on a date. Ruling parties that opposed such a conference included those of China, Albania, Rumania and Yugoslavia. The USSR wanted the conference as a mechanism for reading China out of the world Communist movement or, at the least, for condemning China for refusing to cooperate with other Communist parties. Countries supporting the holding of a conference included Bulgaria, Czechoslovakia, East Germany, Hungary, Mongolia, Poland and the Soviet Union.

YUGOSLAVIA

Mihajlov Convicted

A Belgrade district court Apr. 19 convicted writer Mihajlo Mihajlov, 33, and sentenced him to 4½ years in prison for publishing "hostile propaganda" abroad and disseminating antiregime literature. The court also banned Mihajlov from all public activity, including publishing his writings, for 4 years after his release from prison.

The charges against Mihajlov related (1) to his publication, in the U.S., Austria and Switzerland, of 3 articles in which he had argued for creation of a Yugoslav opposition party and press on the grounds that political liberalization could not come to Yugoslavia as long as the League of Communists held all power; and (2) to his alleged dissemination of emigre leaflets urging creation of an independent Croatian state. Mihajlov had argued during his 2-day trial Apr. 17-18 that he had not approved of the leaflets and had merely passed them on to friends for their comments.

Mihajlov had been sentenced to one year in prison in Sept. 1966 for publishing anti-government articles abroad. The 7 months he had served on that sentence were to be credited toward the new sentence.

Language Controversy

The traditional Serbo-Croatian rivalry flared Mar. 17 when 19 groups of Croatian intellectuals demanded the dissolution of Croatia's linguistic union with Serbia. The Croatian Writers' Association, supported by the Academy of Sciences and 17 other cultural organizations of Croatia, charged federal authorities with favoring Serbian as the official language and relegating Croatian to the status of a provincial dialect. They demanded that the constitution be amended to remedy their grievances. In response, 40 members of the Serbian Writers' Association demanded Mar. 19 that Serbs living in Croatia be allowed to use Serbian and that their children be educated in Serbian. (The Mar. 19 declaration was withheld from publication until Apr. 2, when Serbian Communist party officials consented to its release.)

The 1963 Yugoslav constitution recognized Macedonian, Slovenian and Serbo-Croatian as official languages within the federation. Serbian and Croatian, written respectively in Cyrillic and Latin but considered closely related linguistically, differed only in pronunciation and vocabulary. Among the signatories of the Mar. 17 Croatian declaration were many individuals who had also signed the 1954 Novi Sad Agreement establishing Serbo-Croatian (or Croato-Serbian) as the common name for the 2 variants of the same language.

Both declarations were officially denounced as the work of "a dangerous underground," and reprisals against the initiators were demanded. Meeting separately Mar. 21, the executive committees of the Serbian and Croatian Communist parties branded both sides in the controversy as "nationalist." In several speeches during a tour of the multi-racial region of Kosovo-Metohija Mar. 26-29, Pres. Tito castigated the participants as anti-social and bourgeois elements who wanted to disrupt national unity. But he opposed the use of "Draconian measures" against them.

The Communist League of Croatia Apr. 4 expelled 11 members for openly participating in the dispute. Those expelled included Vlatko Pavletic, chairman of the Croatian writers' union. The author Miroslav Krleza, 74, a close friend of Tito and a signer of the Mar. 17 declaration, resigned as member of the Central Committee of the Communist League of Croatia Apr. 19 in apparent protest against this disciplinary action. The *N.Y. Times* reported Aug. 20 that 3 writers—Matija Beckovic, Brana Crncevic and Dusan Radovic—had been barred from working for Yugoslav radio and TV on charges of helping the U.S. Central Intelligence Agency influence Yugoslav radio and TV. The writers denied the charge, and the *Times* indicated that they were blacklisted for siding with the Croatian intellectuals in the language dispute.

UNREST AMONG INTELLECTUALS

Czechoslovakia

The 4th Congress of the Czechoslovak Writers' Union, held in Prague June 27-29, served as a forum for speeches in which the Communist Party's domestic and foreign policies were criticized and its traditional control over literary activity questioned. The congress was attended by about 500 delegates and a high-ranking party and government delegation led by Communist Party Secy. Jiri Hendrych, a member of the Party Presidium, and by Culture & Information Min. Karel Hoffmann.

The congress June 29 adopted a resolution urging that: (a) literary censorship be restricted to matters of state security; (b) the Press Law be amended to allow authors to defend themselves in person rather than through their respective institutions; (c) closer contacts be established with Czechoslovak writers living abroad, provided that their "activity is not directed against the [Czechoslovak] state."

Kulturni tvorba, the Czechoslovak Communist Party Central Committee weekly, charged in an editorial July 6 that Ludvik Vaculik, Vaclav Havel and Pavel Kohout—3 young writers said to have made critical speeches at the congress—had introduced "politicking" and endangered the congress by "demagogy and anarchism." (According to newspaper reports, a dispute had taken place June 27 between Vaculik, 31, and Hendrych. Vaculik was said to have questioned the competence of the party leadership on the meaning of "true socialism.") *Kulturni tvorba* also said July 6 that a number of delegates who had "misused freedom of expression" had not been elected to the 45-member Central Committee of the union. The official organ of the Slovak Writers' Union, *Kulturny zivot,* stated July 14, however, that the list of candidates "passed the vote in its totality without any changes."

Among highlights of the proceedings:

● Kohout June 27 denounced the government's anti-Israel policy. He said: "A country as small as Israel cannot defend itself otherwise than offensively."

● Kohout June 27 read Aleksandr Solzhenitsyn's letter to the Soviet writers' congress, held in May (the letter was published in the *N.Y. Times* June 5). In the letter, Solzhenitsyn had demanded the abolition of censorship in the Soviet Union.

● The more outspoken delegates were criticized in a letter signed by a group of writers considered loyal to the regime and addressed to the union's Central Committee. The letter was read to the congress June 28.

The party's view of the congress was summed up June 29 in a speech in which Hendrych attacked the "liberals" for their "demand of freedom for hostile views." Serving notice that the party intended to remain as the nation's guiding spirit, Hendrych warned the writers not to yield to "ideological and political infiltration from capitalist countries." In response, Jan Prochazka, a Czech scenarist, defended the writer's prerogative "to express his thoughts" against all official "doctrines and dogmas." He asserted that the congress delegates were "on the side of all those ... who struggle against oppression, persecution, the poison of racism and of anti-Semitism, against chauvinism and narrow-minded nationalism."

Speaking to the graduates of the Party College in Prague June 30, Czechoslovak Pres. Antonin Novotny attacked the writers who had spoken out against past party policy. He rejected their view that the party had gone through a "2d dark age in the recent past." He stressed that the concept of class struggle would not be abandoned and warned the writers that a "3d force" would not be tolerated.

The London *Sunday Times* reported Sept. 3 that more than 300 Czechoslovak writers, artists, scientists and other intellectuals had issued a 1,000-word "writers' manifesto" accusing the Czechoslovak Communist Party of "a witchhunt of a pronounced fascist character" against "the entire Czechoslovak writers' community." (Some American journalists doubted the document's authenticity.) The author of the "manifesto" asserted that party representatives had "expressly ordered the crossing-off at first of 12 and later of 4 of the names of the most courageous colleagues from the list of candidates" for the writers' union's Central Committee. These blacklisted candidates, the manifesto's author charged, had been "put under police surveillance and prohibited from publishing their work" and were "being subjected to persecution." In the manifesto it was reported that the writers' congress had "appealed against anti-Semitism and racism in the official policies of our state in its relationship to Israel." The author called on the "public and writers of the entire free and democratic world" to protest against the repressions in Czechoslovakia. The author addressed this plea "especially [to] ... Western intellectuals who are still subject to dangerous illusions about democracy and freedom in the Socialist countries, who protest against American massacres in Vietnam ... against racism in the United States and tend to overlook what happens there where you are pinning your hopes."

The Prague Municipal Court July 15 sentenced 2 Czechoslovak writers, one a U.S. citizen, on subversive charges. Jan Benes, 31, a dramatist, was given a term of 5 years' imprisonment for "subversive activities against the [Czechoslovak] Republic, speculation and fraud." Pavel Tigrid, 49, a journalist, was tried *in absentia* and sentenced to 14 years in prison for sedition and espionage. Tigrid, a U.S. citizen since 1959 and an editor of an emigre Czech periodical, was said to have been living in Paris at the time of the trial. The court acquitted Karel Zamecnik, 27, a student at the Prague Motion Picture Academy, of charges of having "damaged the interests of the [Czechoslovak] Republic abroad."

The Czechoslovak delegation to the international congress of the PEN Club, held in Abidjan, Ivory Coast July 31, supported a resolution calling for the release of a number of imprisoned writers, including Benes.

It was announced Aug. 16 that Ladislav Mnacko, 48, a Czechoslovak author and journalist, had been deprived of his citizenship and state awards and had been expelled from the Communist Party for his open criticism of Czechoslovakia's support of the Arabs in the Middle East conflict. Defying a travel ban, Mnacko had gone to Israel Aug. 10 to demonstrate his disagreement of his government's anti-Israel policy. Mnacko, not a Jew, had denounced anti-Semitism in Czechoslovakia before he left for Israel. Commenting on Czechoslovak charges that he was a political adventurer and anarchist, Mnacko retorted in Tel Aviv Aug. 16 that: "I would rather be a political adventurer and an anarchist than a publicist who takes orders from above." He said, however, that he would "not stop being a Communist," and that he would return to Czechoslovakia to fight his case.

The Communist Party Central Committee, cracking down on Czechoslovakia's rebellious writers announced Sept. 27 that Jan Prochazka had been removed as a candidate member of the committee and that 3 writers had lost their Party membership. The expelled writers: Ludvik Vaculik, 41, Antonin J. Liehm, 41, and Ivan Klima. The Writers Union journal *Literarni noviny (Literary News)* was transferred to the Culture & Information Ministry and its 17 editorial members dismissed after they refused to work under the new publisher, Culture Min. Karel Hoffmann, 45, a former teacher. Liberals dubbed later issues put out under the culture minister's direction "The Tales of Hoffmann."

Soviet Intellectuals Sentenced

3 Soviet intellectuals, Vladimir Bukovsky, 26, Yevgeny Kushchev, 20, and Vadim Delone, 20, were convicted and sentenced in Moscow Sept. 1 on charges of staging an illegal demonstration Jan. 22. Bukovsky, a biologist, who alone pleaded guilty, received the maximum penalty of 3 years' imprisonment. Kushchev and Delone, both students and poets, were given one-year suspended sentences. Although Soviet authorities said the trial was open, officials and a group of burly men barred foreign newsmen from the court, and no official information on the proceedings was made public.

The Jan. 22 demonstration, by about 50 youths, had been broken up almost before it started. The demonstration was in protest against the arrest of several editors of the underground, typewritten journal *Phoenix 1966* and against Article 70 of the Federal Criminal Code, which provided for long prison terms (up to 10 years) for "anti-Soviet agitation and propaganda." The editors arrested included Yuri Galanskov, Vera Lashkova, Aleksandr Ginsburg and Aleksei Dobrovolsky. *Phoenix 1966* had defended the imprisoned Soviet writers Andrei Sinyavsky and Yuli Daniel.

The trial attracted international attention. Amnesty International, an organization created to aid political prisoners, had said Aug. 30 that it had asked the 800 members of its Postcards-for-Prisoners branch to protest to the Soviet government against the trial. Amnesty revealed that Bukovsky had been arrested on 2 previous occasions and had been sent to a mental institution. British novelist Graham Greene revealed in a letter to the London *Times* Sept. 4 that he had asked the Soviet government to turn over his royalties, seized by Soviet authorities, to the wives of Sinyavsky and Daniel.

4 Soviet intellectuals were reported to have been convicted of treason and sentenced to prison terms ranging from 8 to 15 years in Leningrad late in November. According to the Dec. 22 *N.Y. Times,* the 4, who had been arrested in March as part of a group of 25 to 40 plotters, were charged with acts of "conspiracy for the purpose of seizing power." The unconfirmed reports identified only a Prof. Ogurtsov, a specialist in Tibetan studies at Leningrad University, sentenced to 15 years, and Yevgeny Vagin, a literary editor, who had

received 13 years. The other 2 were not identified. The plotters were said to have assembled caches of small arms as part of a conspiratorial network centered in Leningrad, Sverdlovsk and the Ukraine.

Soviet Art Disputes & Writers' Congress

Communist Party authorities in Moscow closed an art exhibit of abstract and surrealistic works Jan. 22, barely an hour after it had been opened. The brief show exhibited works by 11 Russian painters and was attended by about 500 persons. Party officials gave no reason for closing the show, but Yekaterina Belashova, secretary of the Union of Soviet Artists, issued a warning Jan. 23 to adherents of abstract art not to abandon socialist realism for "empty formalistic exercises."

Aleksandr T. Tvardovsky, editor of *Novy Mir,* came under heavy criticism at a meeting of the secretariat of the Writers' Union for his "one sided" depiction of Soviet society, the Communist Party newspaper *Pravda* reported Mar. 29. The criticism reputedly stemmed from his refusal to discontinue publication of Konstantin Simonov's war memoirs. Simonov's book was believed to have been critical of Stalin's decisions during World War II.

The 4th congress of the Soviet Writers' Union was held in Moscow May 22-27 amid recurring reports of agitation in Soviet artistic circles for tempering of government censorship policies. (It originally was slated for the spring of 1966 but had been postponed, apparently because of the trial of Sinyavsky and Daniel in Feb. 1966 for having smuggled to the West manuscripts judged to be anti-Soviet.) The congress, the first in 6 years, apparently was called to review the official line on the role of literature in portraying Soviet society and to deal with what was termed a "sharp conflict of generations" in Soviet society.

In addition to 500 Writers' Union delegates (representing about 6,500 members), the congress' opening was attended by Communist Party General Secy. Leonid I. Brezhnev, Premier Aleksei N. Kosygin and most Politburo members. Among the foreign visitors attending: C. P. Snow and Pamela Hansford Johnson, his wife, from Britain; Lillian Hellman from the U.S.; Armand Lanoux from France. Absentees noted by observers included Yevgeny Yevtushenko and Ilya Ehrenburg (reported, respectively, to be on visits to Portugal and Italy). Jean-Paul Sartre and Louis Aragon, among other foreign writers, refused to attend in protest against what was described as rigged agenda. It was rumored that the 2 French writers had sought open discussion on the imprisonment of Sinyavsky and Daniel.

The congress was opened by the union's first secretary, Konstantin Fedin, considered a moderate, with the reading of names of members who had died since the 3d congress in 1959. The reading of the list, accompanied by a minute's silence, was considered a semipolitical move; among the names was that of Boris Pasternak, expelled from the union in 1958 after he received the Nobel Prize for his novel *Dr. Zhivago.*

The congress was generally considered to have avoided the issues currently stirring Soviet literary circles. Representative of its tone was an address May 25 in which author Mikhail Sholokhov rebuffed demands for more freedom of the press by quoting Lenin's dictum on the subject: ... What freedom of the press? For whom? For what class? ... We laugh at 'pure' democracy." He called writers who were "hungry for 'freedom'" a danger to Soviet youth.

The congress elected a 79-member Presidium believed to have been made up of writers representing reputedly orthodox (neo-Stalinist) and revisionist (moderate) factions among the Soviet writers. The congress concluded May 27 with the election of a new Writers' Union Secretariat noted for the inclusion of Boris Polevoi and Aleksandr Tvardovsky—editors, respectively, of *Yunost* and *Novy Mir,* considered among the USSR's outspoken "revisionist" publications.

In a letter to the congress, published June 5 in the *N.Y. Times,* Aleksandr I. Solzhenitsyn, known best for his prison-camp novel *One Day in the Life of Ivan Denisovich,* denounced "oppression" by the USSR's system of censorship and demanded its abolition. He argued that censorship was a "survival of the Middle Ages ... illegal [and] unprovided for by the [Soviet] constitution." Western correspondents reported June 9 that a petition, signed by 79 Soviet writers, had been sent to the congress supporting Solzhenitsyn's letter and deploring the failure of the congress to take up the issue. According to unconfirmed reports June 21, the Writers' Union made a gesture toward Solzhenitsyn by returning the manuscript of his confiscated novel *The First Circle* and offering to publish another novel, *The Cancer Ward.* But a London *Times* report said Sept. 24 that Solzhenitsyn had been accused of anti-Soviet propaganda in *One Day in the Life of Ivan Denisovich,* published in the Soviet Union in 1962. The accusation reportedly was made at a Writers' Union meeting Sept. 22, called to deal with the charges contained in his letter to the congress.

The Young Communist League newspaper *Komsomolskaya Pravda* June 30 assailed theatrical censorship officials for incompetence and described them as people who "worry more about safeguarding their bureaucratic careers than about the welfare of the theater." The paper declared that the staging of plays should be decided solely by directors, actors and audiences. The authors of the article—Fyodor Burlatsky, a political analyst, and Lev Karpinsky, a theater critic—later were said to have been reprimanded, and the editor responsible for release of the article was reported to have been dismissed.

Poet Andrei A. Voznesensky, in an appearance July 2 at Moscow's avant-garde Taganka Theater, declared that the modern world wanted and needed the "naked truth." His denunciation of censorship came at the end of a poetry reading session and was greeted with flowers and stormy applause, according to a report in the *N.Y. Times.* It was his first public appearance since a planned trip to New York had been granted and then canceled by Soviet authorities 3 times. Voznesensky was to have read his poetry at an arts festival at Lincoln Center in New York June 21. The *Times* published a letter Aug. 11 in which Voznesensky assailed Soviet literary leaders as "boors" and "chameleons" who were guilty of "lying and total lack of scruples" in their effort to keep him from going to New York. The letter, said to have been sent to *Pravda* June 22, ended: "I am ashamed to be a member of the same union as these people."

DEFECTIONS

Svetlana Alliluyeva Flees to U.S.

Svetlana Iosifovna Alliluyeva, 42, the only daughter of the late Marshal Joseph Stalin and his last surviving child, presented herself at the U.S. embassy in New Delhi, India Mar. 6 and requested U.S. asylum. After a 4-day stopover in Rome Mar. 6-11 and a 6-week stay in Switzerland Mar. 11-Apr. 21, she reached New York Apr. 21. She said on her arrival that she had come to the U.S. to "seek the self-expression that has been denied me for so long in Russia."

Mrs. Alliluyeva * came to the U.S. on a visitor's visa that she had obtained at the U.S. embassy in New Delhi Mar. 6. U.S. State Department lawyers pointed out Apr. 21 that, technically speaking, the U.S. had not granted her political asylum. State Department Spokesman Robert J. McCloskey said Apr. 21 that she was "welcome in this country" and was "free to remain as long as she wishes."

Mrs. Alliluyeva had gone to India Dec. 20, 1966 with the ashes of her late husband, Brajesh Singh, 59, who had died in Moscow Oct. 31, 1966. The Soviet government had granted her permission to take the ashes to India for Hindu burial. Mrs. Alliluyeva spent 67 days in India, for the most part at Singh's family home at Kalakankar. While there she became attached to the Indian countryside and customs and expressed a desire to spend the rest of her life in Kalakankar. She discussed this with Indian government officials, but the Indian government was reluctant to grant her asylum for fear of damaging Indian-Soviet relations.

Failing to obtain asylum and coming under increasing pressure from officials of the Soviet embassy in New Delhi to return to the Soviet Union, Mrs. Alliluyeva agreed to return to Moscow on a flight leaving New Delhi Mar. 8. But the evening

* Mrs. Alliluyeva's surname was variously given as Stalina, the feminine form of the pseudonym under which her father was known, and as Alliluyeva, her mother's maiden name and the name she preferred to use.

of Mar. 6 she apparently had a sudden change of mind. While the Soviet embassy staff was engaged in preparations for a visiting delegation, she summoned a taxi and was driven to the U.S. embassy. There she sought the help of U.S. officials in obtaining asylum in either the U.S. or some other country.

(It was reported Apr. 21 that Mrs. Alliluyeva had argued violently with Ivan A. Benediktov, the Soviet ambassador to India, during a luncheon in her honor Mar. 6. According to the reports, Benediktov chided Mrs. Alliluyeva for having adopted the Indian custom of vegetarianism. Mrs. Alliluyeva became infuriated, asked for her passport and said she would take the next flight out of New Delhi for Moscow. Instead she defected to the West.)*

Because of the delicate problems it posed for U.S.-Soviet relations, U.S. officials reacted cautiously to Mrs. Alliluyeva's request for asylum. But they reportedly felt that her desire to quit the Soviet Union was genuine and that she should be helped to the fullest extent possible. It was therefore decided that the U.S. should facilitate her departure from India but that it should not permit her to come directly to the U.S.

On instructions from the State Department, embassy officials in New Delhi issued a U.S. tourist visa to Mrs. Alliluyeva Mar. 6 and made arrangements for her to leave New Delhi for Rome on a commercial flight. (It was explained in Washington later that a U.S. visa was not required for Mrs. Alliluyeva's departure from India but that it would facilitate her entry into Italy.) She was accompanied to Rome by Robert F. Rayle, the only Russian-speaking official at the U.S. embassy in New Delhi. Officials in Washington refused to confirm press reports that Rayle was a CIA officer.

After 4 days' seclusion in Rome Mar. 7-11, Mrs. Alliluyeva, again accompanied by Rayle, took a chartered flight to Geneva Mar. 11. An official Swiss announcement issued shortly after her arrival said that she had requested "a temporary rest stay" in Switzerland and that this request had been granted "in view of the fact that ... she has never been involved in political activity." A Swiss government spokesman said she was

---

* It was reported from Moscow Apr. 11 that Benediktov had been transferred to Yugoslavia, where he succeeded Alexander Puzanov as ambassador. Puzanov was transferred to Bulgaria and replaced Nikolai Organov as ambassador.

expected to remain in Switzerland "a few weeks" under a 3-month tourist visa that Switzerland had issued to her.

Tass, the Soviet news agency, admitted Mar. 12 that Mrs. Alliluyeva was "now abroad." The terse report noted that she had been granted an exit visa in late 1966 in order to go to India to bury the ashes of her late husband. It added that the duration of her stay abroad was "her private affair."

The State Department acknowledged Mar. 14 that Mrs. Alliluyeva had requested asylum in the U.S. Asserting that this request had been "neither denied nor granted," the announcement said that "the principal concern" of the U.S. in the case "was and is essentially humanitarian" and that this concern had been met "for the time being" through the willingness of the Swiss government to permit her to stay in Switzerland. State Department spokesman McCloskey said Mar. 22 that Mrs. Alliluyeva had requested temporary residence in Switzerland because she had "concluded that her motives for being unwilling to return to the Soviet Union or to remain in India might be misunderstood if she were to proceed directly to the U.S." McCloskey said that, "if in time she should decide her interests would be better served by coming to the U.S., her request would be given prompt and appropriate consideration." He added that the U.S. had "communicated" with the Soviet Union on the case.

Swiss Justice Min. Ludwig von Moos disclosed at a news conference Mar. 13 that the Swiss government had assigned a high-ranking Foreign Ministry official to act as Mrs. Alliluyeva's consultant and companion during her stay in Switzerland. A police guard was also directed "to protect her rest." Swiss officials succeeded in maintaining Mrs. Alliluyeva's privacy, although scores of reporters and photographers scoured the countryside in a search for her. It was reported Apr. 24 that she had stayed initially at the ski resort of Beatenberg in the Bernese Oberland but had left after being recognized. She stayed for awhile at a rest home operated by Catholic nuns at St. Antoni, 7 miles from Fribourg in western Switzerland, and, for the last 3 weeks, she lived at a Catholic convent near Fribourg.

While Mrs. Alliluyeva was in Switzerland, a controversy broke out within the Indian government over her alleged efforts to obtain asylum in India. Indian External Affairs Min.

M. C. Chagla stated in the Lok Sabha (lower house of parliament) Mar. 21 that "there was no question of asylum being refused. She never even suggested she wanted to stay in India to anyone during her stay." But R. M. Lohia, leader of the opposition Samyukta (United) Socialist Party, charged that Mrs. Alliluyeva had "said many times she wanted to stay in India. She has told this to me and to several people, ministers and officials. But for fear of Soviet anger she was told to quit."

Lohia presented to the Lok Sabha Mar. 27 a letter that Mrs. Alliluyeva had written to an Indian friend Feb. 10. In the letter she said she was planning to return to Moscow since she had been unable to obtain permission to stay in India. Lohia Apr. 4 made public a letter that Mrs. Alliluyeva had written to him from Switzerland Mar. 23. In it she related that she had discussed with Singh the "possibility for me to stay in India for the rest of my life" but said that Singh had told her it would be impossible "because of the strong opposition from the Soviet government which would inevitably arise."

Chagla reaffirmed his previously-stated position Apr. 5 and added that, if Mrs. Alliluyeva wanted to reside permanently in India, "we will certainly favorably consider it." A motion presented by Lohia charging that Prime Min. Indira Gandhi, Chagla and Singh had deliberately misled the Lok Sabha was defeated by 236—150 vote Apr. 5.

In conjunction with Mrs. Alliluyeva's arrival in the U.S. Apr. 21, it was disclosed that 2 U.S. citizens had offered to assist Mrs. Alliluyeva in counseling her on her decision to come to the U.S. and in making arrangements for the publication of her memoirs. The 2 were George F. Kennan, former U.S. ambassador to the Soviet Union and currently a scholar at Princeton University's Institute for Advanced Studies, and Edward S. Greenbaum, a lawyer, friend of Kennan's and consultant to publishers Harper & Row. Kennan had read a copy of Mrs Alliluyeva's autobiography (sent to him by the State Department), had described it as a remarkable literary achievement and had decided that every effort should be made to spare Mrs. Alliluyeva from either "cold war" or commercial exploitation. Government officials concurred in this decision and made arrangements for Kennan and Greenbaum to meet her in Switzerland. Greenbaum later made arrangements with Harper & Row for publication of the memoirs Oct. 16.

Kennan Apr. 21 issued a statement in which he appealed to the American people to "rise above the outworn reflexes and concepts of the 'cold war'" and to accept Mrs. Alliluyeva on her own terms, as a "courageous, sincere and talented" human being who desired above all "to lead a normal life and pursue in a normal way the literary interests to which she is devoted." "She has no desire to lend herself either to commercial or political exploitation," Kennan said.

Mrs. Alliluyeva, on her arrival in New York Apr. 21, released a statement in which she explained why she had defected from the Soviet Union. Excerpts from the statement, written in English:

"It is important to me to explain something of the reasons why I decided not to return to Russia but to come to the United States instead. I've read some wrong explanations in newspapers and magazines and I don't want to be misunderstood....

"When I left Moscow last December in order to convey the ashes of my late husband, Mr. Brajesh Singh, to his home in India, I fully expected to return to Russia within one month's time. However, during my stay in India I decided that I could not return to Moscow. It was my own decision, based on my own feelings and experiences, without anyone's advice or help or instruction. The strongest struggle was going on in my heart all that time because I would have to leave my children and not see them for quite a long time....

"But I felt it impossible to go back and went instead to the United States embassy in New Delhi, hoping for help and understanding. Now ... I have come here in order to seek the self-expression that has been denied me for so long in Russia....

"Since my childhood I have been taught communism, and I did believe in it, as we all did, my generation. But slowly, with age and experience I began to think differently. In recent years, we in Russia have begun to think, to discuss, to argue, and we are not so much automatically devoted any more to the ideas which we were taught.

"Also religion has done a lot to change me. I was brought up in a family where there was never any talk about God. But when I became a grown-up person I found that it was impossible to exist without God in one's heart.... Since that moment the main dogmas of communism lost their significance for me.

"I do believe in the power of intellect in the world, no matter in which country you live.... This is the only thing which I can take seriously—the work of teachers, scientists, educated priests, doctors, lawyers, their work all over the world, notwithstanding states and borders, political parties and ideologies. There are no capitalists and Communists for me, there are good people, or bad people, honest or dishonest, and in whatever country they live people are the same everywhere, and their best expectations and moral ideals are the same.... Although I've lived all my life in Moscow, I believe that one's home can be anywhere that one can feel free.

"My late husband ... belonged to an ancient family of India.... Unfortunately the Soviet authorities refused to recognize our marriage officially because he was a foreigner and I, because of my name, was considered as a kind of state property. Even the question of whether I should be allowed to marry a citizen of India was decided by the party and the government. Moreover, we could not travel together to see his homeland, or anywhere else outside of Russia. Mr. Singh had suffered for many years from a chronic illness. Despite my entreaties the government refused to allow me to take him to India, his homeland, before he died. After he died the government finally allowed me to take his ashes home.... My husband's death brought my long repressed feelings about my life to the surface. I felt it impossible to be silent and tolerant any more.

"... 3 years ago I wrote a book about my life in Russia.... Now it will be published in English and Russian, as well as other languages.... I hope that my book will explain more fully than I can in these brief remarks what I felt and what I wanted to, but could not, say while in Russia. The publication of my book will symbolize for me the main purpose of my journey here. The freedom of self-expression which I seek can, I hope, take the form of additional writing, study and reading on the literary subjects in which I am most interested....

"Despite the strong motives and deep desires which have led me to the United States, I cannot forget that my children are in Moscow. But I know they will understand me and what I have done. They also belong to the new generation in our country, which does not want to be fooled by old ideas. They also want to make their own conclusions about life. Let God help them. I know they will not reject me and one day we shall meet...."

Mrs. Alliluyeva had grown up in the secrecy surrounding the Kremlin and little was known of her life. She was born in 1925 to Joseph Stalin and Stalin's 2d wife, Nadezhda Alliluyeva. She had 2 brothers, Yakov, who died in a Nazi concentration camp during World War II, and Vasily, who was killed in an auto accident in 1962. She was 7 when her mother died under mysterious circumstances in 1932; the cause of death was officially given as acute appendicitis, but it was widely believed that she had either been shot by Stalin himself during a quarrel or had committed suicide in protest against the repressiveness of the Stalinist regime.

Mrs. Alliluyeva studied poetry and literature at Moscow State University. While there, at the age of 17, she met and married a fellow student, Grigory Morozov, by whom she had a son, Joseph, currently 21, married and a medical student in Moscow. She later divorced Morozov, reportedly on Stalin's orders. A 2d marriage to Yuri Zhdanov, son of Andrie A. Zhdanov, a leading figure in the Kremlin ruling clique, also ended in divorce; by this marriage she had a daughter, Yekaterina, currently 17 and living with her brother in Moscow. There were unconfirmed reports of other marriages.

After Stalin's death, Mrs. Alliluyeva began to associate with Soviet writers. She taught courses in literature at Moscow State University and later worked as an English translator at the Foreign Languages Publishing House in Moscow. In 1964 she met and married Brajesh Singh, an Indian Communist who was working in Moscow as a Hindi translator. Singh's death in Oct. 1966 precipitated the series of events that led to Mrs. Alliluyeva's defection from the Soviet Union Mar. 6, 1967.

Mrs. Alliluyeva declared at a news conference in New York Apr. 26 that, while she disapproved of many of Stalin's actions, "many other people who still are in our Central Committee and Politburo should be responsible for the same things for which he alone was accused." She said that if she herself felt "somewhat responsible for those horrible things, killing people unjustly, ... [the] responsibility for this was and is the party's, the regime and the ideology as a whole."

Mrs. Alliluyeva, said she had agreed to hold the news conference so that, "after answering all the questions I will have peace and finally will get the quiet life for which I have come here...." Among her other comments, delivered in English: She had joined the Communist Party 20 years ago and had believed in communism, "as everybody, all my friends and people of my generation did." But she became critical as she grew older and began to compare what she had been taught with the "many things which I could see around me ... in our country and in other Socialist countries.... It was not exactly what we were taught theoretically." Her father's death in 1953 had been a contributing factor, "because he was also for me the authority ... and when he was gone I have lost maybe a lot of faith." In the last 15 years "perhaps everybody in our country, especially [the] youngest generation, and also my generation ... became more critical because we perhaps were more free to think and to discuss and to judge about things and events."

Asked what tenets of communism had lost their meaning for her, Mrs. Alliluyeva said that, in the century of the atomic bomb and space flights, "the idea of class revolution which can bring people to progress has lost its significance." She asserted that progress "should be reached by the work of humanity, ... notwithstanding which classes are involved in this work."

Mrs. Alliluyeva said that the death of her husband, Brajesh Singh, in Oct. 1966 was the most important single factor in the events leading to her defection. Since the Soviet government had not recognized their marriage and had not allowed them to return to India after Singh had fallen ill, "his death [in Moscow] ... made me absolutely intolerant to the things to which I was rather tolerant before," she said.

Mrs. Alliluyeva disclosed that she had been baptized in 1962 into the Russian Orthodox Church, "to which my parents and my ancestors belonged." But she said her baptism did not mean that she preferred the Russian Orthodox faith to others, since "different religions are only the different ways to the same God." She said her religious faith was grounded in the belief that "humanity should be one, that mankind should not be divided, that there should be less struggle."

Referring to the situation of the Jews in the Soviet Union, Mrs. Alliluyeva said she knew from personal experience that talented Jewish candidates to the universities and institutes were sometimes passed over in favor of persons of other nationalities who were less talented.

In answer to a question about the rumored assassination of Stalin in 1953, Mrs. Alliluyeva said that, to her, it was "quite evident that he was sick and ... [that] his death was the natural result of illness, nothing else."

Mrs. Alliluyeva said she planned to devote her time to writing, something which would "never be possible for me in the Soviet Union." She referred to the 2 Soviet writers, Andrei Sinyavsky and Yuli Daniel, who had been sentenced in Feb. 1966 to prison at hard labor for publishing "anti-Soviet" works abroad. She said the trial had produced a "horrible impression" on all Russian intellectuals and had caused her to "absolutely disbelieve in justice." From that moment on, she said, "I lost the hopes which I had before that ... we are going to become liberal somehow."

Asked if she intended to take up permanent residence in the U.S., Mrs. Alliluyeva said that "before the marriage it should be love. So, if I will love this country and this country will love me, then the marriage will be settled. But I cannot say now." She said she planned to live "without any political activities" and wished "to preach neither for communism, neither against it."

East German Escapes

3 members of a group of 4 East Germans escaped safely through Czechoslovakia to Austria by swimming across the March River Aug. 27. The 4th, Richard Albert Schlenz, 28, of Leipzig, was killed by a Czechoslovak bullet when already on Austrian soil, Austrian officials charged after an investigation.

Austria Aug. 30 lodged a sharp complaint with the Czechoslovak government again protesting the continued shooting incidents along the border. (The Aug. 30 note followed an earlier protest over a similar shooting Aug. 13 when a Czechoslovak family of 8 crossed the Austrian border near Gmund. All but a boy of 12, who had been captured by Czechoslovak guards, reached Austrian territory under heavy

fire in which several members of the family had been injured.)
In the Aug. 30 note the Austrian Foreign Ministry charged
that the Czechoslovak guards had fired into the Austrian side in
their effort to foil the attempt to flee to the West. The note said
that "under no circumstances can we tolerate killing of this sort
on Austrian territory."

2 East German soldiers, both 21, assigned to patrol duty,
fled to West Germany near Bad Hersfeld Sept. 7 and asked for
asylum.

Other Defections

The U.S. State Department announced May 17 that Janos
Radvanyi, 44, Hungarian charge d'affaires in Washington
since Feb. 1962, had defected to the U.S. and would be granted
political asylum. Radvanyi had requested asylum the previous
day. In a statement issued May 19, Radvanyi gave no reason
for his defection but said that it had become "impossible" for
him to continue to serve the Budapest regime. Radvanyi met
with 2 special Hungarian envoys May 20 to confirm his
decision to defect.

The State Department May 31 announced that Erno
Bernat, 33, 3d secretary in charge of press affairs at the
Hungarian embassy since Aug. 1965, had defected Apr. 21 with
his wife, 3 sons and mother-in-law. The *N.Y. Times* reported
June 1 that Bernat had held the rank of major in the
Hungarian Interior Ministry's State Security Department.

U.S. authorities in West Germany reported June 2 that
Soviet Air Force Lt. Vasily Ilyich Epatko had requested and
been given asylum in the U.S. Epatko, 25, had crash landed his
MiG-17 aircraft May 25 in Hochstadt, West Germany. No
reason was given for his defection.

1968

After 1953 and 1956, the year 1968 provided a 3d climax of dissension in the Soviet bloc. The crisis was precipitated by developments in Czechoslovakia, where the low incidence of open dissent prior to 1967 had created the deceptive impression of widespread conformism. In the opposition movement against the Novotny regime, 3 trends successively merged: (1) the nationalist aspirations of the Slovaks, who resented their alleged treatment as a "2d-rate" people in the country; (2) the desire of intellectuals for the "modernization" of the Marxist doctrine, and (3) the democratic traditions of the Czechs, nourished by memories of their prewar state.

The process of political change began as a struggle of factions within the Communist Party, which led to the replacement of the Czech Novotny by the Slovak Alexander Dubcek as first secretary in January and the announcement of a democratization program in April. The official revelations of scandalous abuses and repressions in the 1950s and during the Novotny era discredited the Communist Party. But the extent of its self-criticism, promoted by intellectuals devoted to the "humanization" of Marxism, convinced the majority of the people that the new leadership wanted radical reforms. These were widely understood as departures from communism—in substance, if not in theory. Such an impression was reinforced by the abolition of censorship and the proposed changes of laws and of party statutes, which would have guaranteed the right of dissent, thus breaking the ideological monopoly of the ruling oligarchy.

Dubcek's resistance to the Soviet-instigated efforts to slow down the democratization process earned him immense popularity. The Czechoslovak government, upholding its right to shape domestic policies without outside interference, received diplomatic support from Tito's Yugoslavia and Nicolae

Ceausescu's Rumania. Dubcek and his colleagues held firm in confrontations with the Soviet and other Warsaw Pact representatives at Cierna and Bratislava in July and August.

During the confrontations, the Soviet leadership became convinced that the new Czechoslovak regime was unable or unwilling to control the democratization trend, which appeared to have acquired a momentum of its own. Moscow's decision to intervene by military force was a result of several factors: first, concern about the adverse effects of the Czechoslovak developments on the European balance of power; 2d, fears that the Czechoslovak example might encourage anti-Russian nationalism in other parts of eastern Europe, notably in the Ukraine; and finally, irritation at the "new" type of Marxism that the Czechoslovak ideologists were expounding with missionary zeal.

The Aug. 21 invasion of Czechoslovakia by the armed forces of the Soviet Union, Poland, East Germany, Hungary and Bulgaria encountered almost unanimous hostility on the part of the population. The widespread nonviolent resistance did not prevent the invading forces from achieving their military objective, but it forestalled the installation of a collaborationist regime such as Moscow had planned.

Despite appearances of officially sponsored resistance, the invasion had caught the Czechoslovak leaders by surprise. They had not been prepared to appeal to the people and the armed forces to deter a possible invasion, and, once the intervention came, it was too late for such actions. In dramatic negotiations with the Soviet leaders in Moscow, Dubcek and his colleagues failed to exact any significant concessions. The Russians, at first, refrained from measures against dissent except for the restoration of censorship. Short of military rule, systematic repression was impossible because of the disintegration of the Czechoslovak party apparatus. In this situation, defiance of the invaders continued, culminating in anti-Soviet demonstrations in October and November.

The intervention in Czechoslovakia widened the split between pro-Soviet East Germany, Poland, Bulgaria and Hungary on the one hand, and the independent-minded Yugoslavia and Rumania on the other. Rumors about the imminent Soviet invasion of these 2 countries led to a quick entente between them and to conspicuous preparations for military and civilian defense. In East Germany, in Hungary and in the Soviet Union itself, groups of dissidents voiced strong sympathy for Czechoslovakia. By the end of 1968, the goal of the intervention, which was to arrest further decline of Soviet power in eastern Europe, appeared elusive.

Manifestations of youthful unrest, which the countries of eastern Europe shared with the advanced nations of the West, complicated the problem of dissent. The influence of the New Left was a decisive factor in the student demonstrations in Belgrade in June, in the disruptions at the Sofia festival in July and August and perhaps in the protests by the sons and daughters of high East German Party officials against the intervention in Czechoslovakia. In contrast, the Polish students demonstrating in March and the Czechoslovak youths resisting the Soviet invaders dissociated themselves from the elitism of the New Left. They seemed to favor a merger of Western ideals of political freedom and economic and social tenets of democratic socialism.

REFORM MOVEMENT IN CZECHOSLOVAKIA

Dubcek Replaces Novotny

Alexander Dubcek, 46, was elected Jan. 5 to succeed Antonin Novotny as first secretary of the Communist Party. Novotny was forced to resign Mar. 22 as president of Czechoslovakia, his last post, which was largely a ceremonial one. Announcing Novotny's resignation, in a communique issued by the Communist Party presidium, the new leadership, however, warned that tendencies threatening the regime "in the guise of democracy" would not be tolerated. It also expressed continuing friendship with the Soviet Union.

Novotny's departure was viewed as marking the end of a 20-year regime widely described as representing Stalinism, resistance to economic reform, tight control over writers and other intellectuals, inferior status for the Slovaks and uncritical devotion to the Soviet Union. Novotny's ouster followed mounting popular pressure against him throughout the country. There were demands, supported by news media already freed from effective censorship, for a revival of the country's democratic traditions by a new generation of Communists, intellectuals and students and a basic reevaluation of the country's political and economic direction.

Demands for the increasing democratization of life and economic reform were believed to have been led by Dubcek. Speaking at a conference in Brno Mar. 16, Dubcek had promised the "widest possible democratization" for the country. He also confirmed that the new leadership would present its political and economic "action program" at the full meeting of the Central Committee, scheduled for Mar. 28. Dubcek, stressing that there would be "cadre changes" in the party to "bring in new people who can carry out the new policies," pledged greater autonomy for the government, the courts, the trade unions and economic enterprises. Referring to foreign policy, he reaffirmed the continuation of "progressive tradition of cooperation" with the Soviet Union but hinted that with greater independence the country would be in a better position "to express its own standpoint" and play a greater role "in the center of Europe ... as an industrialized nation."

It had been disclosed in Prague Mar. 5 that Jiri Hendrych had been dismissed from his post as Communist Party secretary for ideological affairs. A close friend of Novotny's, he was regarded as a firm opponent of liberal ideas. The decision to replace Hendrych was made at the Mar. 4 meeting of the 15-member presidium, which also recommended the transfer of censorship officials from the Interior Ministry to the Culture Ministry and the denial to the censors of their authority to direct the ideological line of the news media.

The Communist Party unit of the Central Publications (censorship) Board Mar. 15 (a) urged an end to secrecy, (b) asked for the abolition of "preventive [prepublication] censorship ... at the present rate of development" and (c) recommended that censorship practices be standardized and the right of appeal be upheld and investigated.

The presidium of the Czechoslovak Communist Party announced Mar. 22 a rehabilitation program involving about 30,000 victims of Stalinism. (The Czechoslovak news agency CTK reported that Novotny's last act as president had been the granting of a pardon to Jan Benes, the author, who had been sentenced in July 1967 to 5 years in prison for "subversion of the republic.")

Informed sources in Prague said Mar. 22 that Soviet Premier Aleksei N. Kosygin had promised not to interfere with the ouster of Novotny. The pledge had been made in Moscow to visiting Czechoslovak officials. They in turn pledged to Kosygin that the current wave of liberalization would not prejudice continued military, political and economic cooperation between Czechoslovakia and the USSR.

The Czechoslovak Communist Party Apr. 9 published its long-awaited "action program" as a basis for reform. The program had been adopted Apr. 5, after it had been debated and amended for a week by the Central Committee. A resolution accompanying the document said its purpose was to purify communism of its "former aberrations" and to "build socialism in this country in a way corresponding to our conditions and traditions."

Repercussions in Soviet Bloc

Party figures of most east European Communist states held a reportedly hastily convened summit meeting Mar. 23 in Dresden, where Dubcek was called on to explain the changes that had taken place in Czechoslovakia since Novotny's ouster.

Participating in the conference were: East German Socialist Unity Party First Secy. Walter Ulbricht, Polish United Workers' Party First Secy. Wladyslaw Gomulka, Soviet Communist Party General Secy. Leonid I. Brezhnev and Premier Kosygin, and Hungarian Socialist Workers' Party First Secy. Janos Kadar. The Bulgarian Communist Party was represented by Stanko Todorov, member of the politburo and secretary of the central committee. Rumania was not represented at the meeting, apparently because of its proclaimed policy of non-interference in the affairs of other Communist parties.

In a communique issued at the end of the conference Mar. 23 the party figures expressed "confidence ... that the proletariat and all working people of Czechoslovakia, under the leadership of the Communist Party, ... would insure further progress of Socialist construction in the country." (This and other passages of the communique were not mentioned in the

Czechoslovak press and TV. The omission was seen by observers as an attempt to avoid protest against the Dresden talks.)

Czechoslovak sources indicated Mar. 23 that the conference had been called by East Germany and Poland in an effort to forestall closer ties between Czechoslovakia and West Germany and to exert pressure on Dubcek to suppress demands for more liberalization. In an interview with CTK, Dubcek confirmed Mar. 26 that "certain worries were expressed at the meeting, mainly to the effect that anti-Socialist elements would take advantage of the democratization process." Dubcek gave the interview after 134 writers and artists had written to the Communist Party presidium about their concern over pressure put on Czechoslovakia by its Communist allies. The letter held that "the communique of the Dresden meeting gave the impression that if we paid heed to other countries it could influence our own development."

In an unusual development between countries of Communist eastern Europe, the Czechoslovak government Mar. 27 protested formally to East Germany over the latter's alleged interference in Czechoslovakia's internal affairs. The protest was against quasi-official criticism of Czechoslovak developments voiced by Prof. Kurt Hager, chairman of the East German Socialist Unity Party presidium's ideological commission, at a congress of Marxist philosophers in East Berlin Mar. 25. Hager charged that events in Czechoslovakia were "in accord with West Germany's alleged policy of trying to 'isolate Czechoslovakia' from East Germany." (Hager reinforced his criticism Mar. 26 with a speech in which he attacked, by name, the then Czechoslovak forestry minister, Josef Smrkovsky, for publicly supporting democratization.)

Commenting on the charge made by Hager, *Rude pravo,* official newspaper of the Czechoslovak Communist Party, declared in a Mar. 27 editorial that there was no reason why the 2 countries should have the same foreign policy toward West Germany. The paper also complained that the Soviet Union and other Communist countries failed to give adequate coverage of Czechoslovak events to their readers. The paper assailed their treatment of Czechoslovak liberalization as "one of the old bad habits" of Communist countries. (It had been reported from West Berlin Mar. 23 that several Czechoslovak newspapers had been confiscated in East Berlin by East German authorities and that Prague students visiting East Berlin had been prevented from participating in discussions with East German youth organizations.)

Further grounds for friction between the 2 countries were provided by Czechoslovak Premier Oldrich Cernik when he declared in a speech to the National Assembly in Prague Apr. 24 that Czechoslovakia would recognize the "existing realities" of a divided Germany. "We are basing our policy on the fact of the existence of 2 German states," Cernik asserted. *Lidova democracie,* organ of Czechoslovakia's newly revived (Catholic) People's Party, said Apr. 24: "The time is ripe to start with Bonn on a resumption of diplomatic relations"; "East Germany must understand that we have to follow our own interest."

Dubcek paid a hurried visit to Moscow May 3-5 in order to allay Soviet fears at his liberalization program and to obtain a $500 million long-term loan to bolster his country's economy. Dubcek was accompanied by Premier Cernik, National Assembly Pres. Josef Smrkovsky and Slovak Communist Party First Secy. Vasil Bilak. In a joint statement issued May 5, the 2 sides described the secret talks as "frank and friendly" and added that "opinions were exchanged." Such phrases were usually used in the Soviet press to signify sharp disagreements.

Czechoslovakia Resists Soviet Pressure

The Soviet Union and its 4 conservative east European allies warned Czechoslovakia July 16 that its liberalization drive was "completely unacceptable" and demanded that Prague end it. The "Warsaw [Pact] 5" charged that liberal elements were endangering socialism in Czechoslovakia. The Presidium of the Czechoslovak Communist Party Central Committee replied July 18 that the Soviet fears were unfounded and that the liberalizing actions in Czechoslovakia would strengthen socialism.

The 5 countries' warning was given in a 3,000-word letter drafted at the conclusion of a hastily convoked 2-day summit conference held in Warsaw July 14-15. The meeting was attended by top party and government delegations from the Soviet Union, East Germany, Hungary, Bulgaria and Poland. Czechoslovakia, the focus of attention at the meeting, declined to participate. The Rumanian Communist Party also stayed away.

The letter's signers declared that the 5 powers "do not want to interfere in your affairs or infringe your sovereignty," but it warned that certain forces in Czechoslovakia had "tried to take the country out of the Socialist camp." In particular, the letter singled out a manifesto, "2000 Words," believed written by the novelist Ludvik Vaculik, clearly signed by 70 Czechoslovak intellectuals and supported by the signatures of some 40,000 people across the country. This manifesto, appealing for a speed-up in democratization, was denounced in the letter as a call for anarchy and counter-revolution. The "Warsaw 5" charged that certain Czechoslovak Communist Party leaders not only failed to fight the manifesto but went so far as to defend it. The leaders of the 5 powers asserted that such manifestations were a threat to the vital interests of the whole Socialist community and that, therefore, it was "something more than only your concern." They also noted that there were within Czechoslovakia "healthy forces" capable of defending "the Socialist system and inflicting defeat on the anti-Socialist elements."

The Soviet leadership agreed July 22 that the entire Politburo of the Soviet Communist Party Central Committee would go to Czechoslovakia and confer with the Presidium of the Czechoslovak Communist Party in an attempt to halt what Moscow and its conservative east European allies had called the growing threat of a "counterrevolution" in Czechoslovakia. The USSR also promised that it would remove its troops that had been left in Czechoslovakia, against Czechoslovak wishes, for 3 weeks after the conclusion of Warsaw Pact maneuvers there in June.

Throughout the week prior to the Soviet agreement to the meeting on Czechoslovak soil, a mood of imminent crisis had prevailed in eastern Europe. Moscow July 19 had issued a summons to the Czechoslovak Presidium, demanding that it meet July 22 or 23 with the Soviet Politburo in Moscow, Kiev, or Lvov to discuss internal Czechoslovak developments. The announcement of the Soviet invitation was unusual since Soviet invitations were normally published only after their acceptance.

The Czechoslovak Presidium did not officially consider the Soviet invitation until July 22, when it announced that, although it agreed in principle to hold bilateral talks with fraternal parties, it would not, however, agree to such a meeting outside Czechoslovakia. Unconfirmed reports said that the Czechoslovak leadership had also refused to meet with the Soviet Politburo until the Soviet troops left the country. Although the number of Soviet troops left in Czechoslovakia was not considered significant from a military point of view, their presence was thought to exert a psychological pressure on the Czechoslovak leadership.

To strengthen its hand for the pending negotiations with the Soviets, the progressive faction of the Czechoslovak Presidium July 19 had convened the Central Committee and had won from it a unanimous indorsement of its plans. The convening of the Central Committee was regarded as a dangerous move because the committee's composition was thought to be divided evenly between the conservative (pro-Moscow) and progressive (pro-Dubcek) factions. In a move to assure support for its tough stand in the coming negotiations with the USSR, the Dubcek leadership invited 40 proven reformists, all delegates to an extraordinary party congress scheduled for Sept. 7, to take part in the Central Committee proceedings as non-voting observers. The leadership also lifted some measure of the secrecy usually surrounding Central Committee meetings and permitted private citizens bringing pledges of support for the Presidium's progressive stand to enter the Spanish Hall of the Hradcany Castle, where the committee met. (An effort of the more radical members to allow live broadcast of the session was rejected.)

Dubcek July 18, the day before the Central Committee session, had made a dramatic radio-TV appeal asking the Czechoslovak people to rally behind the progressive leadership. He declared that "All we wish to do is to create a socialism that has not lost its human character." He continued: "We are determined—in this matter we are counting on public support—to continue the [liberalization] policy we adopted.... This policy is desired and backed by the Czech and Slovak nations." "The Communist Party cannot change the masses, but it can change its leadership."

In his opening speech to the committee July 19, Dubcek reiterated that the party leadership was determined to continue its liberalization program. He declared: "We paid too dearly and are still paying for the methods of the past." But he also renewed the pledge that Prague would remain loyal to communism, to the Socialist camp and, in particular, to the Soviet Union. Only Drahomir Kolder, one of 3 conservatives on the by then 11-man Presidium, spoke against an uncompromising stand against the Soviet Union's military and political pressure.

When the question came up for vote, all 88 Central Committee members approved the progressive line. There were no abstentions.

During a July 14 interview with *Al Ahram,* a Cairo daily, Yugoslav Pres. Tito predicted that the Soviet Union would not be so "shortsighted" as to resort to force to halt Czechoslovak liberalization. He said Yugoslavia and Czechoslovakia were strong enough to resist any danger to their political system from the West.

A resolution of the League of Yugoslav Communists Central Committee, passed unanimously July 16 after Tito had received a letter of invitation from Dubcek, stated that it "firmly believes" in Dubcek's reforms. The League's Central Committee rejected "every outside action" against his leadership by other Communist parties.

The Yugoslav Communist party July 18 issued a declaration, which was transmitted to the USSR and the signatories of the Warsaw letter, in which it gave unconditional support to the Czechoslovak reforms and denounced any threat of interference by the other parties. The declaration termed Dubcek's policy a "significant contribution to the general affirmation of the Socialist system." A July 18 article in *Politika,* a Yugoslav daily, criticized the 5-power Warsaw warning as the "Cominform 1968."

An editorial in the Soviet party daily *Pravda* July 22 charged the Czechoslovak leadership with "failure or reluctance" to meet the dangers "created by the right-wing, anti-Socialist forces." "Is there really any need to wait for the counterrevolutionary forces to become masters of the situation ... before starting to struggle against them?" *Pravda* asked. Charging that anti-Communists had "seized the mass media—

the press, radio and television and [were] using them ... to fan hatred of the Soviet Union," *Pravda* insisted that Prague (a) reimpose censorship, (b) ban anti-Communist activities by suppressing right-wing forces and (c) restore Communist Party discipline and control over the country.

Josef Smrkovsky, president of the National Assembly, appealed to the Soviet Union and its hard-line eastern European allies July 22 to respect his country's sovereignty, "which exclude[s] any kind of uncomradely interference." His appeal, made in *Rude pravo,* was coupled with a renewed pledge that friendship and alliance with the Soviet Union would remain the cornerstone of Czechoslovak policy. "We are and will remain a country that will continue to develop socialism and to deepen Socialist, truly human relations," he declared. "We therefore demand calmly, deliberately but absolutely— from our best friends too—that they respect our rights and positions...."

The surge of popular support for the Dubcek leadership was illustrated by a steady flow of spontaneous rank-and-file comment on Prague TV during interviews following the regular 7 o'clock newscast. Among samples of July 19-20 comment: "If our nation has been divided in the past into party and non-party members, then in this day and hour they are united." "We want to make our own decisions without outside interference."

The Czechoslovak Party Presidium July 25 removed Lt. Gen. Vaclav Prchlik as head of the Central Committee's military department. Prchlik's ouster and the simultaneous abolition of his department were regarded as a concession to Moscow, which had sharply criticized Prchlik for his outspoken anti-Soviet statements in preceding months. Prchlik, however, was given a top command job on Czechoslovakia's border with the USSR.

Krasnaya Zvezda, the Soviet armed forces newspaper, had assailed Prchlik July 23 for his critical remarks about alleged Soviet domination of the Warsaw Treaty alliance. At a briefing for Czechoslovak newsmen July 15, Prchlik had called for (a) the rotation of the top command of the Warsaw Treaty forces among the member nations and (b) a revision of the Warsaw Treaty's structure by the adoption of an amendment to prevent the treaty from being used as an instrument of political goals. These demands were subsequently broadcast by Prague radio.

Cierna & Bratislava Confrontations

As the showdown meeting between the Czechoslovak and Soviet parties' leaderships had neared, Czechs and Slovaks from all walks of life had collected signatures on a patriotic appeal published in a special edition of the liberal weekly *Literarni listy* July 26. The manifesto, drafted by Pavel Kohout, a liberal writer, called on the Presidium of the Czechoslovak Communist Party not to yield to the Soviet Union. By July 29, the day the Cierna talks began, more than one million signatures had been collected in favor of the petition.

The entire Politburo of the Soviet Communist Party and Presidium of the Czechoslovak Communist Party met July 29 in the eastern Slovak village of Cierna on the Tisa River near the Soviet border.

Despite the tight security measures around Cierna, fragmentary reports, mostly from Czechoslovak sources in Prague, gave this account of the 3-day proceedings:

July 29—Dubcek opened the talks with a long speech in defense of the changes that had taken place in Czechoslovakia since the ouster of Novotny in January. Dubcek described the Czechoslovak Communist Party's Action Program and argued that it was neither incompatible with continued Communist rule in Czechoslovakia nor an obstacle to continued friendship with the Soviet Union.

In the afternoon Brezhnev charged that, as a result of loosening Communist control, counterrevolution was afoot in Czechoslovakia. To remedy the situation, Brezhnev demanded that Dubcek (a) restore censorship of all communications media, (b) abolish all "anti-Communist" political clubs that had mushroomed in the country, (c) remove "liberals" from key government positions and (d) allow the stationing of Soviet troops along the Czechoslovak-West German border.

Following Brezhnev, Mikhail Suslov, who was in charge of ideological matters, attacked Czechoslovakia's Action Program, line by line, as heresy. The stormy session ended late in the evening, and the Soviet delegation retired to Soviet soil across the border. (Dubcek was quoted as having told some townspeople in Cierna following the session: "We are dealing with people we call brothers but we cannot get through to them.")

July 30—Pres. Ludvik Svoboda, 72, who had been awarded the title of "Hero of the Soviet Union" for his combat record during World War II, made an impassioned defense of his country's right to carry out its program of liberalization. Observers described Svoboda's address as a turning point in the talks, whose atmosphere was described by Czechoslovak sources as icy until then.

July 31—The 3d day's talks were marked by persistent Soviet efforts to split the Czechoslovak delegation between the conservatives (those who had been known to oppose Dubcek's reform program) and the progressives (who favored the reforms). National Assembly Pres. Josef Smrkovsky was believed to have told the conservative faction prior to the confrontation that "any Czech or Slovak that doesn't back Dubcek at the talks will be known as a national traitor." Dubcek was said to have told the Soviet delegation that he had to leave the talks to meet Yugoslav Pres. Tito, who had openly expressed his support of Dubcek and was said to have been waiting for his call to fly to Prague, on a moment's notice, in a show of solidarity. Brezhnev was said to have retorted to Dubcek: "Let Tito wait." (It was reported in Moscow July 31 that Brezhnev had been suffering from nervous exhaustion.)

A crowd of some 10,000 persons, mostly students, converged at Prague's old city square Aug. 1, the day the Cierna talks ended, and demanded the "truth" about the talks. Smrkovsky told the crowd: "We explained our position [to the Soviets] and succeeded.... We told them our future must be decided by [Czechs].... In the next few days you will learn more and can then judge whether we dealt honestly." The crowd shouted back: "They [the Soviets] are not our friends!" "Long live Tito!"

The first official statement on the outcome of the Cierna talks was made by Pres. Svoboda in a TV address from Kosice Aug. 1. Svoboda admitted that since January there may have been "faults" as a result of the democratization, but he insisted that the reform program had "great strength and [had] taken root so deeply that nobody can reverse it or deflect us from this path." Svoboda said: "Anybody who wants to abuse this [democratization] ... would have no success.... They cannot destroy our sovereignty or independence, which are so dear to us. We spoke openly and frankly to our friends and told them firmly we are determined to continue our policy and not allow anyone to destroy it."

A communique issued at the conclusion of the Cierna meeting Aug. 1 described the talks as "a broad comradely exchange of opinion ... in an atmosphere of complete frankness [and] sincerity" on matters involving the "situation" in both countries. The communique gave no details on the proceedings other than the disclosure that the participants had agreed to meet in Bratislava with representatives of Bulgaria, Hungary, East Germany and Poland. Rumania was not invited.

In a nationwide TV address made before he flew to Bratislava for the next meeting Aug. 3, Dubcek asserted: "We promised you that we would stand fast. We kept our promise."

(The Cierna talks brought a suspension in weeks of attacks by the Soviet press on Prague's reformist policies and by liberal Czechoslovak editors on the Soviet critics of Czechoslovakia. It had been reported in Prague July 31 that Smrkovsky had phoned Communist Party Secy. Cestmir Cisar from Cierna and had asked him to order the liberal editors to tone down their polemics.)

Top party and government officials of 4 of Moscow's most loyal east European allies met with Soviet and Czechoslovak leaders Aug. 3 in Bratislava, Slovakia's capital, and approved the Soviet recommendation that Czechoslovakia be allowed to continue its experiment in democratization according to its own "national specific features and conditions." The Bratislava summit meeting was held as a result of the confrontation in Cierna July 29-Aug. 1.

It was reported in Prague Aug. 4 that the Soviet Union had had difficulty in persuading those of its 4 allies who had taken an open anti-Czechoslovak stand—notably East Germany and Poland—to sign. Hungary, however, was reported to have taken a more sympathetic view of Czechoslovak developments. Hungary's press coverage of Czechoslovak events had been described as balanced; the Hungarian press and broadcasts conspicuously ignored the Soviet/Bulgarian version of the discovery July 19 of an "arms cache" in Western Bohemia and reported instead the Czechoslovak version, which minimized the incident.

In a brief TV address to the Czechoslovak people Aug. 4, Dubcek re-emphasized that "the principle of sovereignty is an indivisible part of our policy." "There is no need to fear for the sovereignty of our country," he declared. Dubcek asserted that the liberalization program "will have far-reaching significance" for the Communist movement all over the world and that "there is no other way, no other route."

Smrkovsky in Prague Aug. 4 called the communique a guarantee of the "sovereignty of our party, of our state and of our government." Replying to a statement that the communique had been received in Prague "without enthusiasm," he offered what he called a "translation [of the communique] into Czech": "We have succeeded not only in defending our policies and preventing a split among the Socialist countries—the double mandate assigned to us when we left—but, what is more, we have succeeded in stopping the interparty polemic."

Tito, Ulbricht & Ceausescu's Visits

The Czechoslovak government received visits in Prague from Yugoslav Pres. Tito Aug. 9-11 and from Rumanian Pres. Nicolae Ceausescu Aug. 15-17. Both visits were made in obvious efforts to bolster the reformist Dubcek regime and served to bracket the chilly visit Aug. 12 of East German party leader Walter Ulbricht in western Bohemia. During the 2d half of July, both Tito and Ceausescu were said to have been ready to fly to Prague to support Dubcek. Dubcek reportedly had asked for the postponement of the visits to avoid offending the USSR.

Tito was accorded a tumultuous welcome in what was generally regarded as Czechoslovak gratitude for his unconditional backing of Dubcek's strong stand against Soviet military and psychological pressures. Tito was accompanied by Mijalko Todorovic, secretary of the Yugoslav party's executive committee, Krste Crvenkovski, chairman of the Macedonian Communist Party, and Stane Kavcic, chairman of the Slovenian Communist Party. These 3 were considered members of the most progressive faction within the League of Yugoslav

Communists. A communique issued in Prague Aug. 10 said that Tito's visit had contributed "in a significant way to further strengthening of all-round comradely cooperation between the 2 countries' Communist parties.

Earlier Aug. 10 Tito had told Czechoslovak and Yugoslav journalists, during a broadcast interview, that Yugoslavia believed in maintaining diplomatic relations with all countries. "No one can prevent us from granting diplomatic recognition to any country," he said. (The remark was considered a reference to the growing rapprochement between Czechoslovakia and West Germany.)

The broadcast was Tito's only public statement during his stay. Commenting on the Bratislava conference, Tito emphasized that, in the document issued at Bratislava, the 6 countries' leaderships recognized each country's sovereignty and lauded the "comradely way" as the best method to solve differences between Socialist states.

(Ex-Vice Pres. Milovan Djilas, who had been imprisoned by Tito for his liberal views but was freed later, said in Belgrade Aug. 12 that he "completely agree[d] with and approve[d] Tito's stand on the democratization trend in Czechoslovakia.")

It was reported in Prague Aug. 11 that among the topics that ranked high on the Tito-Dubcek agenda had been the establishment of close economic ties, including mergers of enterprises, between the 2 countries. The report said that the suggestions for economic cooperation had been initiated by Yugoslavia and that negotiations were to be continued by specialists.

Among the areas of cooperation under discussion were: (a) establishment of a joint banking consortium, with the eventual setting up of a joint Czechoslovak-Yugoslav bank; (b) joint investments in 3d countries; (c) Czechoslovak investment in Yugoslav tourist facilities; (d) Yugoslav aid in the form of know-how and labor to build badly needed housing in Czechoslovakia; (e) the importation of Yugoslav unskilled labor by Czechoslovakia, where the Yugoslav workers would receive specialized training; (f) the elimination of existing barriers to ease the movement of goods, labor and investment funds between the 2 nations.

Observers viewed these prospects of economic cooperation as an attempt to reduce Czechoslovakia's heavy reliance for trade on the Soviet-sponsored Comecon. (Yugoslavia sent only $\frac{1}{3}$ of its exports to east Europe; Czechoslovakia sent $\frac{3}{4}$ of its exports to bloc countries.)

Ulbricht's visit contrasted markedly with that of Tito. The Czechoslovak leadership did not receive Ulbricht in Prague. Instead, Dubcek went to the famous mineral spa of Karlovy Vary, where the 2 men talked Aug. 12. Crowds at the resort cheered Dubcek enthusiastically but were cool toward Ulbricht. The 2 party leaders signed an official communique in which their talks were described as "cordial and comradely" (the Communists' diplomatic euphemisms for controversial and all but unfriendly). Both sides professed continued opposition to "West German militarism" and pledged "full support for the democratic forces" in West Germany.

Ulbricht did not let matters rest at that, however. He appeared before the press corps gathered at the spa and aired his views on West Germany and his differences with Dubcek, in so many words. The East German denounced the German Federal Republic's *Ostpolitik* toward Soviet-bloc members as insincere and said that, to justify it, Bonn would first have to (a) abandon its claim to speak for all of Germany, (b) "regulate" its relations with the Pankow regime and (c) admit the 1938 Munich Agreement's invalidity from its very outset *(ab initio)*.

East Germans, Ulbricht claimed, were sometimes bewildered by the trend of events in Czechoslovakia in 1968 because the German Democratic Republic's regime was Europe's steadiest and East Germans had always exercised "democratic socialism." They also were confused by references in Czechoslovakia to the abolition of censorship, he said; press censorship never existed in the GDR, he claimed.

Czechoslovak party leader Dubcek, the strain of exertions and anxieties visible in his features, greeted the Rumanian head of state and party in the capital Aug. 15. Ceausescu and his delegation, which included Premier Ion Gheorghe Maurer, Foreign Min Corneliu Manescu and Communist Party Politburo member Emil Bodnaras, received an enthusiastic welcome by thousands of Czechoslovaks. Before departing for Prague, Ceausescu had declared in Bucharest Aug. 15 that there could "be no justification for armed intervention in the internal affairs of any Warsaw Treaty member countries."

A 20-year accord renewing the 1947 bilateral treaty of friendship and mutual assistance was signed by Ceausescu and Czechoslovak Pres. Svoboda Aug. 16. Its preamble said that the 2 countries were "firmly resolved to act in keeping with the Warsaw Treaty during the time of its validity." The reference to the validity of the Warsaw Pact, due to expire in 1975, was believed to reflect Ceausescu's repeated calls for the abolition of all military blocs in Europe. Czechoslovak officials had also called for changes in the Warsaw Pact's structure to prevent the treaty from being used as an instrument of political goals within member states. The signing of the treaty was reportedly advanced to provide an occasion for Ceausescu to show support of Czechoslovakia. Rumania had not yet renewed its treaty alliances with Bulgaria, the USSR, Hungary and Poland, all of which had expired.

At a televised news conference following the signing ceremony, Ceausescu asserted Aug. 16 that he favored the continued existence of the Warsaw Pact but only as long as NATO remained in force. Referring to relations between small Communist countries and Western countries, Ceausescu stated that there was a possibility for closer ties, especially economically. (Rumania and West Germany had established diplomatic relations Jan. 31, 1967.)

Referring to the Cierna confrontation, Ceausescu declared at a Prague aircraft factory Aug. 16: "In our opinion, wherever there are differences on this or that problem, it is necessary to resolve these differences in comradely talks, with patience and understanding .... At this time so many differences have amassed between Socialist countries and in the movement that we regard it as a basic and most urgent requirement not to undertake anything that could bring new tensions or increase the present ones."

Dubcek, also speaking at the factory, pleaded with the Czechoslovak people not to drive liberalization too far and too fast. He said: "We need order in our country so that we can be given freedom of action in our democratization process." While he admitted that relations between Socialist countries were "not all that we would want," he stressed that "the alpha and omega of our foreign policy must be unity and alliance with the Soviet

Union." Dubcek's call for order and calm was in response to increasing public demands throughout the country to dissolve the peoples' militia, an armed civilian force created during the Communist takeover in 1948.

SOVIET INTERVENTION
& CZECHOSLOVAK RESISTANCE

Invading Troops Opposed

Armed forces of the Soviet Union, East Germany, Poland, Hungary and Bulgaria invaded Czechoslovakia in a swift military action during the night of Aug. 20-21. The Czechoslovak Communist Party Central Committee declared in a statement broadcast before dawn Aug. 21 that the invasion was taking place "without the knowledge" of Czechoslovakia's leaders. A partial text of the message, broadcast repeatedly by Radio Prague:

"To the entire people of the Czechoslovak Socialist Republic: Yesterday, on Aug. 20, around 2300 [11 p.m.], troops of the Soviet Union, Polish People's Republic, the GDR [German Democratic Republic], the Hungarian People's Republic and the Bulgarian People's Republic crossed the frontiers of the Czechoslovak Socialist Republic.

"This happened without the knowledge of the president of the republic, the chairman of the National Assembly, the premier or the first secretary of the Czechoslovak Communist Party Central Committee....

"The Czechoslovak Communist Party Central Committee Presidium appeals to all citizens of our republic to maintain calm and not to offer resistance to the troops on the march. Our army, security corps and people's militia have not received the command to defend the country.

"The Czechoslovak Communist Party Central Committee Presidium regards this act as contrary not only to the fundamental principles of relations between Socialist states but also as contrary to the principles of international law. All leading functionaries of the state, the Communist Party and the National Front: Remain in your functions as representatives of the state, elected by the laws of the Czechoslovak Socialist Republic.

"Constitutional functionaries are immediately convening a session of the National Assembly of our republic, and the Presidium at the same time is convening a plenum of the Central Committee to discuss the situation that has arisen."

Reports from Czechoslovakia indicated deep, widespread resentment of the invasion. Although there was no organized resistance to the overwhelming occupation forces, Czechoslovak citizens, spearheaded by students, resorted to a wide variety of means to hamper the invaders, and several general strikes of up to an hour's duration took place.

Starting in the early hours of the invasion Aug. 21, crowds roamed the streets of Prague, Bratislava, Kosice and other major towns. They shouted support for Dubcek and insults (in Russian) at the Soviet soldiers. Some citizens, especially older ones, wept in the streets; others, mostly students, painted swastikas on the tanks and armored cars. In open but passive defiance, groups of students repeatedly sat in front of tanks and raised barricades. Angry jeers of "Russians, go home," "Dirty fascists," and "Freedom" could be heard in various parts of Prague and Bratislava Aug. 21-26.

Stubborn, spontaneous resistance was put up in Prague near the radio station, the National Museum and around the statue of St. Wenceslas. Shortly before dawn Aug. 21, students erected barricades in the streets around the radio building. Buses and trolleys were piled up and paving stones dug up to strengthen the defense against the tanks. Students threw stones and garbage at soldiers on the vehicles. Prague radio maintained its program until about 11 a.m., when tanks were able to penetrate the barricades. The broadcasts, however, were resumed later in the day from a secret studio and continued uninterruptedly by constantly switching frequency.

Before the radio building was seized, youths had charged onto the road and set tanks on fire with Molotov cocktails, burning newspapers and branches of fallen trees. Others threw mattresses, wooden crates and garbage cans onto the tanks. One tank was left in flames on the street near the radio building, and 2 flaming Soviet munitions trucks set off a series of explosions, rocking the entire area and injuring several people.

Several buildings near the radio station were burned by tank fire. Store windows were broken by explosions, but there was no report of looting. Except for food stores, nearly all business in Prague was shut; some power lines were down.

Some people during the early phase of the occupation attempted to convince the soldiers that there had been no "provocation" justifying the invasion. An estimated 20,000 peaceful demonstrators marched to St. Wenceslas Square in Prague Aug. 22 and demanded the withdrawal of the occupying forces. Passing in front of the long row of Soviet tanks and soldiers with fixed bayonets beside the tanks, the demonstrators shook their fists and shouted "Russian murderers go home" and "Dubcek, Svoboda." Wall writings denouncing the invasion quickly appeared throughout Prague and other cities. Leaflets circulating throughout Prague urged Czechs and Slovaks to have nothing to do with those who wanted to collaborate with the invaders.

By Aug. 23, rumors spread in Prague of arrests by the secret police. In late morning, lists suddenly went up in the city—scribbled on doorways or in shop windows—giving the license-plate numbers of the cars used by the secret police. Throughout the day, sniper fire could be heard but there were no reports of casualties. A one-hour general strike took place at noon. Later, a throng of long-haired youths, responding to instructions given through the clandestine radio, urged a crowd at St. Wenceslas Square to tear down all street signs to hamper the secret police in their hunt for leaders of the resistance movement.

3 young men were shot and killed by Soviet soldiers in Prague Aug. 24 after they had been caught distributing anti-Soviet leaflets. In defiance of a Soviet-imposed curfew, 30 youngsters Aug. 25 held a 24-hour vigil around the statue of St. Wenceslas in memory of the 3 slain men.

A train coming from the Soviet Union with radio-direction-finding equipment was derailed 60 miles outside Prague Aug. 23 by members of the resistance. The same train was halted Aug. 24 when current on the electrified rail line was cut. Soviet troops finally lifted the equipment into the capital

by helicopters Aug. 25, when, for the 3d time, anti-Soviet
Czechoslovaks had made it impossible to bring it by train.

By Aug. 25 the number of clandestine radio stations was
estimated at 10 to 12. "Radio Free Prague," operating from a
secret location near Prague, gave continuous commentary to
the nation and relayed official messages from the arrested
Czechoslovak leaders negotiating in Moscow. It also
coordinated the other "liberation stations," which formed a
network from Marianske Lazne in the West to Kosice in the
east. Among stations that broadcast almost continuously were
Radio Free Czechoslovakia, operating near Prague, and Radio
Ceske Budejovice, broadcasting from Southern Bohemia, some
30 miles from the Austrian border.

Some 1,200 delegates to the Czechoslovak Communist
Party's 14th congress met secretly Aug. 22-23 and elected a new
144-man Central Committee, which in turn named a new 27-
member Presidium. The congress, it was reported, was held in a
large industrial plant, identified Aug. 23 by the London *Times*
as the CKD factory, in a section of Prague. The delegates
entered the factory clad as workers, doctors, nurses or patients.
According to an Aug. 24 *N. Y. Times* report, the meeting had
been called less than 4 hours after the Soviet invasion had
begun. The congress had been originally scheduled for Sept. 9.

A list of the secretly-elected Presidium was circulated in
Prague Aug. 23. Its members: Alexander Dubcek, Oldrich
Cernik, Josef Smrkovsky, Josef Spacek, Frantisek Kriegel,
Cestmir Cisar, Gustav Husak, Ota Sik, Eduard Goldstuecker,
Bohumil Simon, Vanek Silhan, Peter Colotka, Milan Huebl,
Stefan Sadovsky, Zdenek Hejzlar, Libuse Hrdinova, Vladimir
Kabrna, Josef Zrak, Viktor Pavlenda, Anton Tazky, Jaromir
Litera, Vaclav Simicek, Julius Turcek, Vojtech Matejicek,
Bohumil Vojacek, Zdenek Moc and Andrej Zamek.

(The Paris Bureau of the Assembly of Captive Nations in
Europe reported Sept. 12 that 186 Czechoslovak citizens had
been killed, 362 seriously wounded and several hundred
deported to unknown destinations during the first week of the
"Warsaw 5" forces' occupation.)

Struggle Against Censorship

The Czechoslovak government, under heavy Soviet
pressure since the military occupation began, reimposed

"voluntary" censorship Sept. 4 on the communications media. In announcing the censorship plans Aug. 29, National Assembly Pres. Josef Smrkovsky provided the first detailed account of the conditions accepted by his country's negotiators in their meetings in Moscow with the Soviet leaders.

"We never thought we would have to pay the price we paid the night of Aug. 20-21," Smrkovsky said. "Starting then, not only all our efforts since January but also everything that we cherished—namely, the state and its sovereignty, liberty, the evolution of our internal affairs, even the existence and security of each citizen—have been threatened with a mortal danger.... You know the circumstances under which some of us ... [went to Moscow, as prisoners] and negotiated.... We realized that our decision could be regarded by the Czechoslovak people and by history as a wise solution or as treason.... I beg you to believe that we were not silent, that we clashed hard not only with our interlocutors but among ourselves, and that we made use of every argument within our reach."

The plans to reimpose press censorship and disband non-Communist political clubs were implemented Sept. 4.

Smrkovsky said "special measures" would be taken in the field of radio, TV and the press "to prevent writings against the foreign policy requirements and the interests of the republic." Non-Communist political clubs would be dissolved and the formation of new political parties would be banned, Smrkovsky said. Smrkovsky conceded that "these measures will slow down and make more difficult the process of evolution towards democratic socialism." He appealed to Czechoslovaks to "understand why this must be so and that you will not impute wrong intentions to the party and state leadership."

The press censorship rules announced by the Culture Ministry's new Press Control Office Sept. 4 banned discussion of the Moscow agreement and the use of the word "occupation" in referring to the presence of Warsaw Pact troops in Czechoslovakia. 3 other prohibitions were not disclosed. Under the press control law, government censors were to meet twice a week with newspaper editors; during the 20 years prior to the lifting of press censorship in January, government censors had been stationed at newspaper offices.

The Moscow newspaper *Pravda* had complained Sept. 1
that Czechoslovak newspapers were not adapting quickly
enough to the new censorship rules. *Pravda* singled out
Literarni listy, the liberal weekly of the writers' union, which
had been published clandestinely since the occupation. *Pravda*
assailed the publication as a "wasps' nest" that "continues to
exist somewhere in a backyard and continues to play its abject
role as one of the main ideological centers of
counterrevolution." *Literarni listy* had announced in a one-
page issue Aug. 29 that it would cease publication if censorship
was reimposed.

Pravda Aug. 28 complained of clandestine broadcasts in
Czechoslovakia in which the Moscow agreement between the
Soviet and Czechoslovak leaders had been attacked. The Soviet
newspaper expressed the hope that "the country's working
people, led by their Communist Party, will be able fully to grasp
the complex situation in which the country now finds itself and
deliver a crushing rebuff to its inveterate enemies."

The Soviet press agency Tass charged Aug. 29 that
"counterrevolutionary forces in Czechoslovakia" were
attempting to block the implementation of the Soviet-
Czechoslovak accord. Tass also accused Western radio stations,
which it did not identify, of jamming pro-Soviet stations in
Czechoslovakia while assisting clandestine radio transmitters in
the country. In a situation report on Czechoslovakia, Tass Sept.
3 denounced several Czechoslovak publications for publishing
"anti-Socialist and anti-Soviet" articles. Tass singled out
Kulturny Zivot of Bratislava and *Mlady svet,* a youth
magazine.

Anti-Soviet Demonstrations

Despite pleas of party and government leaders that citizens
refrain from demonstrations, thousands of Czechoslovaks
marched in anti-Soviet protests in Prague Oct. 28, the 50th
anniversary of the founding of the Czechoslovak Republic. This
was the first major protest against Soviet occupation in Prague
since the days following the August invasion.

Celebrating the anniversary for the first time since the
Communist *coup d'etat* in 1948, thousands of angry persons,
mostly youths, surged through various parts of Prague as the

country's leaders were celebrating the 1918 founding of the republic. Beginning late in the morning and continuing late into the night, demonstrators held rallies at the National Theater, Wenceslas Square, near the Soviet embassy and at Hradcany Castle, the presidential palace.

Throughout the day they carried signs and shouted slogans of: "Down with Brezhnev," "Tito yes, Brezhnev no," "Russians go home," "Away with Russian censorship," "We don't want Asiatic culture" and "Masaryk, Svoboda, Dubcek." (Portraits of Thomas G. Masaryk, the republic's founder—and for 2 decades a target of official oblivion—had appeared all over the country, along with portraits of Svoboda and Dubcek. The revival of Masaryk admiration as part of the anniversary celebration was in defiance of a Soviet-waged press campaign. Before the invasion, the Soviet press had denounced Masaryk as a "bourgeois reactionary," who had been acting as a paymaster in a plot to murder Lenin.)

Later in the afternoon, thousands of youths marched to the Soviet military headquarters, where they burned copies of *Pravda,* the Soviet Communist Party newspaper, in front of Soviet soldiers guarding the building. The soldiers looked but did not interfere. Other protesters had attempted to march to the Soviet embassy but were stopped by Czechoslovak police within 500 yards of the building. The group, numbering about 3,000, then sat in the road. This was the only occasion on which demonstrators were opposed by the Czechoslovak police, who remained sympathetic to them throughout the day. (On one occasion in front of the embassy, Czechoslovak policemen pulled a West German tourist from the arms of the Soviet soldiers who had seized him. The West German youth was later released by the police.)

Speaking to party and government leaders in Hradcany Castle, Dubcek was quoted as saying: "We shall preserve the continuity of the policy of the Communist Party of Czechoslovakia on which we embarked after January."

Anti-Soviet demonstrations erupted in Prague again Nov. 6 on the eve of the 51st anniversary of the Bolshevik Revolution. Several hundred persons demonstrated outside the National Theater, which was presenting a commemorative performance of *Swan Lake.* Later, Soviet flags were torn down from buildings and burned.

Chanting "Russians go home" and other anti-Soviet slogans, students and young workers demanded Nov. 7 that all Soviet flags be removed from government buildings. Again, Soviet flags were burned. Later Nov. 7 the police, using clubs and tear gas, broke up a demonstration by 2,000 people in Wenceslas Square. At least 8 persons were reported arrested there and 168 others elsewhere in Czechoslovakia. The demonstrations and the subsequent police action were said to have exceeded the intensity and scope of the Oct. 28 demonstrations.

The Prague government Nov. 8 announced several measures allegedly designed to curb anti-Soviet activity. The measures included: the suspension of *Reporter* and threats of suspension for *Literarni listy* and *Politika,* the Czechoslovak Communist Party Central Committee's organ—3 weekly magazines that reportedly had published anti-Soviet articles and cartoons; the assignment of a deputy premier to oversee press activities; the expulsion of Western journalists who wrote articles contrary to government policies; orders to the Education Ministry to halt student demonstrations.

Another anti-Soviet demonstration took place in Prague Nov. 10 when a crowd of some 5,000 Dubcek supporters jeered at 2,500 pro-Moscow Communists emerging from a Czechoslovak-Soviet Friendship Union meeting in Lucerna Hall and chanted "collaborators" and "the whole nation is against you." Members of the crowds were reported to have thrown garbage at Soviet army vehicles and to have spat at Soviet army officers. As the demonstrators began to attack the "old Communists" (persons over 50 years old) and fist fights developed, police began to escort people to safety.

Massive nationwide demonstrations by university and high school students on school premises took place Nov. 16-21. The students originally had planned a march to commemorate the 29th anniversary Nov. 17 of the closing of the Czech universities by the Nazi occupation forces and the subsequent execution of 9 students. But the Prague government, fearing another outbreak of anti-Soviet demonstrations, refused to allow the march. Premier Cernik said Nov. 11 that the government would use "strength and determination" to prevent anti-Soviet activity because it could result in "chaos and tragedy." Cernik added that "we can enter into the thoughts of the young people, but ... the outstanding principle of our policy ... is that we have to deal with political problems by political means."

Communist Party First Secy. Dubcek issued a similar appeal Nov. 12. Slovak Communist Party leader Gustav Husak, in a stronger warning to students Nov. 13, threatened that "any demonstration will be declared subversive, and we will take steps against them."

Czechoslovak police were ordered on first-degree alert Nov. 15, and Soviet infantry units were reported placed in Czechoslovak police stations to support security forces. Police headquarters appealed to citizens to avoid any "rash or provocative" actions, and mixed units of police and armed Czechoslovak soldiers patrolled Prague's streets. Students, faced with strong government opposition to the march and the threat of reprisals, began a sit-in strike at Prague University Nov. 16. The students, demanding a restoration of the freedoms lost as a result of the Aug. 21 invasion, threatened to remain on strike for a week.

Support of the students by factory workers was reported. At the Skoda automobile and industrial plant in Plzen (Pilsen), workers reportedly prepared to pick a new ruling body to "implement the political and organizational democratization process." At the Kladno steel mills 15 miles west of Prague, 22,000 workers were said to have demanded the removal of leaders opposed to the liberalization program. TV broadcasts in Bratislava reported similar demands from plants in Slovakia. Police and soldiers continued to patrol cities, and National Council Chairman Cestmir Cisar appealed on television Nov. 16 for restraint.

Students in Bohemia and Moravia began Nov. 18 "the legally permissible and peaceful way of making a public stand—a strike in the university buildings." The Union of University Students in Bohemia and Moravia submitted a list of demands to the Communist Party Central Committee, meeting at Hradcany Castle. In the message the students protested against the loss of freedom of the press, of the right to assembly and of freedom of travel. They declared that the Central Committee had to meet demands for the restoration of these freedoms and for the return to the Dubcek reform program if the Party was to retain the people's confidence.

The university students' demands were supported in Prague by high school students, workers, the musicians of the Czech Philharmonic and the Prague Union of Journalists. The Czechoslovak People's Party newspaper *Lidova demokracie* reported Nov. 19 that 40,000 miners in north Bohemia were ready to strike if the students' demands were not met. Workers at the CKD machine factories in Prague and the Kralovo-Polska Zbrojovka arms factory in Brno were also reported to have given support to the student strikes.

The sit-in strikes, scheduled to end Nov. 20, continued in Bohemia and Moravia as students defied a government and Communist Party appeal and warning Nov. 20 that "irresponsible people were seizing the initiative and trying to channel the students' action into a much broader scope" and particularly to involve "the factories, thus dividing the working class and the unity of the workers." (600 CKD factory workers went on an all-day strike Nov. 20.)

The strikes ended quietly Nov. 21, when the students left their university and high school buildings. An estimated 100,000 students had participated in the strikes, which were described as well-organized and peaceful. (According to reports, students refused to permit foreign newsmen to enter university buildings because the demonstrators were afraid that they would be charged with inciting "anti-Socialist propaganda.") Although the students' demands had not been recognized by the end of the strike, the students viewed the strike as a success because, according to some reports, they had been able to make contact "with other strata of the population, chiefly the working class," and had demonstrated their ability to stage an "organized and disciplined protest under difficult circumstances."

Meanwhile, official attacks continued on the media in the Czech lands and Slovakia. These actions excited alarm. In a declaration issued jointly by 9 Czechoslovak cultural organizations Nov. 26, intellectuals warned that the loss of freedom of the press and of expression always led to "the limitation and liquidation" of civil liberties, and they pledged never to repudiate their right to exercise "free and critical thought." The intellectuals, however, did not make public demands on the Prague government but rather sent these in letters to Party First Secy. Dubcek and Premier Cernik. Their public declaration was thus limited to generalities. The intellectuals said they wanted to make their voices heard "after the workers and students" and to assure the continuation of "permanent values" in order to maintain the "humanistic character of our Socialist life."

Originally the intellectuals had intended to publish an 11-point resolution adopted at a meeting of 600 members of various cultural organizations Nov. 22. They key demand of the resolution had been for the establishment of a special committee to investigate and report publicly on who had invited the 5 Warsaw Pact nations to invade Czechoslovakia Aug. 20-21. Other demands criticized the censorship of information media and the loss of freedom of travel. But Dubcek had asked the group to refrain from publishing the resolution pending a meeting held with him Nov. 25.

The Association of the Pastors of the Evangelical Church of the Czech Brethren, in a declaration Oct. 31, had called for the "complete withdrawal" of Soviet troops from Czechoslovakia. The declaration, agreed to unanimously at a meeting in Pardubice, was not published until it was brought to the West by British Council of Churches officials. It declared strong support for the continuation of the reform program. The declaration said: "In the years that have passed we did not do enough to defend the humanitarian principles of T[homas] G. Masaryk. Now our conviction that the truth must finally triumph compels us to struggle bravely with our immediate and urgent problems."

The reasons given by the USSR for invading Czechoslovakia were denounced by the Czechoslovak Academy of Sciences as "lies," "inventions," "distortions of Marxist-Leninist thought" and "schoolboy logic." The statement, circulated Oct. 22 at the academy's annual general assembly, was a 12,000-word rebuttal to the Soviet pamphlet *On the Events in Czechoslovakia,* published in the Soviet Union in September. The statement warned: "Inasmuch as this material [the Soviet pamphlet] contains the twisting or denial of facts that are verifiably known to all our citizens and since this material is distributed here by the Soviet forces, we are seriously worried that it will make considerably more difficult the chances for friendship between Czechoslovakia and the Soviet Union."

Czechoslovak Citizens Flee Abroad

Thousands of Czechoslovak citizens were reported to have fled the country in late August following its occupation by Warsaw Pact forces. The majority of the *emigres* fled to Vienna, where an estimated 12,000-24,000 had gathered by Sept. 2. Thousands of others obtained exit visas as insurance against a possible Soviet suspension of travel out of the country, but the occupying forces were not then impeding exit traffic. Although some 20,000 Czechoslovaks returned home after the invasion from vacations in Yugoslavia, Italy or Austria, there were believed to be some 30,000 vacationers still abroad.

The Czechoslovak Interior Ministry confirmed Nov. 25 that nearly 5,000 Czechoslovak citizens had asked for sanctuary in the West as of Oct. 31. The ministry also reported that 2,067,000 persons (about 15% of the entire population) had made foreign visits, mainly to the West, under liberalized regulations in the first 10 months of 1968. (The Intergovernmental Committee for European Migration had reported Sept. 13 that more than 25,000 Czechoslovaks had left Czechoslovakia since the Aug. 21 invasion. 15,000-20,000 were then in Austria, 5,000 in Switzerland, 4,000-5,000 in West Germany, 1,500 in Italy.)

EAST EUROPEAN REACTION TO INVASION

Immediate Response

The invasion aroused widespread condemnation and resentment in the Communist world and prompted an early justification by the Soviet Union of its role in the matter. The most vehement criticism was leveled by Prague's 2 staunchest allies—Rumania and Yugoslavia—and by Communist China and Albania. Sympathy for Czechoslovakia's plight was also voiced by private citizens in 3 of the invading countries—the USSR, Poland and East Germany. But support for Moscow's move came from Cuba, North Vietnam and North Korea.

Addressing a crowd of more than 100,000 persons in Bucharest's main square, Rumanian Pres. Nicolae Ceausescu Aug. 21 denounced the invasion as "a great mistake and a grave danger to peace in Europe, to the fate of socialism in the world." Asserting that there was "no justification whatsoever" for the invasion, Ceausescu warned that Rumania would use armed force to protect itself from a similar attack. A communique of the Rumanian Communist Party Central Committee read at the rally expressed "profound anxiety" over the invasion, voiced "full solidarity" with the Czechoslovak people and urged the speedy withdrawal of the foreign Communist soldiers from the country. The Rumanian Grand National Assembly (parliament), at a special session held Aug. 22, unanimously approved Ceausescu's reaffirmation of his program of national sovereignty coupled with strict adherence to socialism.

A League of Yugoslav Communists statement issued Aug. 22, following a meeting of the Party Presidium and Pres. Tito, called the invasion an act of aggression. It said: "Involved is not only an attack on the Czechoslovak people but a significant, historical point of rupture, bearing on the relationship among Socialist countries in general,... as well as on peace in Europe and in the world." A rally in support of Czechoslovakia was held in Belgrade Aug. 22. Organized by the League of Yugoslav Communists, an estimated 200,000 persons marched for hours through the streets shouting "Freedom for Czechoslovakia," "Tanks Must Go" and "Tito-Dubcek." Demonstrators gathered in front of the Czechoslovak embassy and were greeted by Foreign Min. Jiri Hajek, who expressed gratitude for their display of sympathy. (Hajek had arrived in Yugoslavia with other Czechoslovak officials Aug. 21 for a vacation.)

A resolution adopted by the League of Yugoslav Communists' Central Committee Aug. 25 called for an immediate end of the Soviet occupation of Czechoslovakia. It warned that Yugoslavia was ready to put up armed resistance to any threat against its territorial integrity.

Presidents Tito and Ceausescu were reported to have discussed the East European crisis Aug. 24 at Vrsac, a Yugoslav border town.

The Kremlin took refuge in its own version of ideological orthodoxy as a defense of its action. The Soviet government newspaper *Izvestia* charged Aug. 24 that Ceausescu's speeches had given aid to "the Czechoslovak counterrevolution." Ceausescu's speeches also were assailed by 2 Hungarian newspapers Aug. 24. One paper, *Magyar Nemzet,* said: "There is a strange similarity between the tone and content of Ceausescu's [Aug. 21] speech and the phrases repeated a hundred times a day by Western radio stations."

Ceausescu softened his criticism of Moscow in a speech delivered in the industrial city of Brasov Aug. 26. He said all Communist states must seek common cause in opposing imperialism and must try to smooth over their differences. Ceausescu reaffirmed Rumania's friendship with the USSR, Hungary, Bulgaria and Yugoslavia as well as with Czechoslovakia. The Rumanian leader's apparent retreat from his rigid position followed a meeting he had held Aug. 25 with Soviet Amb.-to-Rumania Aleksandr V. Basov.

The Albanian government Aug. 23 had condemned the Soviet-led invasion but also denounced Czechoslovak Communist Party First Secy. Dubcek as a traitor "to the interest of his people."

East German workers were said to have refused Aug. 23 to sign petitions "approving" the invasion of Czechoslovakia. The petitions were said to have been circulated by Socialist Unity Party officials among factory, office and farm workers. East Berlin citizens were said to have signed a document at the Czechoslovak embassy expressing sympathy with the Prague regime.

The Polish United Workers' Party organ *Trybuna Ludu* Aug. 29 assailed what it dubbed Rumania's "blind alley of nationalism." The paper charged that Rumanian support for Czechoslovakia "indicates that the objective was not 'defense of democracy and sovereignty' but disintegration of the Socialist commonwealth." For the first time since the invasion of Czechoslovakia, the paper attacked Rumanian Pres. Ceausescu by name, charging that he was too "eager to give advice." The paper also criticized Rumania for having established relations with West Germany in 1967 and for failing to break relations with Israel following the 1967 Arab-Israeli war.

Trybuna Ludu Aug. 31 attacked Yugoslavia for opposing the Warsaw 5's action in Czechoslovakia. The paper charged that Pres. Tito's concept of national sovereignty and independence was "detached from the conditions, place, time and reality of the present world."

Rumania Asserts Independence

According to rumors circulating in the West late in August, the Soviet Union was planning to follow up its invasion of Czechoslovakia with a similar drive into Rumania.

In a speech delivered at Cluj Aug. 29, Rumanian Communist Party leader Nicolae Ceausescu repeated his call for the earliest possible withdrawal of Warsaw Pact troops from Czechoslovakia. He added: "The word freedom can be said in many languages, but it has the same meaning. What is understood is that people must be fully equal, have the right to express their opinion, be able to take part in the guiding of society in accordance with their capability and knowledge."

Thousands of Rumanian citizens underwent para-military training Aug. 31—Sept. 1 amid new reports of Soviet troop movements behind the Prut River in Soviet Moldavia (northeastern Moldavia and Bessarabia).

British Foreign Secy. Michael Stewart conferred with Rumanian party and government leaders in Bucharest Sept. 9-10. A joint communique issued Sept. 11 noted that they had discussed "current international issues" and had "restated their convictions regarding the necessity of continuing efforts to ensure detente and cooperation in the spirit of the UN charter."

Ceausescu said at a Bucharest rally Sept. 9 that "nothing in the world can sway the Rumanian people from the path of socialism and communism.... The Socialist countries must know that we are their friends and that we will never betray the cause of Communist unity."

The U. S. and Rumania signed a 2-year cultural exchange agreement Nov. 26. The cultural agreement was the most extensive ever signed by the U.S. with a Communist country. Under the terms of the accord, the 2 countries would exchange both undergraduate and graduate students for 4-year study programs. 50-60 students would be involved in the exchange, 30-40 of them to work on scientific and technical projects.

Another novel feature was a provision for the exchange of radio and TV coverage of public events.

Officials in Washington said that if Rumania had joined in the Aug. 21 occupation of Czechoslovakia, the agreement would have been unlikely. The U.S. had cancelled projected exchange programs with the Soviet Union, Bulgaria and Poland, 3 nations participating in the invasion.

The U.S. and Rumania signed an agreement Nov. 22 for the exchange of information on the peaceful uses of atomic energy. The pact provided for the exchange of unclassified technical films and literature, study by Rumanian graduate students in U.S. universities and laboratories and the exchange of scientific delegations.

The Rumanian government Nov. 11 formally applied for full membership in the General Agreement on Tariffs & Trade. (Rumania, as did Bulgaria and Hungary, held observer status in GATT.) Mircea Petrescu, director of Rumania's Foreign Trade Ministry, told the GATT council that 5% of the country's foreign trade was with GATT members and that "Rumania follows a policy of developing trade and economic cooperation with all countries, irrespective of their social systems, on the basis of independence and non-interference in the internal affairs of other countries." Rumania's application was warmly received by the U.S. and other GATT members, but U.S. GATT representative Henry Brodie cautioned that current U.S. law prevented Washington from extending "most-favored-nation" treatment to Rumania. (This guaranteed that trade concessions made to one GATT nation would be made to all 75 other GATT member-states.) The U.S. had granted "most-favored-nation" treatment to Yugoslavia and Poland but had not extended it to Czechoslovakia. All 3 were GATT members.

Yugoslavia Strengthens Defenses

The Yugoslav leadership took the occupation of Czechoslovakia as, in effect, a renewal of the Cold War. It responded accordingly.

In a resolution adopted Sept. 4 at a joint meeting of its Presidium and Executive Committee, the Yugoslav Socialist Alliance expressed "profound indignation" over the occupation of Czechoslovakia and affirmed the right of each nation to independent development. With respect to the Yugoslav nation, the Alliance declared: "It has always been clear that there can be no compromise or bargaining over the independent internal development of our country or of its sovereignty with anyone or at any price. The defense of the country is a sacred thing for every citizen of Socialist Yugoslavia, in the constitution of which it has been stated that nobody has the right to sign or to recognize capitulation or occupation of the country." The Alliance affirmed the intention of the Yugoslav leadership to do everything in its power to strengthen the defensive capability of the country.

Pres. Tito Sept. 5 reiterated his demand for an "urgent withdrawal" of Warsaw Pact forces from Czechoslovakia so as to "create conditions for establishing the indispensable trust for development of equal cooperation among Socialist countries and Communist parties." "We believe that the fraternal peoples of Czechoslovakia should alone be in charge and that they themselves could have solved their problems," Tito said.

The Soviet military reacted sharply to the Yugoslav criticism. *Krasnaya Zvezda,* the armed forces newspaper, Sept. 6 referred to anti-Soviet attacks in the Western press as being "facilitate[d] by the actions of the Chinese splitters, headed by Mao Tse-tung, and of the Yugoslav revisionists, whose anti-Soviet themes are taken up by imperialist propaganda." The attack, with its use of the word "revisionists," reportedly was the sharpest leveled against Yugoslavia since the partial reconciliation between Moscow and Belgrade 6 years before.

The Yugoslav party sought other allies besides Rumania's Communists. Representatives of the Yugoslav and Italian Communist parties conferred in Belgrade Sept. 7 on the Czechoslovak situation. The conferees reportedly agreed to boycott a planned Soviet-sponsored conference of the world's Communist parties if Moscow insisted on holding the meeting while Czechoslovakia was still occupied. (The Italian Party did not in fact keep to this agreement—if, indeed, it ever made the agreement.)

Vice Adm. Bogdan Pecotic said in a navy day speech Sept. 9 that the combat readiness of the Yugoslav navy had been raised to the point where it could fulfill "all necessary tasks."

The admiral noted that the need for such readiness was greater than before.

Tito called on all nonaligned and small and medium-sized countries Sept. 23 to close ranks against tendencies that, he indicated, carried the seeds of a world conflict. Speaking at a banquet in honor of Emperor Haile Selassie of Ethiopia, who was visiting Yugoslavia, Tito said: "Some big powers are striving to impose by force on other peoples what is contrary to their aspirations, independence and own roads to a better future." Some countries interfered in the affairs of "African, Asian and now, unfortunately, European countries, too," so it was "again necessary to unite to avert a catastrophe which could envelop the entire world."

Speaking to the Yugoslav Federal Assembly Sept. 24, Yugoslav Premier Mika Spiljak said that an intensification of Yugoslav military readiness had become imperative as a result of the Czechoslovak invasion. He asserted that a big-power intervention in a small country "made more acute the question of security of small- and medium-sized countries." Spiljak also denounced an anti-Yugoslav press campaign waged "particularly in the Soviet Union, Bulgaria and Poland." Spiljak said that he attached "great significance" to relations with the U.S. and that "these relations can be further widened on the basis of mutual interest and mutual respect."

(According to Western reports Sept. 11, Italy and Greece had assured Yugoslavia that they would not rekindle old disagreements in the face of the current Soviet pressure. As a result of these unofficial guarantees, Yugoslavia regrouped its armed forces, deployed mostly along the Greek and Italian frontiers, to reinforce Yugoslav borders with Hungary and Bulgaria.)

(Austrian Pres. Franz Jonas visited Belgrade Sept. 30-Oct. 5 to discuss closer Yugoslav-Austrian cooperation in the aftermath of the Czechoslovak invasion. Jonas was accompanied by Foreign Min. Kurt Waldheim.)

Ex-Yugoslav Vice Pres. Milovan Djilas said in London en route to the U.S. Oct. 4 that if the Soviet Union invaded Yugoslavia the West should give Yugoslavia all possible help, "including military power."

U.S. State Under-secy. Nicholas deB. Katzenbach visited Belgrade Oct. 17-18 to demonstrate U.S. concern over the increasing Soviet pressure on Yugoslavia. Observers agreed that the talks centered largely around Yugoslavia's economic and security position in the wake of the Czechoslovakia invasion.

Tito told an audience of about 100,000 Oct. 20 that any attack on Yugoslavia from any source would be "sharply received." Tito issued the warning in Leskovac, southern Serbia, at a rally marking the 25th anniversary of the formation of a wartime partisan brigade. Rejecting Soviet assertions that sovereignty was not too important to small Communist countries, Tito assailed what he termed a Soviet theory of conditional sovereignty. Tito declared: "We said 'no' in 1948 [the year Tito broke with Stalin] to all pressures against our sovereignty and freedom, and we have done so again, this time in connection with Czechoslovakia." "We shall stick to this position forever."

Deriding Soviet and east European attacks on Yugoslav economic policy, Tito said: "The very ones who criticize us come here to do their shopping and charge into our stores like bees after honey." Answering attacks from Bulgaria, widely regarded as Moscow's spokesman on Balkan issues, Tito said: Any unsolicited help from Socialist countries would be rebuffed; "if you are not invited, it means that you are not wanted ... and that we alone will take care of our own affairs."

In a speech Nov. 29, Tito, without specifically mentioning the Soviet Union or the Czechoslovak invasion, attacked Soviet foreign policy by asserting that "those who do not respect their own country and their own people cannot respect other countries or other peoples." He added that cooperation had to be based on the concept of "independence and full equality of all peoples" and not on subservience to any country.

Yugoslavia's defense minister, Gen. Nikolai Ljubicic, announced Nov. 18 that his country's defense budget would be increased by 532 million dinars to 7.31 billion dinars ($585 million) in 1969. The figure represented 61% of Yugoslavia's total budget but only 6.2% of its national income, a decrease from the percentage for 1968.

Djilas asserted in a Nov. 15 *N.Y. Times* interview (published Nov. 27) that the Soviet Union had reverted to 19th century tsarist imperialist ambitions and should no longer be considered a revolutionary society. Djilas saw little to distinguish Soviet east European policies from Russian imperialist policies. He said: "There are only differences in ideas and forms. In the earlier period we had Pan-Slavism and [Russian] Orthodoxy as instruments. Today we have Leninism. But in essence this is a continuation of Russian imperialism, Russian tendencies, tsarist imperialism." Soviet bureaucracy was a "continuation of the tsarist bureaucracy." If the U.S. remained a military power, it would find it easier to coexist with the Soviet Union as a traditional imperialist military power.

Questioned on whether he thought the USSR was returning to "Stalinism," Djilas replied: "There is some going back to Stalinism, but I think this formulation of neo-Stalinism is too strong. They take some steps backward, but at the same time they take opposite steps from Stalinism." Djilas said the Soviet Union feared Germany as a power only when Germany was united with another power. But the Soviet Union did fear China: "China is a potential power. She shares historical rights to some parts of Russia.... I know very well that this split in communism between China and them is definite.... And they cannot find, I am convinced, compromise on an ideological basis. That means they never will be people with the same ideas."

Asked whether he thought the USSR would intervene in Yugoslavia as it had in Czechoslovakia, Djilas said that Yugoslavia was in no immediate danger, but "we will fight" a Russian attack.

Albania Consummates Break with Soviet Bloc

Albania Aug. 28 assailed the Aug. 26 Moscow-Prague agreement as a "foul compromise" between the "revisionist Soviet aggressors and the revisionist Czechoslovak capitulators ... to salvage their positions to the detriment of the Czechoslovak people and socialism." The official press agency charged that the accord had placed the Prague leadership in the "shameful role of a puppet government."

Radio Tirana carried the announcement Sept. 13 that Albania had formally withdrawn its membership in the Warsaw Pact. The broadcaster said that the action, the 2d by any member of the pact, had been approved that day by unanimous vote of the Albanian People's Assembly. (Hungary withdrew breifly late in 1956.) Albanian Premier Mehmet Shehu had called on the assembly Sept. 12 to approve the withdrawal since Albania had "long been excluded" from the treaty and Moscow had changed the pact from one of "defense against imperialist aggression" into one that was "aggressive ... against the Socialist countries themselves."

In an Albanian language report broadcast by Moscow radio Sept. 14, the Soviet Union asserted that Tirana's withdrawal from the Warsaw Pact was the "price which Albania paid to its masters in Peking." Albania had been excluded from Warsaw Pact meetings since 1962 for its support of Communist China.

In a reversal of their country's isolationist policy in Europe, Albanian diplomats accredited to Vienna, Belgrade, Rome and other European capitals were reported to have sought closer contacts with foreign Leftists. One action in this new policy was the sudden dropping of Radio Tirana's customary attacks on Yugoslav "revisionism."(Communist China had also been reported Oct. 15 to have stopped its attacks on Yugoslavia.)

Albania was reported Sept. 23 to have sent to Bulgaria a protest telegram requesting the immediate withdrawal of the "huge concentration of Soviet forces" that had allegedly been stationed in Bulgaria. It was reported from Vienna Oct. 6 that Albania had reinforced its coastal defenses with Chinese help to counter alleged Soviet-Bulgarian designs on its sovereignty. Albanian government spokesmen and Radio Tirana had repeatedly charged the Soviet Union and Bulgaria with aggressive plans against Albania.

Diplomatic sources in Vienna said Sept. 29 that Albania had made diplomatic overtures to Yugoslavia as a result of their common distrust of Bulgaria.

Hungarian Protesters Expelled

3 members of the Hungarian Academy of Sciences were expelled from the Communist Party Dec. 13 on charges of criticizing Hungary's participation in the Czechoslovak invasion. Those expelled were Vilmos Sos and Gyorgy Markus,

both staff members of the Institute of Philosophy, and Mrs. (Maria) Markus, party secretary of the Social Science Research Group. Andras Hegedus, who had been replaced as premier by Imre Nagy Oct. 23-24, 1956 during the abortive Hungarian rebellion, was reprimanded on similar charges. He was currently head of a research group of the Institute for Social Sciences.

YOUTH UNREST

Belgrade Students Riot

Students and faculty members at the University of Belgrade seized and occupied several university administration buildings June 3-11 in protest against police brutality against students. Following the disruption of classes and as a result of a series of teach-ins, the students, backed by the League of Young Communists, soon raised other demands. The sit-in strike ended only after Pres. Tito pledged to deal honestly with student grievances or resign from office.

The events leading to the 8-day sit-in occurred June 2, when some 1,000 university students tried to enter a suburban Belgrade hall where a concert was being held for volunteer construction workers. When the police intervened to bar the students, they rioted and set fire to cars and trucks. Order was restored early June 3, but an estimated 3,000 students assembled again later that day for a protest march in downtown Belgrade. Charging the government radio with "false reporting" of the previous night's clashes, the students demanded the dismissal of Nikola Bugarcic, Belgrade's police chief.

Clashes erupted on a larger scale when police prevented the marching students from reaching the downtown section of the city. The police used tear-gas grenades, clubs and pistol fire; more than 60 students were injured in the fighting.

The protesting students occupied the university's administrative offices and the building of the school of philosophy June 3. But the police, who drew a cordon around the buildings, allowed students to move freely in and out. Inside, students and faculty held discussions and drew up wide-ranging demands. These included: (a) improved housing conditions at universities; (b) better jobs for university graduates (many of whom had had to emigrate to Western Europe to obtain jobs); (c) higher faculty salaries; (d) abolition of what they termed the Communist "establishment"; (e) an end to police brutality and the dismissal of the federal and Serbian interior ministers and the Belgrade police chief.

The students June 4 proclaimed that Belgrade University had been renamed the "Red University of Karl Marx." They displayed a banner reading: "We have had enough of the Red bourgeoisie." Leaflets demanded the introduction of "real democracy" in the Communist Party and the admission of working-class students into the universities in greater numbers.

By June 6, expressions of support were reported from other university cities, among them Zagreb, Skoplje, Sarajevo, Ljubljana and Novi Sad. In many factories across the country, workers joined in expressing support for the striking students.

In an effort to prevent the spread of unrest to other universities, the Serbian government June 5 proposed an increase in minimum wages and unemployment payments, the introduction of progressive income taxes and more jobs for young graduates. The authorities also lifted the ban on *Student,* a university magazine, which had charged the police with brutality "crueler than before the war [World War II]"

Ignoring the conciliatory gesture, the students appealed directly to Pres. Tito. In a letter to Tito June 7, they declared that their action had been inspired by his "revolutionary thought and supports the great struggle that you guide." "We have always been with you and we are with you now as well," the letter asserted.

Tito responded to the students June 9 in a nationwide TV address in which he espoused their demands. He declared that "90% of the students are honest youngsters" and that most of their demands were justified. In an unusual statement of support for the movement to liberalize Yugoslav society, Tito said: "This time I promise the students that I will wholeheartedly strive for solutions, and the students should help me. Moreover, if I am not capable of settling these questions, then I should no longer be in this position." But, despite his conciliatory tone, Tito warned oppositionists not to attempt to make political capital out of the current unrest. He addressed the warning specifically to followers of Milovan Djilas and

Aleksandar Rankovic, former colleagues who had been dismissed for opposing him.

According to the London *Times* July 23, Professor G. Petrovic, editor of the Zagreb review *Praxis,* had been expelled from the League of Yugoslav Communists. *Praxis* had supported left-wing Communists during the Belgrade University student uprising June 3-11.

Polish Demonstrations

Massive student demonstrations broke out in Poland in Mar. 1968. They were said to have had their genesis in the Arab-Israeli conflict of 1967 and their model in the Czechoslovak demonstration of Oct. 31, 1967 in Prague, where students marched in a demand for better living and study conditions at their dormitories. The inner-party friction and "anti-Zionist" campaign that followed the June 1967 war had keyed social tensions up to a new pitch by late January. As dissatisfaction in cultural and school circles grew, the position of liberal journalists was shaken by the inroads of Interior Min. Mieczyslaw Moczar's "Partisans"—an organization of former anti-Nazi resistance fighters—into control of Polish TV and of the most important newspapers.

Observers generally agreed that the spark for the demonstrations was furnished by an official ban on further presentations in Warsaw of the Romantic poet and exile Adam Mickiewicz' famous play *Dziady (Ancestors),* which was censored after playgoers applauded its anti-Russian lines. (Mickiewicz, who died in exile in 1855, had been in a Russian prison with other students from Wilno's university, and he had put some of the memories of his sufferings into the poetic fantasy-drama. The play took its title from "the half-pagan religious commemoration of their ancestors practiced among the peasantry of the Slavonic nations," according to Prof. Roman Dybosi of Cracow University.) The students, many of whom were the children of liberal figures of the intelligentsia and the government (and some of Jewish origin), demonstrated Jan. 29, but police and university authorities took immediate measures against them and expelled 2 students. In the next few weeks, student meetings were broken up by shock forces from the workers' militia, and in March the city of Warsaw experienced riots. Schools throughout the country took up the students' cause.

The disturbances started in earnest after a student uprising began at Warsaw University itself Mar. 8. 4,000 students were dispersed by militia before it subsided. But the student action received early support from students at other universities and continued to spread to other Polish cities. The protesting students generally expressed sympathy for democratization movements in Communist-bloc countries and demanded a voice in their universities' educational and disciplinary systems. Government reaction included actions widely interpreted as anti-Semitic. Official spokesmen and the press repeatedly denounced the student protests as Zionist-inspired, and Jews were prominent among professors and alleged demonstrators' parents who were ousted from their jobs.

In Cracow, Jagiellonian University students Mar. 11 approved a resolution expressing solidarity with the Warsaw demonstrators. A reported 3,000 of them demonstrated Mar. 13 and boycotted classes Mar. 14-19. The Nowa Huta steelworkers joined the Cracow students for a solidarity strike Mar. 18. During a 2-day sit-in Mar. 21-22, the students again refused to attend classes. In Lublin, Poznan, Lodz and Wroclaw similar student solidarity demonstrations took place. In Lodz, students declared their "support of the Socialist system, solidarity with all the progressive movements in the world, with the struggle of the Vietnamese people, with the struggle of Czech, Slovak, and Russian students and intellectuals, and also with the movement of young Communists of the Western countries."

At an unauthorized Warsaw University meeting Mar. 26, students demanded the reinstatement of 6 professors and lecturers dismissed for allegedly inciting demonstrations.

The university administration began Mar. 28 to institute measures to suppress the rebellion. University Rector Stanislaw Turski closed 6 departments (economics, philosophy, sociology, psychology, mathematics and physics) and, according to the London *Times* Apr. 17, expelled 34 students and suspended 11 others. More than 1,300 students in the closed departments had to reapply for admission. The process of readmission was apparently regarded by the administration as an expedient means to remove student agitators. (Classes in the departments were resumed in May.) The university further warned Apr. 22

that the school would be closed until October if more student demonstrations occurred. An unknown number of students who participated in the demonstrations were inducted into the army.

In the wake of the student demonstrations, Polish university officials instituted 2 reforms designed to provide greater control over students and professors. A new admissions policy favoring worker and peasant children was adopted. About 17% of these favored students would receive extra grants raising their monthly allotments to 1,050 zlotys ($42), instead of the 600-700 zlotys received by other students, as long as they showed "irreproachable moral standards and acute political consciousness." A 2d reform reintroduced a mandatory Marxist-Leninist course that had been abolished in 1956. The universities also replaced scores of purged professors with politically reliable teachers.

Outspoken "anti-Zionism" reemerged in Poland following the outbreak of the student demonstrations. The new wave of attacks on Jews was coupled with the apparent power struggle between United Workers' (Communist) Party First Secy. Wladyslaw Gomulka and Interior Min. Moczar. The campaign resulted in the dismissal of numerous Jews from party and government posts, repeated denunciations of Jews in the press and other communications media, the suppression of literature offering sympathy and support to Jews and the exodus of some Jews from Poland.

The attack on Jews began Mar. 11 when, according to the Polish news agency, Warsaw auto workers, at a meeting organized by the United Workers' Party to demonstrate solidarity with the government, carried banners stating: "Warsaw wants order"; "Rid the party of Zionists." The Jewish poet Antoni Slonimski was singled out by *Kurier Polski* Mar. 13 as a key leader of the student demonstrations. The paper charged Slonimski with being "in the ranks of the friends of Israel" and denounced him for writing a poem that "slandered the Polish nation." In a speech in Katowice Mar. 14, Silesian party leader Edward Gierek outlined a party line on the disturbances in which "Zionists" and liberal intellectuals were branded as the instigators.

According to a *N.Y. Times* report Nov. 2, about 2,000 Jews had emigrated from Poland since March. During September and October the rate was 500 a month.

A Warsaw provincial court Dec. 12 sentenced 2 Warsaw University students, Seweryn Blumsztayn and Jan Litynski, to 2- and 2½-year prison terms, respectively. The students had been convicted of "taking part in a secret organization" during the March student uprising in Warsaw.

(Ex-Yugoslav Vice Pres Milovan Djilas said in a Nov. 15 *N.Y. Times* interview that the student and youth movements of Eastern Europe "are more democratic" than the New Left in the West. The Eastern movement—"democratic socialism"— might lead to "some new form of transition to ... some new form of society," he predicted. But although the Western movement had "some things positive," Djilas said that the movement, as seen in France, was "without any perspective to essentially change society of today.")

Disorders at Sofia Festival

The 9th World Youth Festival was held in Sofia, Bulgaria July 28-Aug. 6 under the slogan, "solidarity, peace and friendship." Although carefully scheduled and planned by the Bulgarian government, the festival, attended by nearly 18,000 delegates from 143 countries (Cuba, Communist China and Albania refused to send delegates), ended with angry dissension among the participants. The focus of the gathering, the Vietnam question, was submerged in the conflict between New Left students from Western Europe and the Communist delegates who controlled the festival.

The dissension erupted July 29 when the young East German Karl Dietrich Wolff, leader of the German Socialist Student League, led 150 students in an unauthorized demonstration near the U.S. embassy. Shortly afterward, some 300 Bulgarians arrived to take control of the demonstration, completely displacing the students. The students, according to the London *Times* July 31, believed that many of the Bulgarians were policemen in disguise.

Western journalists and a team of NBC newsmen were publicly assaulted Aug. 1 when they attempted to photograph 15 Maoist students led by Wolff emerging from the Chinese embassy. The newsmen were first pushed aside by Bulgarian plainclothesmen. When photographers began to take pictures of the police action, they were attacked while uniformed police stood nearby without intervening. Several of the plainclothesmen were recognized as the same men who had taken control of the July 29 demonstration.

The hostility between the New Left students and the Bulgarians was intensified Aug. 3 when Wolff was denounced as a Nazi at the conference and was beaten by the Bulgarian secret police when he attempted to answer the charge. Officials refused to apologize publicly and instead blamed the New Left Aug. 4 for instigating the incidents. Decrying the authoritarian and pro-Soviet attitude of the festival organizers, the New Left students complained that "imposed unanimity, controlled discussions and empty cries of friendship are now substitutes for critical analyses of the forces of capitalism and the means and strategy of combatting them."

Yugoslav students voted Aug. 3 to leave the festival (the Confederation of Iranian Students had already left the festival, charging that the Bulgarians had molested them), but they reversed their decision Aug. 4 in order "not to leave the Czechs here alone." The Czechoslovak students had been a continual source of irritation to Bulgarian officials, who had attempted to isolate them, fearing they would use the meeting as a forum for liberal Communist ideas. (CTK, the Czechoslovak news agency, reported July 27 that 31 of the Czechoslovak youths had been refused entry to Bulgaria.) But the Czechoslovak students retaliated by forming a coalition with German, Dutch, English and Yugoslav delegates, organizing unofficial teach-ins and distributing literature critical of the festival.

The French Students' Union announced Aug. 5 that its delegates had been expelled from the festival. The expulsion was the result of a conflict between the union and the Communist-dominated French committee for the festival over the selection of student delegates. The union nevertheless had sent 10 delegates to Sofia. 9 were admitted to the country and went to the meeting as "tourists" but were later expelled by the police.

The Tunisian news agency reported Aug. 5 that the Tunisian delegation had protested to the Bulgarian government over attacks by the police Aug. 3 on members of the delegation. Later, Tunisia officially announced its withdrawal from the festival.

At an unofficial teach-in organized by the New Left students, the students and orthodox Communists Aug. 5 openly debated the questions of China, peaceful coexistence and parliamentary democracy. But when the Bulgarians realized that they could not control the talks, they attempted to close the meeting.

At a news conference Aug. 5, Yugoslav delegation leader Janez Kocijancic, summarizing the events at the festival, denounced "the effort to impose on the festival certain concepts of a narrow ideological and sectarian unity." He criticized the sponsors for "undemocratic procedure," "limited freedom of speech," "unwarranted security measures" and the "exertion of pressure."

East German Youths Jailed

The East German news agency ADN reported Oct. 28 that 7 youths (4 boys and 3 girls) had received prison terms of up to 27 months for protesting against the Czechoslovak invasion. At the 7-day trial in an East Berlin court, the youths were charged with publishing and distributing literature condemning East German participation in the invasion, inciting people to take "actions hostile to the state" and aiding West German policy. They were freed on probation Nov. 14.

The defendants included Frank Havemann, 19, and his brother Florian, 16, sons of Robert Havemann, alleged "revisionist" who had been ousted from the Socialist Unity (SED) Party, from the East German Academy of Science and as a Humboldt University chemistry professor Dec. 24, 1965. Charging that the youths had been "systematically inspired by their father" and by singer Wolfgang Biermann, the court sentenced Frank to a 27-month jail term and Florian to a reform center.

Other youths jailed included children of long-time SED Party officials. Thomas Brasch, 23, son of Deputy Culture Min. Horst Brasch, was sentenced to a 27-month term. Erika Berthold, 18, daughter of Prof. Lothar Berthold, director of the Institute of Marxism-Leninism, received a suspended 22-month sentence.

SOVIET DISSENTERS

Intellectuals Jailed

Following a 5-day trial in Moscow City Court, 4 members of Moscow's "literary underground"—Yuri Galanskov, 29, Aleksandr Ginsburg, 31, Aleksei Dobrovolsky, 29, and Vera Lashkova, 21—were convicted Jan. 12 on charges of anti-Soviet activity. 3 were sentenced to terms at hard labor: Galanskov to 7 years, Ginsburg 5 years, Dobrovolsky 2 years; Miss Lashkova was given one year (but was reportedly released Jan. 18 because of her year-long pretrial detention).

The 4 were charged and convicted under Article 70 of the Federal Criminal Code, which forbade any "agitation or propaganda carried out with the purpose of subverting or weakening the Soviet regime." They were tried after a year of detention and investigation during which they were not allowed visits from anyone but their lawyers or to write to their families. (Article 97 of the Criminal Procedure Code limited the length of pre-trial detention pending investigation to not more than 9 months.) Their arrest was reported to have taken place Jan. 18-19, 1967 or earlier.

The trial, ostensibly open to the public, was closed to all but about 7 relatives of the defendants and others with special passes. No coverage of the trial appeared in Soviet news media until Jan. 13, when Tass and the Moscow evening newspaper *Vechernaya Moskva* briefly reported the trial and sentences. The report said the defendants' guilt had been proven but gave no details.

Western correspondents received their accounts of the trial mostly from relatives of the defendants and from friends who stood outside the court throughout the trial. According to these reports, the 4 were accused of: (1) editing a paper in defense of imprisoned Soviet writers Andrei Sinyavsky and Yuli Daniel (published only in the West and entitled *The White Book on the Sinyavsky-Daniel Affair*); (2) publishing *Phoenix 1966,* an underground typewritten literary journal; (3) other charges related to ties with an anti-Bolshevik emigre organization called the Popular Labor Alliance (NTS), with headquarters in West Germany, which had been accused of links with the U.S. Central Intelligence Agency. Galanskov was also charged with illegal possession of and transactions in foreign currency.

Friends and relatives said that Dobrovolsky had turned state's evidence during the pre-trial period, had admitted his guilt and had testified against the others. Ginsburg and Galanskov reportedly pleaded not guilty; Miss Lashkova admitted that she had typed manuscripts for the 3 but denied that her act constituted a crime against the state. *Komsomolskaya Pravda,* official organ of the Young Communist League, reported Jan. 18 that Dobrovolsky and Lashkova "have confessed their guilt and told the court everything." The paper said, however, that Ginsburg and Galanskov "continued in every way to dodge, wriggle, and cringe, and resorted to trickery."

The arrest and subsequent conviction of the 4 intellectuals provoked widespread criticism and protest both inside and outside the Soviet Union. Pavel Mikhailovich Litvinov, grandson of the late Soviet foreign minister, and Larissa Daniel, wife of the imprisoned writer Yuli Daniel, issued an appeal to world opinion denouncing the trial as a "wild mockery ... no better than the celebrated trials of the 1930s." Litvinov and Mrs. Daniel, who were among the several sympathizers refused admission to the trial, demanded in their appeal that (a) the trial be condemned, (b) those "guilty of perpetrating it [the trial]" be punished and (c) the 4 be released and a "new trial with the observance of all the legal norms and with the presence of international observers" be held.

(It was reported Jan. 17 that Litvinov had lost his job as a lecturer at Moscow's Institute of Precision Chemical Technology Jan. 3. The dismissal was apparently a punishment for his defiance of the Soviet security police [KGB], which had warned him against publicizing testimony he had gathered on the trial of a young dissident writer, Vladimir I. Bukovsky, who had been sentenced to 3 years' imprisonment Sept. 1, 1967. Litvinov's investigation of the testimony disclosed that Bukovsky had not pleaded guilty at the trial as the Soviet press had reported.)

Ex-Soviet Maj. Gen. Pyotr Grigorenko, denied admission to the trial Jan. 9, said "12 of us" had signed a petition protesting the "illegal transformation of a judicially open trial [of the 4 intellectuals] into a factually closed one." (Grigorenko, a veteran of the Civil War and World War II, had been dismissed as a Frunze Military Academy professor in 1964 and confined for 2 years to a mental hospital because, friends said, he had protested against the Khrushchev regime's discrimination against Jewish officers.)

31 Soviet writers and other intellectuals were reported Jan. 10 to have sent to the Moscow City Court an appeal demanding "full public airing" of the trial in the press. The letter asked for impartial selection of the witnesses for the defense. Signatories of the appeal were said to have included Vasily Aksyonov, a novelist, Bella Akhmadulina, a poetess, and Igor R. Shafarevich, a mathematician and winner of the 1959 Lenin Prize.

About 180 intellectuals sent a letter urging the Supreme Soviet (parliament) to abolish press censorship.

A wave of protests against the trial was reported Feb. 6. Most of the protests, said to have been sent to Moscow newspapers and government officials, deplored the procedure used in the trial of the 4. A Jan. 7 protest, reportedly signed by 52 writers, scientists and others, condemned the court officials and the secret police for conducting the trial behind closed doors.

3 Moscow intellectuals circulated a petition calling on other intellectuals to speak out against "inhuman reprisals" by the authorities. The 1,700 word document also warned of the dangers of Stalinism, which was being "slowly but surely" restored in the country. The 3 signatures were those of Pyotr Yakir, a historian (reportedly the son of a Soviet Army commander, Iona E. Yakir, who had been one of the victims of the 1937 Stalinist purges); Yuli Kim, a teacher; Ilya Gabai, an editor.

22 Moscow writers sent a letter asking Premier Alexei N. Kosygin, Communist Party General Secy. Leonid I. Brezhnev, Pres. Nikolai V. Podgorny and Chief Prosecutor Roman A. Rudenko for a new trial of the 4. The signers included writers Konstantin Paustovsky, 75, Vasily Aksyonov, 35, Veniamin Kaverin, 65, and Pavel Antokolsky, 71.

Aleksandr S. Yesenin-Volpin, 43, a leading mathematician who had participated in protests over the trial, was summoned to the KGB headquarters Feb. 15 and subsequently committed to a mental institution. 99 mathematicians, including some members of the elite Academy of Sciences and 7 Lenin Prize winners, protested that he had been taken "forcibly, without preliminary examination and without the consent of his relatives." (He was reported discharged May 12.) It was reported in London Apr. 23 that the Soviet Communist Party had expelled several of the protesters against Yesenin-Volpin's detention. Among those reported expelled: mathematician-biologist Israel M. Gelfand and mathematicians Yuli I. Manin and Igor R. Shafarevich, all Lenin Prize winners.

Komsolmolskaya Pravda had denounced the protesters Feb. 28 for not learning the truth about the trial and for letting themselves be duped by "the misinformation of bourgeois propaganda."

Ivan A. Yakhimovich, once hailed by *Komsolmolskaya Pravda* as a model collective farm chairman, said the trial was "causing enormous damage to our party and to the cause of communism, both in our country, and elsewhere." In a letter to Soviet Politburo member Mikhail A. Suslov, reported in the *N.Y. Times* Mar. 8, Yakhimovich said: "I believe that the persecution of young dissenters in a country where more than 50% of the population is younger than 30 years of age is an extremely dangerous line."

A defense lawyer in the trial, Boris A. Zolotukhin, was reported Mar. 26 to have been expelled from the Communist Party and from his position as chairman of a district legal consultation bureau in Moscow. The *N.Y. Times* Mar. 27 reported that these 5 other Communists who had protested against the trial had also been expelled from the party: Boris G. Birger, a painter; Lev Z. Kopelev, a historian; Boris Shragin, an esthetics specialist; Yuri F. Koryakov, a literary figure; Lyudmila Alekseyeva, an editor in the Nauka publishing house.

Intellectual dissent became increasingly apparent throughout the spring of 1968. Much of the protest focused on the alleged injustice of the trial of the 4 dissident writers. This dissent was met by constant threats and rebuffs by the Soviet government.

In a speech Mar. 29, Brezhnev warned intellectuals who stepped out of line that their "shameful acts" would not go unpunished. He called for "iron discipline" within the party. "Renegades cannot expect immunity," he said. He condemned the appearance of "ideologically and artistically immature works" in the Soviet literature and other areas of culture. He added that official organizations should exercise more control over the works of writers and other intellectuals.

The head of the Writers' Union, Sergei V. Mikhalkov, demanded Mar. 30 that Soviet authors pay more attention to the ideological content of their work. He noted that some writers, whom he labeled "freaks" in Soviet society, had ignored warnings and were continuing to protest against the January trial.

In a move to counter the wave of protests over the trial, the Communist Party held a series of local and regional meetings at which writers and party officials spoke against dissidents. Stepan P. Shchipachev and Aleksei Surkov, writers who had been victims of a 1963 crackdown on liberals, Apr. 3 denounced those who protested against the trial of the 4 writers. Shchipachev said of the defendants: "They were not writers. They are ordinary scum, whom we do not know and do not want to know." Viktor Telpugov, a writer, also criticized "those few writers who put their signatures under unsubstantiated letters which try to defame the trial of the Ginsburg-Galanskov anti-Soviet group."

In view of the increasing protests over the trial and of the liberalization developments then taking place in Czechoslovakia, intellectual dissent was a major issue of the Apr. 9-10 Communist Party Central Committee meeting. (The meeting was the first working session since Sept. 1967.) In a resolution adopted Apr. 10, the Central Committee demanded more ideological control over Soviet literature and art in order to further strengthen the patriotism of the Soviet people. The duty of party organizations, the resolution stated, "is to wage an offensive struggle against bourgeois ideology, to actively stand up against attempts to drag views alien to the Socialist ideology of Soviet society into individual works of literature, art and so forth."

The resolution also reflected concern over unrest in Poland and Czechoslovakia. Speaking of a conflict between capitalism and communism, the statement declared: "The entire huge apparatus of anti-Communist propaganda is now directed at weakening the unity of Socialist countries, the international Communist movement, at splitting the front-ranking forces of our time, at undermining the Socialist society from inside."

The Supreme Court of the Russian Republic Apr. 16 confirmed the sentences of the January trial. The appeal of 4 defense lawyers was rejected at a 4-hour hearing that only a few persons were allowed to observe.

It was reported Apr. 17 that 17 Leningrad intellectuals, accused of conspiring to replace the Soviet government with an Orthodox Church-led democracy, had been convicted and sentenced to prison terms of one to 6 years after a 3-week trial ended in early April. The 17 were said to be members of a group of 60, whose 4 leaders had been sentenced in Nov. 1967 to 8-to-15-year labor-camp terms on treason and conspiracy charges. The alleged conspirators, calling themselves the All-Russian Social-Christian Union for the Liberation of the People, included university lecturers, scientists, engineers and students from Leningrad and the Siberian cities of Tomsk and Irkutsk. At their trial, the defendants had denied charges of connection with the Munich-based Narodno-Trudovoi Soyuz, or Popular Labor Alliance, which was dedicated to the overthrow of Communist rule in the USSR.

The *N.Y. Times* reported Apr. 19 that author Yuri V. Maltsev, 36, had appealed to the UN Human Rights Division to help him leave the Soviet Union. Maltsev said his "last hope" was the UN, that he had been trying unsuccessfully to live where he wished in realization of "one of the basic rights of man."

At a meeting of the Moscow regional party committee Apr. 23, Vsevolod A. Kochetov, editor of *Oktyabr,* blamed ex-Premier Khrushchev for the current dissent among Soviet writers. He said: "Literature must be watched over in a Leninist way—it is a mighty and massive weapon." "It has prepared the way to revolution. But, as we know, it also prepares the way to counterrevolution."

Literaturnaya Rossiya (Literary Russia) reported Apr. 28 that the Moscow branch of the Writers' Union had ordered investigations of the "unprincipled actions" of at least 22 of its members who had signed petitions protesting the January trial. The article singled out writers Yuri Pilyar and L. Kopelev for criticism. Included among those who signed petitions but reportedly were not mentioned in the article were the novelists Paustovsky, Kaverin and Aksyonov and the poetess Akhmadulina.

Ex-Maj. Gen. Pyotr G. Grigorenko, speaking Nov. 14 at burial rites for Soviet writer Aleksei Y. Kosterin, who had died Nov. 10 at 72, charged the Soviet Union with "totalitarianism that hides behind the mask of so-called Soviet democracy" and warned that "Leninist democracy" was turning into a "bureaucratic machine." He held the government responsible for Kosterin's death. Kosterin, who had joined the Bolshevik party in 1916, had spent 17 years in a labor camp before being released in 1953. Kosterin was expelled from the Communist Party Oct. 17 for criticizing the Soviet invasion of Czechoslovakia and for calling for broader democracy in the USSR. Without his knowledge, he was expelled from the Union of Soviet Writers Oct. 30. Grigorenko noted at Kosterin's funeral: "They forget that neither [Alexander] Pushkin nor [Lev] Tolstoy was a member of the union ... and [Boris] Pasternak was expelled."

In an article in the December issue of *Kommunist,* the Communist Party ideological magazine, young scientists and engineers were criticized for "naive" views about the West. It cited a report in the newspaper *Vpered (Forward),* published in Obninsk, a scientific research town 60 miles southwest of Moscow. The report, written by a scientist after visiting Denmark, had praised Western technology and achievements. The author of the *Kummunist* article said: "Unfortunately, political naivete and a lack of a class approach to the evaluation of capitalist reality also distinguish reports in the same newspaper by several other scientists who decided to share their impressions gained during trips abroad." The author assailed older scientists for failing to indoctrinate their younger colleagues properly in ideological matters.

Sympathy for Czechoslovakia

It was reported from Moscow July 29 that, as the Cierna talks began, a delegation of Soviet dissidents, including artists and scientists, visited the Czechoslovak embassy in Moscow to show support for Prague's democratization program. Among members of the dissident delegation were Pyotr G. Grigorenko, the former major general, and Ivan A. Yakhimovich, the former collective farm chairman. Both had lost their positions for their repeated demands for fair trials of accused writers in the USSR.

The *N.Y. Times* reported Oct. 14 that a Soviet dissenter, Anatoly T. Marchenko, 30, had addressed an open letter to Czechoslovak and Western Communist newspapers in protest against the Kremlin's attempt at reimposing orthodox-style communism in Czechoslovakia. In his letter, handed to the Czechoslovak embassy in Moscow July 29, Marchenko declared: "I am ashamed for my country, which is once more assuming the shameful role of policeman of Europe." Marchenko's protest coincided with the dramatic Cierna confrontation between the Czechoslovak and Soviet Communist Party leaders. (Marchenko, who had served 6 years in political prison camps, was arrested, tried and sentenced Aug. 5 to one year at hard labor.)

88 Soviet writers protested the invasion of Czechoslovakia in a letter dated Aug. 23 and subsequently smuggled to the West, where it was disclosed Sept. 10 by a British author, Lord Bethell. In the letter, which Bethell said had been given to him during a recent European tour, the 88 told Czechoslovak writers that "since January of this year we observed your struggle with envy, and we are delighted to see that in at least one Slavonic country there existed freedom of thought, speech and behavior." Unfortunately, the letter continued, "freedom today is being stifled not only in Czechoslovakia but in our country also." The writers said they were "ashamed of the fact that on this occasion the suppressors of freedom are men of our own country."

Several Soviet intellectuals preparing a Moscow rally to denounce the invasion of Czechoslovakia were arrested in Red Square Aug. 25. Police seized 9 persons, including Mrs. Yuli M.

Daniel, wife of the imprisoned writer, and Pavel M. Litvinov. 5 women in the dissident group, with the exception of Mrs. Daniel, were released. But one of the freed women, poetess Natalya Gorbanevskaya, was rearrested Aug. 26. The Soviet action against Czechoslovakia had been denounced earlier Aug. 25 at a meeting of the Academy of Sciences' Russian Language Institute. Similar rallies had been staged by Soviet intellectuals at other institutes, including one in Leningrad where 4 persons were arrested.

The 5 detained protesters were convicted in a 3-day trial in Moscow Oct. 9-11. Litvinov, 30, Larissa Bogoraz Daniel, Konstantin Babitsky, 40, Vadim Delone, 23, and Vladimir Dremlyuga, 28, were sentenced Oct. 11 to terms of up to 5 years in exile to a remote area of the Soviet Union and of up to 3 years at hard labor.

The 3 sentenced to exile were: Litvinov, a physicist and grandson of pre-World War II Soviet Foreign Min. Maksim Litvinov (who had denounced the 1939 Nazi invasion of Czechoslovakia), to 5 years; Mrs. Daniel, a linguist, to 4 years; and Babitsky, a literary critic, to 3 years. The 2 defendants sentenced to hard labor were Delone and Dremlyuga. Delone, a poet who had already received a one-year suspended sentence in 1967 for protesting against the Sinyavsky-Daniel trial, was sentenced to 34 months. Dremlyuga, an unemployed worker with a previous conviction for "speculation," received the maximum sentence of 3 years.

Charges against the 5 included "systematic slander" and "group activities aimed at undermining the public order" under paragraphs 1, 2 and 3 of Article 190 of the Russian SSR's Criminal Code. (The Soviet constitution permitted civil, nonviolent demonstration.) The indictment charged them with a "criminal conspiracy" as well as with spreading "false views" about the Soviet Union's "fraternal aid to the Czechoslovak government." During the trial, all 5 denied any conspiracy but reiterated their disapproval of the invasion of Czechoslovakia.

The 5 defendants, along with Natalya Gorbanevskaya and Viktor Feinberg, an art critic, had protested near St. Basil's Cathedral at noon Aug. 25. The group had carried banners reading: "Long live free and independent Czechoslovakia," "Shame on the occupiers," "Hands off Czechoslovakia," and "For your freedom and ours." According to Mrs.

Gorbanevskaya's account, the group had been immediately seized, beaten, denounced as enemies of the Soviet Union and carried off in waiting police vans. (Mrs. Gorbanevskaya was subsequently freed to attend to her 3-month old son; Feinberg was said to have been confined to a mental institution.)

The trial, in a 40-seat courtroom, was ostensibly open to the public, as provided for by Article 18 of the Soviet Procedural Code, but actually it was closed to all but 12 close relatives of the defendants. About 150 of the defendants' friends and supporters stood outside the courthouse throughout the trial; many of them engaged in open arguments with a handful of persons, reportedly belonging to KGB, who were hostile to the accused. Western newsmen were barred from the trial.

In their final pleas, all 5 defendants denied that they had violated public order. As they attempted to expound the political motives behind their opposition to the Kremlin's policies toward Czechoslovakia, they were interrupted repeatedly by both the prosecution and the judge.

Litvinov was said to have stated: "Liberty is important for us. In a great Socialist country like ours, the freer each one of us is, the better it will be for all of us." When the judge interrupted Litvinov and said that his arguments about civil liberties were irrelevant, Litvinov was reported to have retorted: "This [liberty] is relevant. Who is to judge what is in the interest of socialism and what is not? Perhaps the prosecutor, who spoke with admiration ... of those who [had] beaten us up and insulted us. And he is a legal expert. This is what I find ominous. Evidently it is these people who are supposed to know what is socialism and what is counterrevolution. That is what I find terrible and that is ... what I shall continue to fight against for the rest of my life, by all lawful methods known to me."

In her plea, Mrs. Daniel denied the charge that the slogan "Freedom for Dubcek," which had been carried by the demonstrators, was slanderous. She declared that Dubcek had not been at liberty Aug. 21-25. Speaking of her motive for opposing the government's policy on Czechoslovakia, Mrs. Daniel said: "It was all the meetings and information in the press telling of uniform [Soviet] support that caused me to say openly that I was against the action [to invade Czechoslovakia].

I would have had to consider myself responsible for the error of our government. Feeling as I do about those who [had] kept silent in a former period [the reign of Stalin], I consider myself responsible." On public opinion she declared: "I do not doubt that public opinion will support this verdict, as it would approve any other verdict. They [the defendants] will be depicted as social parasites and outcasts and people of various ideologies." (Mrs. Daniel's son, Aleksandr, 17, was reported to have been barred from Moscow's mathematical schools, despite superior grades.)

Babitsky said in his plea: "Look at us not as enemies of socialism but as people who have a different opinion of it. The court must decide what is to win in our society: Respect for the views of others or hatred for all independent thinking."

Delone, who was ordered to serve 4 months of a one-year suspended sentence, told the court: "For 3 minutes on Red Square I felt free. I am glad to take your [the judge's] 3 years for that."

Moskovskaya Pravda (Moscow Truth) Oct. 12 charged the 5 dissenters with "alcoholism, debauchery and idleness" and with "concocting dirty, slanderous lampoons that regularly appeared in the Western yellow press." It did not mention Czechoslovakia.

The *Washington Post* reported Oct. 13 that 6 intellectuals—5 in Leningrad and one in Moscow—had been arrested on charges of "anti-Soviet agitation and propagation." They were also charged with publishing underground material. The Leningrad group, identified by last name only: Danilov and Gendra, both lawyers; Shashenkov, Krachevsky and Studenkov, all engineers. The 5 had been accused of having sent a letter to Dubcek in support of his reform program. The man arrested in Moscow, Viktor Krasin, 40, an economist and friend of Larissa Daniel's, was one of the 12 signers of a February appeal addressed to the Budapest preparatory conference of 65 Communist parties and in protest against "the trampling on man" in the Soviet Union.

Yevgeny Yevtushenko, Soviet poet who had been a symbol of de-Stalinization during the Khrushchev regime, had protested Aug. 22, in a telegram to Premier Kosygin and Communist Party General Secy. Brezhnev, against the Soviet intervention in Czechoslovakia (reported Sept. 29). Describing the intervention as both a "personal tragedy" and a "gift for all reactionary forces," Yevtushenko said: "I am deeply convinced that our action in Czechoslovakia is a tragic mistake and a bitter blow to Soviet-Czechoslovak friendship and the world Communist movement.... It is a setback for all progressive forces, for peace in the world and for humanity's dreams of future brotherhood."

39 of the 42 members of the secretariat of the Union of Soviet Writers charged certain Czechoslovak writers with having joined "anti-Socialist destructive forces" and urged them to help correct "mistakes in Czechoslovak development." In an open letter in the union's *Literaturnaya Gazeta* Oct. 23, the Soviet writers defended the Aug. 21 invasion. Signers included novelist Mikhail Sholokov and playwright Alexander Korneichuk. The 3 nonsigning members were poet Aleksandr Tvardovsky, editor of *Novy Mir,* and novelists Konstantin Simonov and Leonid Leonov.

The Soviet Supreme Court Nov. 18 rejected an appeal by the 5 intellectuals sentenced Oct. 11 for participating in a Moscow demonstration against the Czechoslovakian invasion.

95 Soviet artists and cultural figures sent a letter to the Supreme Soviet Dec. 1 denouncing the Oct. 9-11 trial of the 5. The signers, who included the writer Viktor P. Nekrasov, the movie actor Igor Kavsha and pianist Mariya Yudinna, said that the 5 had been tried and convicted merely for exercising their constitutional rights of peaceful demonstration and free speech.

Unrest Among Nationalities

The *Toronto Telegram* reported Jan. 6 that at least 15 Ukrainian intellectuals had been sentenced to terms of up to 6 years at forced-labor camps in Siberia at secret trials in the Ukrainian cities of Kiev, Lvov, Ternopol and Ivano-Frankovsk during the winter of 1965-6. They were charged with "anti-Soviet nationalistic propaganda and agitation." These "anti-Soviet" activities included reading prerevolutionary Ukrainian books and writing material in which they quoted such Western leaders as Pope Paul VI and Dwight D. Eisenhower.

News of the secret trials reached the West through smuggled manuscripts written by Vyacheslav Chornovil, 30, a former TV newsman, who had been sentenced to 3 years in a secret trial held in Lvov Nov. 15, 1967 for "anti-Soviet activities" after he had refused to testify for the prosecution at the secret trial of a Lvov University lecturer, Mykhaylo Osadchy. Chornovil had been initially assigned to cover the trial for his employer.

It was reported May 3 that 12 Ukrainian writers had been threatened with disciplinary action for joining 126 other Ukrainian intellectuals in sending to Brezhnev, Kosygin and Podgorny a strong protest over secret trials of Ukrainian intellectuals that had taken place in 1965-6.

The Presidium of the Supreme Soviet was reported June 15 to have issued a decree permitting members of 4 Moslem minorities to end their exile and to return to their homes in the Georgian Republic. The 4 minorities—Turks, Kurds, Hemshils (Armenian Moslems) and Azerbaijanians—had been evicted in 1948 from the Adzhar Autonomous Republic and 5 other districts in Georgia as security risks and sent into exile in Soviet Central Asia. The minorities had been rehabilitated less than 10 years later along with other minorities that had been exiled during the Stalin rule, but they had not been permitted to return to their homes. The Presidium's decree restored their full rights.

The Soviet government was reported May 3 to have received a protest over the arrest Apr. 21 of 300 Crimean Tatars in Chirchik, in the Soviet Central Asian District of Tashkent. According to a statement submitted by a group of 16 Tatars residing in Moscow, (a) Soviet authorities had denied the Tatars permission to assemble to celebrate the 98th anniversary of the birth of Lenin and (b) the arrests were carried out after the ban was defied. The protesters charged that in dispersing the gathering, police and troops had assaulted the crowd and tank trucks had sprayed "poisonous liquid." The complaint demanded the release of those arrested and an official investigation of the incident. The Tatars had been exiled to Central Asia from their autonomous republic in the Crimea toward the end of World War II for collaborating with the German invaders.

Sakharov Statement

Prof. Andrei Dmitriyevich Sakharov, 47, a prominent Soviet nuclear physicist, proposed and predicted wide-ranging collaboration between the U.S. and the Soviet Union. He stated his views in an essay that had been circulating unofficially in unpublished manuscript form in the USSR. The essay, entitled *Thoughts About Progress, Peaceful Coexistence and Intellectual Freedom,* was completed in June and was published by the *N.Y. Times* July 22.

Sakharov, a member of the Soviet Academy of Sciences, called an ultimate "convergence" of the capitalist and Communist systems not only inevitable but the only solution to the dangers threatening the future of mankind. Sakharov, who had been a leader in Soviet development of thermonuclear energy, listed these dangers as the threat of thermonuclear war, famine and population crises in less-developed nations, chemical pollution of the environment, police dictatorships and infringement of intellectual freedoms. Sakharov proposed a 4-point timetable for U.S.-Soviet rapprochement by the year 2000. He held that there was actually little difference in the effectiveness of the U.S. and Soviet systems—each had moved towards the other, and each had achieved measurable economic progress.

The Soviet scientist condemned the trials and imprisonment of Soviet writers and other intellectuals, and he urged the release of all political prisoners. (Sakharov had signed several petitions and even appealed directly to the Communist Party's Central Committee on behalf of writers and intellectuals who had been tried.)

Excerpts from Sakharov's essay, as translated by the *N.Y. Times:*

Introduction—"The division of mankind threatens it with destruction. Civilization is imperiled by: a universal thermonuclear war, catastrophic hunger for most of mankind,— stupefaction from the narcotic of 'mass culture' and bureaucratized dogmatism, a spreading of mass myths that put entire peoples and continents under the power of cruel and treacherous demagogues, and destruction or degeneration from the unforeseeable consequences of swift changes in the conditions of life on our planet.

"In the face of these perils, any action increasing the division of mankind, any preaching of the incompatibility of world ideologies and nations is madness and a crime. Only universal cooperation ... will preserve civilization...."

"Millions ... are striving to put an end to poverty. They despise oppression, dogmatism and demagogy.... They believe in [scientific] progress....

"... Intellectual freedom is essential to human society—freedom to obtain and distribute information, freedom for openminded and unfearing debate and freedom from pressure by officialdom and prejudices. Such a trinity of freedom of thought is the only guarantee against an infection of people by mass myths, which, in the hands of treacherous hypocrites and demagogues, can be transformed into bloody dictatorship. Freedom of thought is the only guarantee of the feasibility of a scientific democratic approach to politics, economy and culture."

Changes proposed—"Certain changes must be made in the conduct of international affairs, systematically subordinating all concrete aims and local tasks to the basic task of actively preventing an aggravation of the international situation, of actively pursuing and expanding peaceful coexistence to the level of cooperation, of making policy in such a way that its immediate and long-range effects will in no way sharpen international tensions and will not create difficulties for either side that would strengthen the forces of reaction, militarism, nationalism, fascism and revanchism....

"The international policies of the world's 2 leading superpowers (the United States and the Soviet Union) must be based on a universal acceptance of unified and general principles, which we initially would formulate as follows:

"(1) All peoples have the right to decide their own fate with a free expression of will. This right is guaranteed by international control over observance by all governments of the 'Declaration of the Rights of Man.' International control presupposes the use of economic sanctions as well as the use of military forces of the United Nations in defense of 'the rights of man.'

"(2) All military and military-economic forms of export of revolution and counterrevolution are illegal and are tantamount to aggression.

"(3) All countries strive toward mutual help in economic, cultural and general organizational problems with the aim of eliminating painlessly all domestic and international difficulties and preventing a sharpening of international tensions and a strengthening of the forces of reaction.

"(4) International policy does not aim at exploiting local, specific conditions to widen zones of influence and create difficulties for another country. The goal of international policy is to insure universal fulfillment of the 'Declaration of the Rights of Man' and to prevent a sharpening of international tensions and a strengthening of militarist and nationalist tendencies."

Police dictatorships—"An extreme reflection of the dangers confronting modern social development is the growth of racism, nationalism and militarism and, in particular, the rise of demagogic, hypocritical and monstrously cruel dictatorial police regimes. Foremost are the regimes of Stalin, Hitler and Mao Tse-tung, and a number of extremely reactionary regimes in smaller countries, Spain, Portugal, South Africa, Greece, Albania, Haiti and other Latin-American countries....

"Fascism lasted 12 years in Germany. Stalinism lasted twice as long in the Soviet Union. There are many common features but also certain differences. Stalinism exhibited a much more subtle kind of hypocrisy and demagogy, with reliance not on an openly cannibalistic program like Hitler's but on a progressive, scientific and popular Socialist ideology....

"Our country has started on the path of cleansing away the foulness of Stalinism.... We are learning to express our opinions, without taking the lead from the bosses and without fearing for our lives....

"The exposure of Stalinism in our country still has a long way to go. It is imperative, of course, that we publish all authentic documents, including the archives of the NKVD [secret police], and conduct nationwide investigations. It would be highly useful for the international authority of the Soviet Communist Party and ideals of socialism if, as was planned in 1964 but never carried out, the party were to announce the 'symbolic' expulsion of Stalin, murderer of millions of party members, and at the same time the political rehabilitation of the victims of Stalinism....

Threat to intellectual freedom—"This is a threat to the independence and worth of the human personality, a threat to the meaning of human life.

"Nothing threatens freedom of the personality and the meaning of the life like war, poverty, terror. But there are also indirect and only slightly more remote dangers.

"One of these is the stupefaction of man ... by mass culture with its intentional or commercially motivated lowering of intellectual level and content, with its stress on entertainment or utilitarianism, and with its carefully protective censorship.

"Another example is related to the question of education. A system of education under government control, separation of school and church, universal free education—all of these are great achievements of social progress. But everything has a reverse side. In this case it is excessive standardization, extending to the teaching process itself, to the curriculum, especially in literature, history, civics, geography, and to the system of examinations.

"One cannot but see a danger in excessive reference to authority and in the limitation of discussion and intellectual boldness at an age when personal convictions are beginning to be formed....

"Modern technology and mass psychology constantly suggest new possibilities of managing the norms of behavior, the strivings and convictions of masses of people. This involves not only management through information based on the theory of advertising and mass psychology, but also more technical methods that are widely discussed in the press abroad. Examples are biochemical control of the birth rate, biochemical control of psychic processes and electronic control of such processes....

"We cannot completely ignore these new methods or prohibit the progress of science and technology, but we must be clearly aware of the awesome danger to basic human values and to the meaning of life that may be concealed in the misuse of technical and biochemical methods and the methods of mass psychology...."

"At this point we must touch on some disgraceful tendencies that have become evident in the last few years. We will cite only a few isolated examples.... The crippling censorship of Soviet artistic and political literature has again been intensified. Dozens of brilliant writings cannot see the light of day. They include some of the best of Solzhenitsyn's works....

"The Daniel-Sinyavsky trial, which has been condemned by the progressive public in the Soviet Union and abroad ... and has compromised the Communist system, has still not been reviewed. The 2 writers languish in a camp with a strict regime and are being subjected (especially Daniel) to harsh humiliations and ordeals....

"Was it not disgraceful to allow the arrest, 12-month detention without trial and then the conviction and sentencing to terms of 5 to 7 years of Ginzburg, Galanskov and others for activities that actually amounted to a defense of civil liberties and (partly, as an example) of Daniel and Sinyavsky personally....

"Today the key to a progressive restructuring of the system of government in the interests of mankind lies in intellectual freedom. This has been understood, in particular, by the Czechoslovaks, and there can be no doubt that we should support their bold initiative, which is so valuable for the future of socialism and all mankind....

"The situation involving censorship ... in our country is such that it can hardly be corrected for any length of time simply by 'liberalized' directives. Major organizational and legislative measures are required, for example, adoption of a special law on press and information that would clearly and convincingly define what can and what cannot be printed and would place the responsibility on competent people who would be under public control. It is essential that the exchange of information on an international scale (press, tourism and so forth) be expanded in every way, that we get to know ourselves better, that we not try to save on sociological, political and economic research and surveys, which should be conducted not only according to government-controlled programs."

The Soviet government newspaper *Izvestia* Aug. 11 published an indirect rebuttal to the Sakharov essay. In an article entitled *Problems of the Last 3d of the Century,* a Soviet economist, Dr. Viktor A. Cheprakov, predicted that instead of collaboration and ultimate convergence of capitalism and communism over the next 3 decades, an intensification of the struggle between them would ensue with communism emerging as the victor.

Cheprakov did not discuss Sakharov's insistence on intellectual freedom, his denunciation of neo-Stalinists nor his condemnation of the trial and imprisonment of intellectuals.

1969

Despite the setback to democratization in Czechoslovakia, vocal dissent persisted throughout eastern Europe. Because many Communist parties condemned the occupation in Czechoslovakia, the Soviet leaders encountered difficulties in preparing a summit conference that would sanction the intervention and reaffirm Moscow's supremacy. Rumania successfully resisted Soviet pressure for closer participation in the economic and military organizations of the bloc. It joined with Yugoslavia in rejecting the "Brezhnev doctrine" of limited sovereignty, which claimed Moscow's right to intervene in the internal affairs of other Communist countries if deemed justified by alleged danger to the status quo. When the summit conference finally took place in the Soviet capital in June, dissent was more conspicuous than unity among its participants.

Reports multiplied during 1969 about acts of defiance by individual dissenters in the Soviet Union and about widespread circulation of underground antigovernment publications. Although some of the publications may have been disseminated by the police in an effort to identify the members of the opposition, others were indicative of grave dissatisfaction among the intellectual elite. Whereas unrest did not noticeably affect other classes of the Russian people, it was evident among the non-Russian nationalities, particularly the Tatars, Tadzhiks, Baltic peoples and Jews. The prison sentences given to the leading protesters resulted in no significant decline in the incidence of dissent.

Czechoslovak resistance toward the Soviet occupation and toward the pro-Moscow policies of the government continued during the first 8 months of 1969 despite the tightening of controls and the purges of "liberal" Communists. The popular opposition movement culminated in anti-Soviet demonstrations *in March and August, although some of the incidents that took place may have been instigated by the authorities to provide a pretext for the repression of dissent. The most dramatic acts of protest were self-immolations of the student Jan Palach, Jan Zajic and other Czech youths. Intellectuals and workers rallied in an impressive display of solidarity against censorship and restrictions of the labor unions. Resistance in Czechoslovakia began to decline rapidly after the police and the army used massive force to suppress demonstrations during the first anniversary of the occupation.*

In other countries of eastern Europe, dissent was less conspicuous than in the Soviet Union and Czechoslovakia. Poland, Bulgaria and East Germany took stiff administrative measures to discourage opposition among intellectuals. In Yugoslavia, intellectual dissent was not so disruptive as agitation by the nation's Albanian minority, suggestive of the latent nationality conflict in the Yugoslav federal state.

SOVIET INTEGRATION DRIVE OPPOSED

Economic Integration Stalemated

Writing in the Soviet journal *Voprosy Ekonomiki (Economic Questions)*, G. M. Sorokin, an economist and member of the Soviet Academy of Sciences, proposed a long-range plan for complete economic and political integration of the Communist world. The features of Sorokin's plan, reported Jan. 7 in the London *Times:*

● Establishment of supranational agencies to supervise industrial production. Each member-nation would contribute to the total output based on a quota system that would include an international division of labor.

● Adoption of similar trade and fiscal policies by all bloc nations. Ultimately, there would be one socialist common market with a uniform price system.

● Revaluation of Soviet-bloc currencies to more realistic rates than those currently in effect.

• Establishment of one supranational agency to integrate and promote technological and scientific research and development. The member-states would pool their efforts in these fields.

Sorokin cautioned, however, that some Communist countries had not yet reached the stage at which they could fit their economies into an integrated system. He was also critical of certain Yugoslav and Czechoslovak economists who, he said, "openly revise Marxism" under the guise of a "so-called theory of nonadherence to any bloc, socialist or capitalist."

In an article in the Polish newspaper *Zycie Warszawy,* A. Kruczkowski argued for closer economic collaboration in eastern Europe within the Council for Mutual Economic Assistance (Comecon), it was reported Jan. 9. He claimed that such cooperation would give "a clear-cut vision of the progress of economic integration of the countries of our camp...." He said that it also would restrain West German influence in eastern Europe.

The 22d session of the Council of Comecon, held in Berlin Jan. 21-23, ended in disagreement over several major issues. The meeting, chaired by Herbert Weiz, deputy premier of the German Democratic Republic, failed to enact policy on currency convertibility, price coordination and centralized control of trade.

The Hungarian delegation, led by Deputy Premier Antal Apro, called for an agreement whereby Comecon countries' currencies would be convertible on the basis of the Soviet ruble. But East Germany successfully resisted the move, claiming that as the richest Comecon country it would be forced to underwrite currencies of poorer member nations. (Sources in Berlin said that the lack of currency convertibility was the main obstacle to closer ties among the Comecon states.)

In the matter of trade, Hungary and Rumania strongly opposed a move by East Germany, Poland and the USSR to advance tighter control on integration. Rumania's main objection to the plan, it was reported, was that integration would entail the establishment of supranational agencies to supervise trade policies and relations among the Comecon countries. This, the Rumanians maintained, would run counter to the principle of national sovereignty and would also adversely affect the interests of less-developed member states. Commenting on the trade integration plan, Radio Bucharest said Jan. 26: "On the basis of established principles, it is natural that recommendations and decisions of Comecon be adopted only with the consent of the countries interested, each country being entitled to express its interest in any problem, and that the decisions and recommendations adopted not be extended to noninterested countries."

Communist sources in Berlin also reported that Poland, East Germany and the Soviet Union had decided not to press their demands on major issues for fear of raising additional difficulties prior to the conference of Communist parties scheduled for May. This decision, and the discord at the meeting, were reflected in the concluding address by Polish Vice Premier Piotr Jaroszewicz. "In spite of the existing differences of opinion," he said, "the unity of ideals and principles of Socialist cooperation are stronger than any difficulties and discrepancies."

Yugoslavia & Rumania Bolster Defense

The Yugoslav Federal Assembly Feb. 11 approved a law creating territorial defense units throughout the country. Defense Min. (Col. Gen.) Nikola Ljubicic said that the law would provide defense against all types of potential invaders. "It is aimed at turning every part of the country, every city and every village into a center of resistance, and the whole country into a fortress."

Under the law, all males up to age 65 and every woman from 19 to 40 would be assigned to military, parliamentary or civil defense units. The guerrilla units would be composed of both sexes, students, workers, peasants and intellectuals, and would be trained by the army. The creation of the civil defense units reportedly was prompted by the invasion of Czechoslovakia in August.

The Zagreb newspaper *Vjesnik u Srijedu* disclosed that Yugoslavia and Rumania had agreed to strengthen their military defenses. The newspaper reported Feb. 6 that the topic had been discussed by Pres. Tito and Rumanian Communist Party General Secy. Nicolae Ceausescu at a meeting in Timisoara, Rumania Feb. 1-2. An official announcement after the meeting said that the 2 countries had reiterated the principles of sovereignty and noninterference. Whether they intended to coordinate their defense policies remained unclear. (Premier Mika Spiljak shortly thereafter made a 4-day unofficial visit to Hungary for talks with Hungarian Premier Jeno Fock. This was the first time the 2 countries had held high-level meetings since the invasion of Czechoslovakia.)

The Soviet press agency Tass reported Apr. 1 that Rumanian, Soviet and Bulgarian forces had taken part in Warsaw Pact exercises in Bulgaria the previous week. This was Rumania's first participation in pact maneuvers since Aug. 1967.

The Rumanian government asserted Apr. 12 that it would not permit the Warsaw Treaty command to give orders to Rumanian troops or to send other troops into Rumania. An editorial in the Rumanian Communist Party newspaper *Scinteia* declared: "The sole bodies entitled to engage the Rumanian armed forces in any action, to decide on or to approve the presence on Rumanian territory of foreign troops, are the legally elected, constitutional bodies that represent the will of the entire Rumanian people." It added that the Warsaw Treaty alliance had been established as a defense against "imperialist aggression" and that in no case "can action be expanded to other areas."

In an authoritative editorial in the Albanian Labor Party newspaper *Zeri i Popullit* in late April, the Albanian leadership pledged support for Rumania and Yugoslavia against Soviet military aggression. The editorial said that Tirana "will support without any hesitation the resistance of the people of Yugoslavia toward aggression." It declared that the Albanian party "powerfully back[s] the just resistance of the Rumanian fraternal people ... against the aggressive aims of the Soviet chauvinists and their followers."

An editorial in *Zeri i Popullit* Sept. 4 again affirmed Albania's solidarity with Yugoslavia and Rumania against Soviet military pressures in the Balkans. It said: "The peoples of Yugoslavia have proved during their whole history that they are not afraid, nor do they, as [does] the chief of Soviet revisionist diplomacy, [deal] only in words, for in fact it [the Yugoslav people] has the cannons behind it." The editorial also indicated that Communist China would support Rumania against Soviet pressures, stating that "all the progressive peoples of the world" would back Rumania against aggression.

Yugoslav Party Congress

The 9th Yugoslavian Communist Party Congress was held in Belgrade Mar. 11-15. The congress, boycotted by all Warsaw Pact nations except Rumania, was marked by a reaffirmation of Yugoslavia's ideological independence from the Soviet Union. Its sessions were attended by 1,261 delegates and by representatives from 64 foreign Communist, Socialist and Social Democratic parties.

In an address opening the congress Mar. 11, Pres. Tito was highly critical of Stalin and his attempt to impose Soviet domination on other Communist Parties. He condemned Stalin for his intervention "in the discussion on the national question in our country" and for his purges of the Yugoslav Communist Party, in which, Tito said, "innocent victims" "were tortured on the false accusation that they were spies and traitors ... [and] were taken to their death under monstrous accusations of ill-deed which they had never committed."

Tito denounced the USSR's attempts to subordinate Yugoslav interests to the needs of Soviet foreign policy. He charged that such policy "caused ... enormous damage to individual Communist parties. Such policy created bureaucratic relations in the party leaderships, hampered their initiative and, what was even worse, led them into isolation from their own working class and people of their country." Tito warned: "We continue to be witness to the practice whereby, in the relations between Socialist and between Communist Parties, the principle of internationalism is at times misused for the purpose of imposing unilateral obligations on individual parties."

In an apparent reference to the Czechoslovak invasion, Tito declared: "In the name of higher interests of socialism, attempts have been made to justify even the open violation of the sovereignty of a Socialist country and the resort to military force to prevent its independent Socialist development." Tito said that Yugoslavia was "very sorry" that some Communist parties had failed to attend the congress, "including the Communist Party of Czechoslovakia."

(Yugoslavia had invited all Communist parties except those of China and Albania. The Soviet Union, Hungary, Poland, Czechoslovakia and East Germany had informed Yugoslavia Mar. 6 that they would not attend the congress, reportedly because of Yugoslavia's criticism of the Czechoslovak invasion and of the Soviet doctrine of "limited sovereignty." Bulgaria and Mongolia cancelled their participation Mar. 7.)

(An estimated crowd of 5,000 demonstrators marched through Prague to the Yugoslav embassy Mar. 14 in protest against Czechoslovakia's "forced" exclusion from the Yugoslav congress. The demonstrators shouted "Long live Tito" and "Tito yes, Brezhnev no.")

In his address concluding the congress, Tito declared that Yugoslavia would not be "isolated." Alluding to pressure from the USSR, he said: "We want to have relations even with those with whom our relations are not the best.... We do not want to give cause for attacks ... [so] that it might be said that we are breaking up some international movement. But we shall never renounce our principles."

Preparations for Summit Meeting

The 7 member states of the Warsaw Treaty Organization met in Budapest Mar. 17, for the first time since the invasion of Czechoslovakia in Aug. 1968. During the 2-hour meeting, Communist party leaders of the 7 countries, constituting the alliance's Political Consultative Committee, unanimously adopted a resolution appealing for "peace and good neighborly relations with other European peoples" and for strengthening of efforts to achieve "European peace and security." The resolution also called for an all-European conference "to discuss questions of European security and peaceful cooperation," but it emphasized that "the inviolability of existing frontiers in Europe, including the Oder-Neisse frontier and the frontiers between the GDR [German Democratic Republic] and the Federal German Republic, is a fundamental condition of Europe's security; so is recognition of the existence of the GDR and the Federal German Republic."

The meeting, presided over by Czechoslovak Communist Party First Secy. Alexander Dubcek, had begun 5 hours late. Western observers attributed the delay to last-minute attempts by the Soviet Union to persuade Rumania to accept a resolution condemning the Communist Chinese as the "aggressors" in the recent border clashes between Chinese and Soviet forces. The Rumanians reportedly refused to support the resolution, declaring that the border incidents should be more thoroughly investigated. The final resolution contained no mention of China.

Details of the meeting were not made public until 2 days later. In an interview with the Czechoslovak Communist Party newspaper *Rude pravo* Mar. 19, Dubcek disclosed that the purpose of the Budapest meeting had been to improve "the organization of the combined command of the Warsaw Pact forces." 2 military documents were signed, establishing a Committee of Defense Ministers and adopting a "statute on the Combined Armed Forces and Combined Command." Dubcek said that the establishment of a joint command and multinational staff "will make it possible to settle more purposefully the military affairs of our defense community, to improve the system of equipment of our armies and achieve higher efficiency of expenditure on the defense of our countries." (In the official report on the proceedings Mar. 17, it was said only that the documents establishing the defense committee and joint command had been "unanimously adopted.") Dubcek also denied Western speculation that relations with China had been discussed.

The agreement for creation of a joint command was regarded as a concession to Rumania and other countries that had long demanded a greater voice in the activities of the Warsaw Pact. Since its establishment in 1955, the Warsaw Pact forces had been headed by a Soviet supreme commander and a Soviet chief of staff. The pact's forces had been nationally separate, associated only by the treaty. The new structure of the Warsaw Pact forces reportedly would resemble that of NATO. (According to the *Washington Post* Mar. 19, the USSR's purpose at the Budapest meeting had been to strengthen supranational control over the military forces of the member states.)

Tass announced Mar. 22 that the long-heralded World Conference of Communist & Workers' Parties would begin in Moscow June 5. The announcement also said that the Preparatory Committee for the conference, which had met in Moscow Mar. 18-22, would hold its final meeting May 23 in Moscow. The Moscow preparatory meetings had been boycotted by Albania, Communist China, Cuba, North Korea, North Vietnam and Yugoslavia.

(The Rumanian delegation at the International Conference on Prosecution of Nazi Criminals refused Mar. 28 to sign a Soviet-backed resolution that attacked the U.S., West Germany and Israel. The purpose of the conference, held in Moscow Mar. 25-28, had been to persuade West Germany to rescind its Dec. 1969 deadline for the prosecution of war criminals. But besides adopting an appeal for the continuation of the war trials, the conference adopted a resolution denouncing U.S. "aggression" in Vietnam, Israeli "aggression" in the Middle East and the "fascist" regime in Greece. Justice Min. Andrian Dimitru, speaking for the Rumanian delegation, said that while the delegation supported the appeal for the continuation of the war trials and for the condemnation of U.S. "aggression," the Rumanians did not have the authority to sign either the appeal or the resolution. Observers viewed Rumania's refusal as part of the country's policy of maintaining good relations with both Israel and West Germany.)

Moscow Conference

The long-postponed World Conference of Communist & Workers' Parties was held June 5-17 at the Kremlin.

The congress, attended by representatives of 75 Communist parties, was the first international Communist conference since Nov. 1960. The parties, invited to discuss the "urgent tasks of the struggle against imperialism and problems of united action by Communists," registered their most marked dissension over the questions of policy toward Communist China (not present at the conference), the Soviet-led invasion of Czechoslovakia and the independence of national Communist parties. A final declaration, signed June 17, was entitled "The Tasks of the Struggle Against Imperialism at the Present Stage, and the Unity of Action of the Communist & Workers' Parties and of All Antiimperialist Forces."

Soviet Communist Party General Secy. Leonid I. Brezhnev had welcomed the delegates June 5 with an appeal to Communists to close ranks, because "the pooling of their efforts ... [was] and remain[s] an important condition of success in the antiimperialist struggle, an important prerequisite of new victories for socialism." Brezhnev expressed the hope that the meeting would "rally the international Communist movement on the principles of Marxism-Leninism and proletarian internationalism."

In response to a Paraguayan delegate's charge that China was trying to split the world Communist movement, the Rumanian president and Communist Party general secretary, Nicolae Ceausescu, warned delegates June 6 that persistent attacks on other Communist parties would jeopardize the success of the conference. Ceausescu said that preparatory conferences had indicated that such criticism would be avoided at the summit meeting. Both Polish United Workers' Party First Secy. Wladyslaw Gomulka and French Communist Party General Secy. Waldeck Rochet, however, openly attacked China June 6. Gomulka said: "They [Chinese leaders] have betrayed internationalism, have spoken from positions of anti-Soviet nationalism and have split the world system of Socialist states. They have espoused political struggles in other fraternal parties and have created splinter groups."

In another speech June 9, Ceausescu warned that attacks on China and other countries not represented in Moscow were having "an adverse effect" on the conference. He disclosed that the Rumanian delegation June 6 had considered walking out of the meeting in protest but had decided to remain "in order to express our position." Ceausescu stressed Rumania's neutrality in the Sino-Soviet dispute and its disapproval of polemics by both sides. He urged negotiations to resolve differences among the parties.

Without specifically mentioning Czechoslovakia, Ceausescu called for acceptance of the principle of noninterference in the affairs of other countries. Disclosing that a draft declaration submitted to the conference by the USSR contained condemnations of nationalism, Ceausescu said that "independence and national sovereignty, equal rights and noninterference in internal affairs" were equally important and valid principles.

Ceausescu also rejected the idea that a "leading center" (Moscow) existed in the world Communist movement, and he asserted that the movement's meetings should not "establish directives and normative lines" but should provide for a free exchange of views, "after which each party can independently decide on its concrete way of action." The latter statement was an apparent reference to a speech the same day by East

German Socialist Unity Party First Secy. Walter Ulbricht, who had declared that international meetings should be held regularly to work out "common principles."

Dissenting views on the invasion of Czechoslovakia were placed before the conference June 6 by Laurie Aarons, secretary general of the Australian Communist Party, and June 11 by Enrico Berlinguer, deputy chairman of the Italian Communist Party. Aarons declared that the invasion had "damaged the cause of struggle for ... socialism in the whole world." He implied that Moscow had acted in its own national interest under the guise of "proletarian internationalism," which, Aarons said, should not "be separated from respect for the rights of all nations." Berlinguer reaffirmed his party's opposition to the invasion and rejected suggestions that raising the issue meant interfering in Czechoslovak affairs.

The conference ended June 17 with the formal signing of a 4-part declaration. The original draft, which had indorsed the Soviet viewpoint, had been the subject of nearly 1½ years of preparatory meetings and a principal object of debate at the conference. The authors of the final document, who diluted it by hundreds of amendments, significantly refrained from directly criticizing China and did not explicitly mention the invasion of Czechoslovakia.

Although the document's authors recognized Rumania's position on "noninterference in each other's internal affairs," they also incorporated a generalized version of the Brezhnev doctrine on limited sovereignty. They said: "The development and strengthening of each Socialist country [must] ... conform both to the interests of each people separately and the common cause of socialism." The document's authors also bowed to the Rumanian viewpoint in their admission that the world Communist movement had no "leading center." They said: "All parties have equal rights. As there is no leading center of the international Communist movement, voluntary coordination of the actions of parties in order effectively to carry out the tasks before them acquires increased importance."

The delegations from Rumania, Switzerland and Spain signed with reservations that were not incorporated into the document. Ceausescu appended a statement criticizing the declaration for exaggerating the threat of Western imperialism. In addition to the Chinese party, 4 other ruling parties did not send representatives to the conference: the parties of Albania, North Vietnam, North Korea and Yugoslavia.

Nixons' Visit Buoys Rumanians

The Rumanian commitment to national sovereignty was strikingly underscored by the reception accorded U.S. Pres. Richard M. Nixon and his wife as they stopped for 2 days in Rumania (at the invitation of Pres. Ceausescu) during their worldwide tour in midsummer of 1969.

The largest and most enthusiastic crowds encountered during the world tour greeted Pres. and Mrs. Nixon in Rumania Aug. 2-3. Estimates of the size of the crowds lining Bucharest's streets on their arrival ranged from a quarter of a million to 900,000. Many Rumanians waved American and Rumanian flags (distributed by authorities prior to the Nixons' arrival). The first American President in nearly a quarter of a century to visit a Communist nation, Nixon Aug. 2 expressed the belief that "nations can have widely different internal orders and live in peace." While the U.S. believed that "the rights of all nations must be equal," he said, "... we do not believe that the character of all nations must be the same." If international amity were to prevail, he said, the nations of the world must be prepared "to see the world as it is—a world of different races, of different nations, of different social systems—a real world, where many interests divide men and many interests unite them."

Rumanian Pres. Nicolae Ceausescu responded "that in the complex conditions of international affairs today, the development of relations between states on the basis of the principles of peaceful coexistence and respect for independence, sovereignty, equal rights and non-interference in the internal affairs, represents the safe way toward promoting a climate of confidence and understanding among peoples and of peace and security in the world."

It was announced Aug. 3 that the 2 leaders had agreed to reopen formal negotiations on a consular convention and hoped that negotiations for a civil air agreement could be resumed "at an appropriate opportunity." A U.S. library was to be opened in Rumania and a Rumanian library in the U.S. In a joint statement, the 2 leaders further asserted agreement to "look for new ways" of increasing economic exchanges between the 2 countries.

(A scheduled trip by Soviet leaders to Rumania just prior to the Nixon visit—in mid-July to sign a 20-year friendship treaty—had been postponed until fall. The postponement was attributed to the President's visit.)

Presidential Press Secy. Ronald Ziegler told reporters in Washington, D.C. Aug. 4, after Nixon had briefed 22 Congressional leaders on his trip, that the President had told Rumanian officials that the U.S. could move to open trade with eastern Europe after the end of the Vietnam war. Nixon's position at the White House meeting was that the U.S. should not furnish strategic materials to countries supplying arms to North Vietnam.

GROWTH OF SOVIET DISSENT

Attempted Assassination of Brezhnev?

According to Soviet reports, several shots were fired Jan. 22 at a motorcade carrying 4 astronauts on their way to a Kremlin celebration. The incident took place in the Borovitsky Gate to the Kremlin. Western observers believed that the attacker, whose identity was not disclosed, had aimed at the 2d car in the motorcade and that he believed that this was the car in which the top Soviet leaders were traveling. The leaders, headed by Brezhnev, were actually traveling further back in the motorcade of about 20 vehicles.

According to Tass, the bullets wounded the chauffeur of one of the cars and a motorcycle guard. The assailant was promptly seized. A Russian source described the attacker as an approximately 25-year-old man wearing a police uniform. Another source identified him as an army deserter. He was supposedly firing 2 pistols at the same time. No foreigner was said to have witnessed the shooting, which the Kremlin walls also concealed from pedestrians on adjoining streets. The incident took place in an area of the Kremlin ordinarily open to visitors.

The London *Sunday Times* Jan. 26 reported that the assailant had been dressed in a uniform of the special Kremlin guard. According to the paper's Moscow correspondent, he emerged from a sentry box and then fired 5 shots at the 3d car in the motorcade. The correspondent further asserted that the cars had changed place shortly before the incident. In the cold weather, all occupants of the cars were dressed in heavy coats and caps that made their identification difficult. It was later reported in Moscow that the chauffeur wounded in the shooting had died Jan. 27.

According to further reports that reached the West Jan. 31, the attacker was supposedly an army lieutenant in his 20s, absent without leave from a Leningrad unit. He was said to have obtained a policeman's uniform from Moscow relatives on the false pretext that he wanted to get a better view of the parade. Other sources reported his name to be Ilyin. The rumor that he had taken a cyanide capsule and committed suicide was denied.

Theodore Shabad of the *N.Y. Times* reported from Moscow Feb. 4 that no evidence of political conspiracy had been discovered. Ilyin's behavior was considered amateurish. According to some rumors, he was a member of a fanatical religious sect and fired the 2 pistols haphazardly, without aiming them. Anatol Shub, former Moscow correspondent of the *Washington Post,* asserted in his book *The New Russian Tragedy* (published in 1970) that the target of the attack had been Brezhnev. Shub said that he considered it indicative of unrest in the Soviet armed forces. He compared it to the Decembrist revolt of 1825, in which army officers had played a prominent role, and he predicted further conspiracies against the Soviet regime by members of the Soviet elite.

Dissidents Jailed

Irina Belgorodskaya, 29, received a one-year jail term Feb. 19 for spreading slander against the Soviet Union. Miss Belgorodskaya had been arrested in Aug. 1968 after 60 copies of a petition demanding the release of a political dissident, Anatoly T. Marchenko, were found in her handbag in a Moscow taxicab. The daughter of a retired KGB (State Security Committee) colonel, Miss Belgorodskaya, an engineer, was a cousin of Mrs. Larissa Daniel, who had been sentenced to exile in Siberia in Oct. 1968 for protesting the Czechoslovak invasion.

Ilya Burmistrovich, charged with possessing writings of 2 imprisoned authors, Andrei D. Sinyavsky and Yuli M. Daniel, was sentenced May 21 to 3 years in prison. He had spent more than a year in jail awaiting his trial.

The *N. Y. Times* had reported Mar. 14 that the writers Yuli Daniel, Yuri Galanskov and Aleksandr Ginsburg and other inmates of a prison camp had threatened a hunger strike unless their status was changed from that of common criminals to political prisoners. The camp, located near Potma, 250 miles east of Moscow, reportedly had 15,000 prisoners, including several hundred foreigners. The *Washington Post* reported Mar. 17 that the hunger strike had actually begun Mar. 14. In a letter to the Supreme Soviet reported June 2, Daniel, Galanskov, Ginsburg and 3 other inmates (Valery Ronkin, Sergei Mashkov and V. Kalninsh) protested against allegedly intolerable living conditions at the prison. They charged that they had been subjected to physical maltreatment, cold and hunger and had been deprived of their limited legal rights as political prisoners. In their appeal, the writers said: "Today it is in your power to confirm and strengthen the existing situation or change it towards some other direction—to regularize the lawlessness or to restrict it by effective control so that our human and civic rights are observed."

(Ginsburg was permitted to marry his common-law wife, Irina Zholkovskaya, Aug. 21. The marriage was performed at a "private" house outside the perimeter of the Potma prison camp. Ginsburg had gone on hunger strikes in June because authorities would not recognize Miss Zholkovskaya as his wife and, therefore, would not allow her to visit him twice a year as the rules permitted.)

Sources in Moscow reported Sept. 4 that Daniel had been moved from Potma to Vladimir Prison, 100 miles east of Moscow. The move followed a trial in July in which Daniel was accused of anti-Soviet protests at the prison camp. His wife, Larissa Daniel, in exile in Siberia, reportedly had been given a supervisory position in July. Mrs. Daniel, who had been suffering from fatigue and acute gastritis, had been forced to work as a laborer in a sawmill.

The London *Times* reported Dec. 19 that a new hunger strike at the Potma prison camp had been begun in early December to protest the transfer of Daniel and Ronkin to Vladimir Prison in July. The strikers included Galanskov, Ginsburg and 4 others.

Ex-Maj. Gen. Pyotr Grigoryevich Grigorenko, a leading political dissenter, was reported Mar. 7 to have circulated to Soviet citizens an appeal for the withdrawal of Soviet troops from Czechoslovakia. Grigorenko, 62, citing the suicides of the Czech students Palach and Zajic in protest against the occupation, said in his appeal: "We call upon all Soviet people, without doing anything rash or hasty and by all legal methods, to bring about the withdrawal of Soviet troops from Czechoslovakia and the renunciation of interference in her internal affairs."

Grigorenko, was arrested in Tashkent May 7 on charges of slandering the USSR and its social system. He had arrived in the Uzbek Republic May 3 to provide nonprofessional legal advice for a group of 11 Crimean Tatars accused of anti-Soviet offenses. Internal security agents reportedly had warned Grigorenko, who had spoken out for restoration of Tatar national rights, that he would be arrested if he tried to take part in the Tashkent trial. He was reported Oct. 30 to have been committed to a mental institution. His family reported Dec. 12 that doctors at a Moscow mental institution had declared him insane and suffering from a "paranoid development of his personality."

Ivan A. Yakhimovich, arrested in Riga, Latvia Mar. 25 on charges of spreading anti-Soviet material, was reported June 2 to have been ruled psychiatrically unfit to stand trial. Yakhimovich was a leading Russian critic of the Soviet invasion.

Informed sources in Moscow reported Aug. 27 that Anatoly Marchenko, jailed since Aug. 5, 1968, had been sentenced to an additional 2 years in a "corrective labor" camp for slandering the Soviet Union. Sources said that Marchenko, 31, had been sentenced for "slanderous and anti-Soviet propaganda while in prison." His original sentence of one year at hard labor, imposed Aug. 21, 1968, had been for protesting Soviet pressure on Czechoslovakia.

Moscow sources reported Oct. 23 that 3 unidentified Soviet naval officers had been arrested in June in Tallinn, Estonia, in connection with their plans to distribute an appeal calling for the democratization of Soviet society. The officers, who were reported to have signed an earlier petition denouncing the Czechoslovak invasion, were arrested before the appeal was widely distributed. The sources also said that the officers had written a commentary on the 1968 "convergence" theory of Andrei D. Sakharov.

Appeal to UN

55 Soviet dissidents appealed to the UN Commission on Human Rights for an investigation of "the repression of basic civil rights in the Soviet Union." The petition was disclosed May 22, and the dissidents signing it included Pyotr I. Yakir, 46, the son of the late Gen. Iona E. Yakir (executed June 11, 1937, during Stalin's purge of the army). The signers declared themselves "deeply indignant over unceasing political persecutions in the Soviet Union, perceiving in them a return to Stalin's times, when our whole country was in the grip of terror."

The signers said: "Recent arrests have compelled us to think that Soviet punitive organs have decided finally to bar the activity of people protesting against arbitrariness in our country." The petitioners said they were appealing to the UN because their protests and complaints to Soviet organs had been unsuccessful. Officials at the UN said May 22 that the dissidents' appeal had not reached the New York headquarters.

(10 Soviet dissidents appealed to the world conference of Communist parties, which opened June 5 in Moscow, to consider "the rebirth of Stalinist methods in our country." In their appeal, the dissidents, who included Yakir, said: "Again as under Stalin, the alternative is silence. Again as in those terrible times we are deprived of the possibility of expressing our convictions.")

Sources in Moscow reported June 18 that several of the Soviet dissidents who had appealed to the UN commission had been punished. Some of them had lost their jobs and others had been reprimanded; one reportedly was committed to a psychiatric hospital.

The dissidents, learning that their petition had not been received at the UN in New York, had attempted in mid-June to present copies to the UN Information Center in Moscow. UN officials said in New York June 19 that they were investigating to determine why the petition had not been forwarded by the Moscow office.

A petition with an appeal to the UN Commission on Human Rights to investigate "violations of human rights" in the USSR was signed by 46 Soviet dissidents and delivered to the UN Information Center in Moscow Sept. 26. The dissidents, including some of the signers of the May petition to the UN, were informed that the petition could not be accepted because the signatures were typewritten. (The original allegedly had been sent through the Soviet postal system to the UN.) When the dissidents returned Sept. 29 they were told that the center was not competent to forward their petition and to use usual telegraphic or postal systems.

The UN Office of Public Information Oct. 3 supported the decision of the Moscow center not to forward the petition. A new regulation stated that the 50 UN information centers would no longer accept petitions for the secretary general. The new order reportedly broke a 20-year tradition.

Anatoly Y. Levitin, a former Russian Orthodox priest, was reportedly arrested in Moscow Sept. 11 on charges of anti-Soviet activity. It was reported that Levitin, 54, had been arrested for signing the May petition. Levitin, whose works had been published in the West under the pen name Krasnov, had joined 14 other dissidents early in 1969 in forming the Initiative Group for the Defense of Civil Rights in the USSR. Sources in Moscow reported Oct. 30 that another signer of the May appeal, Vladimir Gershuni, a mason, had been arrested Oct. 18. 6 other signers already had been detained, including Yuri Maltsev, a translator, who had been committed to a mental hospital in October. Maltsev also belonged to the Initiative Group for the Defense of Civil Rights in the USSR.

A petition signed by 11 Soviet dissidents and supported by 36 others was received at the UN Oct. 29. The document, in which the 11 called on the UN to speak out against further repression of human rights in the USSR, contained the assertion that several of its authors had been either forcibly placed in mental institutions or arrested. The 11 also protested against the arrest of Levitin.

Genrikh Altunyan, an engineer who had signed the May appeal, was sentenced Nov. 26 to 3 years in prison on charges of defaming the Soviet social system and state. The charges included 3 specifications: signing of the appeal, protesting against the treatment of Ex-Maj. Gen. Grigorenko, and asserting publicly that anti-Semitism existed in the USSR. Altunyan's sentencing was made public Nov. 27 in a letter to the UN.

Sources in Moscow reported Dec. 26 that the economist Viktor Krasin had been sentenced by a Moscow court Dec. 23 to a 5-year term in exile on charges of being "an antisocial parasite." Under a 1961 act, administrative action, as distinct from criminal action, could be taken against persons who "avoid socially useful work ... or commit other antisocial acts that enable them to lead a parasitic way of life." Krasin, who had been dismissed from his post at the Moscow Economics Institute earlier in 1969 for his support of dissidents, had refused on principle to take any menial jobs and was thus charged with being unemployed. Krasin, who reportedly had spent several years in a Soviet concentration camp in the early 1950s for criticizing Stalin, had been a signer of petitions to the UN protesting the lack of civil liberties in the USSR.

Kuznetsov Defects

The defection to Britain of the Soviet author Anatoly V. Kuznetsov was revealed July 30 in London. Kuznetsov, who shortly before had been named to the editorial board of the youth magazine *Yunost,* received permission to remain in Britain indefinitely. The permission, however, did not involve political asylum, granted only to those in danger of political persecution on return to their own country. Kuznetsov, 39, had gone to London July 24 at the invitation of the British Society for Cultural Relations with the USSR. He left behind in Russia, his wife, common-law wife, son and mother.

In a statement published Aug. 3 in the London *Sunday Telegraph,* Kuznetsov renounced all his published works as ideological pot-boilers that had been distorted beyond recognition by Soviet censors. Since his first work appeared 25 years ago, Kuznetsov said, not one work had been published in its original form. He declared: "For the past 10 years I have been living in a state of constant, unavoidable and irresolvable contradiction. Finally, I have simply given up." Kuznetsov also renounced his name as that of a "dishonest conformist, cowardly author." He said that he would use the pen name A. Anatol.

The *Telegraph* also published Kuznetsov's letters of resignation from the Soviet Communist Party and the Soviet Writers' Union. He declined to meet with Soviet officials in London until the Soviet Union withdrew from Czechoslovakia. He denounced Marxism-Leninism as an ideology "utterly incapable of resolving the contradictions in society today."

Kuznetsov's 2 novels, *Babi Yar* and *The Fire* (published that past winter in *Yunost)*, had been sharply criticized by Soviet conservatives for unflattering portrayals of life in the USSR. *The Fire* had depicted demoralized people in a metalworks town; *Babi Yar* described the Nazi massacre of most of Kiev's Jewish population

The first official Soviet acknowledgment of Kuznetsov's defection appeared in the Aug. 6 issue of the weekly newspaper of the writers' union, *Literaturnaya Gazeta (Literary Gazette),* which announced that the union had expelled Kuznetsov Aug. 3 "for betrayal of the motherland, for betrayal of socialism and for political and moral double-dealing." The weekly said that Kuznetsov's trip to Britain had originated out of his own proposal to the editors of *Yunost* that he do a book about Lenin in honor of his 100th birthday.

Kuznetsov said in an interview in the West German weekly *Der Spiegel* Sept. 1 that he expected that his defection would set off a purge of intellectuals in the Soviet Union. He said: "My flight to the West has made a big impression on the Russian intellectuals. The reprisals will thereby be intensified. The pressure will become greater. Perhaps it will reach the point where thoughts that someone has sheltered deep inside himself will come more boldly to expression. Perhaps then he will not be afraid that communism is evil."

In an article in the London *Daily Telegraph* Aug. 9, Kuznetsov told how the KGB controlled and used writers. He said he didn't know any writer in the USSR who had not had some connection with the KGB. Some writers, he said, collaborated enthusiastically or indirectly, while others were approached and rebuffed all advances. The latter writers would not be published and might even find themselves in concentration camps. Kuznetsov said a KGB "comrade" always accompanied Soviet travelers: "If 5 people are traveling abroad, at least 2 of them are informers. If 2 are traveling, at least one must be an informer. And if there's only one person, then he is an informer on himself."

Kuznetsov reported that at Yasnaya Polyana, Leo Tolstoy's estate 7 miles south of Tula, where he had gone in 1963 to write a novel, all writers were kept under surveillance. He said: "One of the 'scholars' at Yasnaya Polyana was an officer of the KGB, and everyone, from the director down to the guides, had to report to him. Every foreigner who visited Yasnaya Polyana was kept under specially strict surveillance."

(Kuznetsov disclosed Aug. 6 that he had begun action to reopen a literary suit won by him in France. His first novel, *The Continuation of Life,* had been translated in France by the Rev. Paul Chaleil and had appeared under the title *L'Etoile dans le Brouillard* [*The Star in the Mist*]. In 1961 Kuznetsov had sued the French publishing house for distorting and falsifying his work for ideological reasons. In 1965 the French courts awarded Kuznetsov $200 in damages, which he claimed he had never collected. In a statement to the *Daily Telegraph,* however, Kuznetsov said Chaleil had "simply not bothered to translate those optimistic chapters which had been forced out of me." He said he had written to French Justice Min. Rene Pleven requesting that the verdict be reversed. "Living as I was," Kuznetsov wrote, "in that monstrous state, the Soviet Union, under pressure from Soviet officials and at their dictation, I made an insincere application to your court.")

Solzhenitsyn Controversy

Literaturnaya Gazeta confirmed Nov. 12 that novelist Aleksandr I. Solzhenitsyn had been expelled Nov. 4 from the branch of the writers' union in Ryazan, 110 miles southeast of Moscow, where he lived. The secretariat of the writers' union of the Russian Republic approved the local union's decision Nov. 10. The journal said Solzhenitsyn, 51, had been charged with conduct antisocial in character and "contrary to the principles and tasks formulated in the rules of the Union of Soviet

Writers." It added that "the name and works of Solzhenitsyn have been actively used by hostile bourgeois propaganda in recent years for a slanderous campaign against our country."

Sources in Moscow reported Nov. 12 that Solzhenitsyn had denied charges that he had "blackened" the USSR by stressing the worst aspects of life under Stalin's rule. He reportedly said: "One cannot succeed indefinitely in keeping quiet about Stalin's crimes, for they were the crimes committed against millions of human beings. To pretend that they did not exist is to pervert millions of other human beings."

(Of Solzhenitsyn's major works—*The First Circle, Cancer Ward* and *One Day in the Life of Ivan Denisovich*—only the latter had been published in the Soviet Union; since 1966 his works had been banned.)

In a letter sent to the writers' union of the Russian Republic Nov. 10 and made public Nov. 14, Solzhenitsyn, considered by many as the greatest living Soviet novelist, termed the USSR a "sick society."

In an article in the *Literaturnaya Gazeta* Nov. 25, the union's board charged that Solzhenitsyn had taken sides "with those who are acting against the Soviet social system." The union denied that he had not been given a chance to defend himself before the secretariat of the union approved his expulsion. Referring to the letter in which he described the USSR as a "sick society," the board said that it was "pretentious, full of curses and threats and of pseudo-theoretical deliberations." The board suggested that Solzhenitsyn leave the Soviet Union. "No one intends [to stop him]," it said, "not even when Solzhenitsyn wishes to go where his anti-Soviet works and letters are always met with such enthusiasm."

The Nobel Prize winner Mikhail A. Sholokhov indirectly joined the campaign of denunciation against Solzhenitsyn Nov. 27. The orthodox Soviet novelist castigated certain writers as "Colorado beetles—those who eat Soviet bread but who want to serve Western bourgeois masters and send their works through secret channels."

The secretariat of the Moscow branch of the Soviet Writers' Union "unanimously approved" the expulsion of Solzhenitsyn Dec. 2. The decision by the 22 minor literary figures was viewed as a rebuff to a number of writers, including Aleksandr T. Tvardovsky and the poet Yevgeni Yevtushenko, who had written to the union requesting a review of the decision to expel Solzhenitsyn.

39 dissidents Dec. 20 protested the expulsion of Solzhenitsyn from the union. The protesters, including Pyotr Yakir, said the ouster represented "another major manifestation of Stalinism, a reprisal against a writer who embodies the conscience and mind of our people." Culture Min. Yekaterina A. Furtseva said Dec. 26 that if Solzhenitsyn wrote "good works" he would be published in the USSR despite his expulsion from the union.

Other Disputes over Art & Ideology

An article in the Communist Party newspaper *Pravda* Feb. 17 attacked literary critics who had lauded the works of writers and poets of the immediate prerevolutionary period and the 1920s without regard for their positions toward communism. The article, written by P. Vikhodtsev, charged that critics had emphasized the personality of the writer while neglecting the "social and historical aspects of his work." "This leads," Vikhodtsev said, "to an appreciation of his artistic merits separately from his opinions."

Sovetskaya Rossiya, the newspaper of the Communist Party central committee of the Russian Republic, May 29 assailed Soviet intellectuals who remained neutral in the class struggle, promoted "imperialist slogans" of freedom of criticism, sought to expose Stalinism, and smuggled unpublished works to the West.

Kharif Sabirov, a Kazan philosophy instructor, said in an article that intellectuals could not remain ideologically neutral without betraying society. He conceded, however, that the reindoctrination of intellectuals would not be easy: "It is known that survivals of individualist morality and psychology—the placing of the individual in opposition to the collective, and elements of a semianarchist, lordly attitude toward discipline—are harder to overcome in the ranks of the intelligentsia." Sabirov did not call for the suppression of any authors but rather for "patient ideological work with the disoriented part of the intelligentsia."

Sabirov wrote that intellectuals had been adversely influenced by the concept of freedom of criticism. He argued that this freedom could only be understood in a class context. "In a Socialist society," he said, "criticism cannot depart from the sharp class question; it is either a powerful weapon for strengthening socialism, or a weapon for undermining its foundation." Sabirov complained that certain unnamed intellectuals had persisted in publishing works critical of Stalin and "collecting examples of the harmful consequences of the [Stalin] personality cult." He said this fascination with Stalin had turned intellectuals away "from the main goal of participating in the great problems of building communism."

Sabirov held that the same problems existed in other Communist nations, but to a greater degree. He said: "In other Socialist countries, the main mass of the old bourgeois intelligentsia is active [yet], ... and far from all of it has been freed of bourgeois ideas, views, habits and prejudices."

Sabirov's article was regarded by Western sources as the fullest and most honest treatment of intellectual unrest in the Communist world for some time.

Pravda had attacked *Novy Mir* Mar. 6 for publishing a novel on hardships under Stalin's rule. (The novel, *Youth in Zheleznodolsk,* by Nikolai Bronov, had been published in the past 2 issues of *Novy Mir.*) The book described the plight of kulaks (well-to-do peasants) in the Urals during the first 5-Year Plan (1929-33). Referring to an earlier criticism of *Novy Mir,* considered a liberal Soviet publication, the author of the *Pravda* article said: "This criticism is all the more well founded because the editors of *Novy Mir* in the past have been subject to criticism more than once for publishing a number of works that contained ideological mistakes and that denigrate our way of life." (*Pravda* published extracts from a new Sholokhov novel in which it was alleged that Stalin had been "running the country with his eyes shut" prior to 1941. The book, entitled *They Fought for the Fatherland,* described life in the Soviet Union during the purges of the 1930s; it implied that Stalin had allowed the secret police to imprison innocent people. *Pravda* reportedly published the extracts to dispel rumors of a dispute between Sholokhov and literary and ideological leaders.)

The London *Times* reported May 26 that Aleksandr T. Tvardovsky, editor of *Novy Mir,* had been asked to resign. The request reportedly was made by the board of directors of the union. Tvardovsky suffered from a chronic liver ailment and had been unable to work for long periods. Tvardovsky, editor of the monthly since 1958, had lost his candidate-membership in the Communist Party Central Committee Apr. 8, 1966.

Novy Mir was attacked in an open letter published July 26 in the popular weekly magazine *Ogonyok.* The letter accused *Novy Mir* of promoting "cosmopolitan ideas" and minimizing the dangers of bourgeois ideology at the expense of Soviet patriotism. "Cosmopolitanism" was the Stalinist term for foreign or Jewish influences. The 11 conservative writers who signed the letter were: Lenin Prizewinner Sergei Smirnov, Mikhail Alekseyev, Sergei Vikulov, Sergei Voronin, Vitaly Zakrutkin, Anatoly Ivanov, Sergei Malashkin, Aleksandr Prokofiev, Pyotr Proskurin, Vladimir Chivilikhin and Nikolai Shundik. The letter centered its attack on a *Novy Mir* article by Aleksandr G. Dementyev, 65, a well-known liberal writer. Dementyev reportedly had sharply rebuked the monthly Young Communist League publication *Molodaya Gvardia (Young Guard)* for over-zealous treatment of Soviet patriotism and the dangers of foreign ideological influences.

Novy Mir's editor, Tvardovsky, was criticized by the newspaper *Sotsialisticheskaya Industriya (Socialist Industry).* An open letter published July 31 denounced him for permitting *Novy Mir* to print unpatriotic works.

In the July issue of *Novy Mir,* which appeared in Moscow Aug. 29, the editors rebuked their critics. The editors, under the leadership of Tvardovsky, denounced the "crude demagogy and unbridled tone" of the conservative attacks and said: "The editors of *Novy Mir* do not consider their work free of mistakes and are prepared to listen to any, even the most strict, comradely criticism, but they decidedly reject attempts to blacken one of the oldest Soviet journals—attempts bordering on political accusations."

The editors continued: "Soviet patriotism and love for the motherland cannot be the privilege of one narrow group of writers. In the final count, only by means of the national recognition and longevity of books, poems and articles can the real as opposed to the pretentious love of the writer for his homeland be measured."

The July issue also contained 3 new poems by Andrei Voznesensky. This was the first time in more than a year that his work had appeared. Voznesensky, widely regarded as the most brilliant young Russian poet, reportedly had refused to submit his work to ideological considerations.

3 prominent liberal writers had been dropped from the editorial board of the magazine *Yunost,* it was disclosed July 21. The names of poet Yevgeni Yevtushenko, playwright Viktor S. Rosov and short story writer and playwright Vasily P. Aksyonov did not appear in the magazine's July issue. A 4th member of the board, E. B. Vishnyakov, was reported to have retired. A *Yunost* spokesman declined to give reasons for the dismissals. The *N.Y. Times* reported July 22 that Yevtushenko had been ousted because he had criticized the invasion of Czechoslovakia and had published a series of poems about Spain in the *Novy Mir* in which he had rebuked his critics. Aksyonov was also believed to have been dismissed for his negative views on the invasion.

Prof. Pyotr L. Kapitsa, 75, a leading Soviet nuclear physicist, criticized Soviet ideologists for not competing freely with other world philosophies and for falling behind the times. His criticism, which appeared in the Soviet Academy of Sciences' philosophy journal *Voprosy Filosofii (Philosophical Questions)* May 27, stressed the need for the USSR to emerge from self-isolation. Soviet ideologists, he said, "stood isolated" from the student revolutionary movement in the West. Kapitsa said that while the capitalist world was reexamining its ideology and looking for possible alternatives, the Soviet theorists had remained unmoving. He advocated that ideologists take an active part in showing how the Soviet example could influence revolutionary movements.

The USSR was on almost even terms with the U.S. in the political, cultural and economic fields and lagged behind only in technological development, Kapitsa declared. The "battle of the century" had thus become an ideological one "between 2 systems of organized society—the capitalist way and the Socialist way."

Kapitsa indorsed the theory of the ultimate "convergence" of the Soviet and U.S. systems. Speaking at a news conference in Washington Oct. 9, Kapitsa supported the concept, first advanced by Prof. Andrei D. Sakharov in 1968, that only through collaboration could the 2 great powers avoid the dangers threatening mankind. Kapitsa assailed the development of anti-ballistic-missile systems, arguing they were costly and ineffective. Kapitsa also said he favored cooperation in fields too costly or vital for competition, such as cancer research and the development of a large particle accelerator or atom smasher.

An article in *Sovetskaya Rossiya* warned Dec. 3 against the corruption of young writers, and it blamed the West for spurring "ideologically immature" works that "blacken" Soviet achievements. The article called for tighter party control of literature.

In a letter to 6 Western newspapers published Dec. 3, writer Andrei Amalrik said the Soviet Union had refused to give him part of the royalties awarded by Western publishers because he had published abroad. Amalrik requested that further royalties be retained in the West.

It was reported Dec. 8 that Yuri Rybakov, editor of the leading theatrical journal *Teatr,* had been removed from his post. The journal had come under attack in October for displaying ideological "inexactness."

At a 2-day ideological conference in Moscow Dec. 10-11, Soviet intellectuals were warned against Western influences and admonished to "fight bourgeois reactionary culture." Reflecting the general tone of the conference, Sergei Mikhalov of the Moscow branch of the writers' union said: "The majority of us realize that tolerance to the intolerable turns out to be harmful to our general cause.... There is no place for any all-forgiving liberalism and bleeding hearts." In addition to attacking the writers Solzhenitsyn and Kuznetsov and *Novy Mir,* most of those voting at the conference supported a resolution asserting that "the intellectuals of the country, true as they are to the Leninist principles of party-mindedness and folk character of art, will discharge their supreme civic duty with honor."

Unrest Among Soviet Nationalities

Leaders of the Central Asian republic of Tadzhikistan were strongly criticized in the Soviet Communist Party Central Committee journal, *Partiinaya Zhizn (Party Life),* for not implementing economic reforms, for corruption and for allowing Moslem customs and nationalism to continue. According to the article, Tadzhik ministries had not developed the economic reforms applied in other areas of the Soviet Union but rather had continued the "inadequate use of economic management methods and unnecessary regimentation of factory operations, curbing the initiative of plant managers and staffs." Moscow leaders charged that Tadzhik authorities had not sown crops in large areas of irrigated land, that "many farms [relied] widely on manual labor and [made] poor use of machinery" and that manpower resources were not efficiently used. Moscow authorities further charged that some Tadzhik officials were corrupt and unqualified as leaders. They also said that propaganda efforts had been unsuccessful mainly because of inadequate facilities for disseminating information; the result was that Moslem customs continued to exist.

Sources in Moscow reported May 7 that a student in Riga, Latvia, had slain himself in protest against the Czechoslovak invasion. Ilya Reus, 20, was said to have hung a sign on his body reading "Interventionists Out of Czechoslovakia" before he burned himself to death Apr. 27 in Riga's main square.

The underground news sheet called the *Chronicle of Current Events* carried Apr. 30 a report on the trial of a Crimean Tatar, Gomer Bayev, in Simferopol. Bayev received a 2-year sentence at forced labor for advocating the right of his people, deported during the Stalin regime, to return home. The *Chronicle* estimated that since the publication of the Sept. 1967 decree rehabilitating the Tatars, about 12,000 of those who went back to the Crimea had again been evicted.

6 Crimean Tatars were arrested in Mayakovsky Square in Moscow June 6 for alleging government persecution of their nationality group. The demonstrators carried banners calling for the release of ex-Maj. Gen. Grigorenko, arrested in Tashkent, Uzbekistan May 7 on the charge of slandering the USSR in championing the Tatar cause.

After a month-long trial, 10 Crimean Tatars Aug. 5 received jail sentences that were described by Moscow dissenters as "showing some flexibility on the part of authorities." 4 defendants received the maximum prison term of 3 years, less the 11 months they had already spent in jail, while the remaining 6 were given sentences equal to the time already spent in jail. The defendants had been charged with violating a law dealing with "falsehoods derogatory to the Soviet state and social system." (In recent years, 200 Tatar leaders reportedly had received the maximum prison sentences.) The verdict led to a protest by about 600 Tatars who assembled outside the court and marched to the Uzbekistan party central committee's offices. Many of the demonstrators were arrested; 4 of the leaders were subsequently sentenced to 15 days in jail and the rest were released.

According to a later issue of the *Chronicle,* a number of mass meetings of Uzbek nationalists had taken place in May under the slogan "Russians, Get Out of Uzbekistan!" The capital city, Tashkent, was surrounded by troops, and about 150 persons were arrested. 30 of them received sentences to 15 days for "petty hooliganism." One unconfirmed rumor was that the daughter of the party first secretary of Uzbekistan was among those detained. In Bukhara, many Tadzhiks living in the city reportedly had been described in their passports as "Uzbeks" by the authorities. The Tadzhik reaction was said to have led to 8 murders.

Boris Kochubyevsky, a Jewish engineer from the Ukraine, was sentenced to 3 years in prison May 16 on charges of slander against the Soviet state and social system. The charges stemmed from a speech Kochubyevsky made at a memorial service in 1968 at Babi Yar, the ravine outside Kiev where most of the city's Jewish population had been slaughtered by the Nazis. Kochubyevsky reportedly had said that the Babi Yar victims were victims not only of fascism but also of genocide. A Kiev court was said to have ruled that his remarks were of a bourgeois-nationalist-Zionist nature and not in keeping with the Soviet policy of memorializing Babi Yar's victims as Soviet citizens, rather than as Jews. Kochubyevsky and his wife had attempted to emigrate to Israel in 1968 but had been refused permission to leave the USSR. Kochubyevsky's friends said that he had been forced to leave his job as a radio engineer and that his wife, who was not Jewish, was expelled from a teacher's college. (More than 40 persons picketed near the Russian embassy in Washington June 12 in protest against Kochubyevky's jailing.)

CZECHOSLOVAK RESISTANCE

Protests Against Ouster of Smrkovsky

The Czechoslovak Communist Party (CPCS) Presidium Jan 7 relieved Josef Smrkovsky, 57, a Czech, from his post as chairman of the old National Assembly and named him to head the People's chamber in the country's newly formed bicameral legislature. The Presidium chose Vice Premier Peter Colotka, a Slovak, to head the entire new parliament as chairman of the new Federal Assembly.

Because of his liberal views, Smrkovsky had received wide support from workers and students for the post eventually received by Colotka. The 900,000-member Czech Union of Metal Workers had threatened to strike, and students to demonstrate, if Smrkovsky was not appointed Federal Assembly chairman.

In response, the Presidium, in a radio broadcast Jan. 4, had warned the people to stop agitating for political and economic reforms and, by implication, had raised the possibility of another Soviet intervention. The Presidium said: "These campaigns are driving our society into conflicts whose consequences it is possible the initiators cannot even imagine unless of course they themselves wish it. We therefore consider it necessary to warn citizens of the gravity of the situation and the consequences that could result from any unconsidered steps...." "There is no truth in speculation about attempts to remove Comrade Smrkovsky from party and state functions and to exclude him from political life."

The Presidium simultaneously defended Gustav Husak, the Slovak party leader who had been one of the leading Presidium members to urge the replacement of Smrkovsky by a Slovak in the post of Assembly chairman. (Husak had been assailed Jan. 3 by Vlastimil Toman, chairman of the Metal Workers Union, for making "extremist" statements against Smrkovsky's appointment.)

On a TV broadcast Jan. 5, Smrkovsky pressed his supporters not to strike on his behalf. The Union of Metal Workers, after a two-day meeting, decided Jan. 9 not to strike in support of him. But it called for a "democratic election" in the Federal Assembly to select the Assembly's chairman.

Members of the Czech Trade Union of Printers Jan. 11 refused to print the first issue of the new party weekly *Tribuna,* a publication of the CPCS Central Committee's Bureau for Party Affairs in the Czech Socialist Republic. The union also named Smrkovsky its honorary chairman.

Lidova Democracie, the newspaper of the People's (Catholic) Party, printed Jan. 11 a resolution of printers that "recogniz[ed] the work of journalists" and proclaimed "astonishment that millions of people in the country are seen as 'pressure groups,'" as the occupiers styled all political opposition.

The Printer's Union refused to distribute in Ostrava a brochure, entitled "2-Faced Politics," which criticized Smrkovsky. The brochure reportedly had been ordered by conservatives wanting to discredit Smrkovsky.

Some 2,000 students and workers met in Prague Jan. 15 and adopted a "Prague manifesto" that condemned the Soviet-led occupation of Czechoslovakia. The manifesto declared that good relations could be restored between Czechoslovakia and the five invading nations (the USSR, Poland, Hungary, Bulgaria and East Germany) only when full sovereignty was restored and the "humiliating consequences" of the invasion ended. The manifesto demanded that Peter Colotka, chairman-designate of the Federal Assembly, withdraw in favor of Smrkovsky, and it called for an immediate restoration of all political freedoms. Speakers, who included leaders of the Union of Printers and the Metal Workers Union, asserted that they would never relinquish their right to participate in policy-making.

Self-Immolations

Jan Palach, 21, a student at Charles University in Prague, set himself afire near a fountain before the National Museum in *Vaclavske namesti* (Wenceslas Square) Jan. 16 in protest against the Soviet occupation. He died of his burns Jan. 19 in a

Prague hospital. Before his death, Palach told a friend, in a statement later broadcast by Prague radio, that "my act has achieved its purpose. But it would be better if nobody repeats it. Lives should be used for other purposes. We are involved in a great struggle today."

In a note found in his jacket, the student demanded the end of government censorship and a ban on the distribution of the Soviet Czech-language newspaper, *Zpravy*. The note was posted in Wenceslas Square. It said: "With regard to the fact that our nations are at the edge of hopelessness, we decided to express our protest and awaken the people of this country in the following way: Our group is composed of volunteers who are ready to burn themselves for our cause. I had the honor to draw the first lot and I have gained the right to write the first letter and set the first torch.... Should our requirements not be fulfilled within 5 days [by Jan. 21], and if the people will not come out with sufficient support (such as a strike for an indefinite period), further torches will go up in flames." The letter was signed "Torch Number One."

Palach's burning and subsequent death touched off a wave of student and worker protests. In a statement by students at Charles University Jan. 17, Palach was described as a "deeply human, thoughtful, political thinking man." The statement denounced the Soviet Union and the Prague government: "We accuse the Soviet leadership of adding by its policies yet one more victim of the 21st of August [date of the Soviet invasion]. We accuse the political leadership of the Czechoslovak Communist Party of dragging, in the name of so-called political realism, the people of Czechoslovakia into this situation by the smallness of its policy and by treason of the previously proclaimed ideals." The Communist Party responded to student demands by issuing a statement that expressed sympathy and concern for students and the liberalization movement.

As news of Palach's death spread in Prague the afternoon of Jan. 19, thousands of people crowded into Wenceslas Square. Students carried the Czechoslovak flag and the black flag of mourning; others carried candles and wreaths. 4 persons set up a tent in the square and began a hunger strike. Posters compared Palach to Jan Hus, the Czech religious reformer who had been burned at the stake in 1415. Elsewhere in Prague,

1,000 Prague University students drew up a new list of demands which included the immediate withdrawal of Soviet troops.

In a telegram sent to Palach's mother CPCS First Secy. Alexander Dubcek and Pres. Svoboda said: "We know well that he was led to this by his genuine and honest love of his country." On a TV broadcast later that evening Cestmir Cisar, chairman of the Czech National Council, declared: "This was not the act of an individual psychotic. The state of mind which led to this act is shared by quite a proportion of our youth. But the ideas of the youth are not very far from those of us who are not so young." Nevertheless, government officials told students and others at meetings that Palach's demands could not readily be met.

During the afternoon of Jan. 20, a crowd estimated at more than 100,000 gathered in Wenceslas Square. A march, organized by Charles University students, began at the square and proceeded to the university. The procession was led by a student carrying the flag of the first (1918-39) Czechoslovak Republic. Before leaving Wenceslas Square, the students posted paper signs changing its name to "Jan Palach Square."

In a TV address that evening, Svoboda announced that another youth, Josef Hlavaty, 25, had set himself aflame in Pilsen, 50 miles southwest of Prague. Hlavaty, a brewery worker, was described as in serious condition, suffering from 2d-degree burns. Svoboda continued: "This is a tragic event. As a soldier I appreciate his personal courage and sacrifice, but as president I cannot agree.... On behalf of your parents, of all the people in the country, and myself, and in the name of humanity, I urge you to stop these terrible acts." (The Interior Ministry reported Jan. 21 that Hlavaty had been treated several times as an alcoholic, had family problems and had told people "of his intention to commit suicide.")

In Budapest, Sandor Bauer, 17, an industrial apprentice, set himself on fire Jan. 20. A passing soldier smothered the flames with his coat, but Bauer received burns over 60% of his body. The reason for his act was not known. He died Jan. 24.

More than 1,300 delegates attending the first congress of the Czech regions' trade unions in Prague Jan. 21 expressed their support for the students' demands. Karel Polacek, chairman of the group, said: "We can assure the public that the trade union movement will do all possible for realization of the hopes of citizens. We believe working people ... will support the students and will find means of achieving solidarity which will not harm our common interests and aims.... We shall not wait with folded arms for the miracle which would fulfill our targets."

The meeting was attended by Premier Oldrich Cernik, who called for moderation and an understanding of the Nov. 1968 Central Committee resolution, pledging "normalization," which he and Dubcek had presented to Soviet leaders in Warsaw. "Some demands and attitudes in the given circumstances cannot be fulfilled, and they are creating serious situations of conflict," Cernik said.

Rudolf Pacovsky, the congress' chairman, said that unions would cooperate with the government, but workers would not give up their right to strike. "We shall not strike indiscriminately," Pacovsky declared, "but only in extreme cases, and then only if the aim of the strike is greater than the losses that would arise from it."

Hunger strikes in support of Palach's demands spread to several Czechoslovak cities Jan. 22. While police were trying to quell the strike in Prague, students began hunger strikes in Brno, Bratislava, Ceske Budejovice and Karlovy Vary.

Prague Radio reported Jan. 22 that 2 more youths had attempted suicide by fire. In Brno, Miroslav Malinka, 23, a mechanic, set himself afire and received 2d-degree burns covering 12% of his body. In Leopoldov, in western Slovakia, Frantisek Bogyi, 23, who was serving a prison sentence, attempted to commit suicide by fire. His condition was described as not serious. Official reports said that the motives of the 2 men were personal rather than political.

(The *Washington Post* reported Jan. 22 that anti-Semitic slogans had appeared on billboards in Bratislava, the capital of Slovakia. The slogans were erased by soldiers, but not before they had been seen by large crowds. The slogans read: "The Jews are with the Russians" and "Slovaks united against the Jews." Since the Aug. 20-21, 1968 invasion, many prominent Jews reportedly had left Slovakia. Some Slovak intellectuals allegedly were concerned over anti-Semitic remarks in speeches by Slovak Communist Party leader Gustav Husak, who had said that extremist groups were being controlled by international groups in Vienna—a city to which many Czechoslovak Jews had fled.)

Palach received a hero's funeral in Prague Jan. 25. At brief ceremonies in the courtyard of Charles University, Prof. Oldrich Stary, rector of the university, delivered the eulogy. He said: Palach's death was "an expression of a pure heart and the highest degree of love for country, freedom and democracy. Jan Palach brought to the altar of his home the highest possible sacrifice which will remain in the memory of Czechs and Slovaks and millions of people elsewhere."

After the ceremonies, the long cortege proceeded to the Old Town Square and Wenceslas Square. The Czech government was represented in the procession by Emanuel Bosak, minister of youth and physical education, and Vilibald Bezdicek, minister of education. In the procession walked 3 men closely identified with the Czechoslovak liberalization movement: Jiri Hajek, ex-foreign minister; Vladimir Kadlec, ex-education minister; Eduard Goldstuecker, chairman of the Czechoslovak Writers' Union. A crowd estimated at 500,000 lined the streets and squares to watch the procession. At Wenceslas Square, the Czech National Anthem was played; afterwards, Stary thanked the audience for its support and calm behavior and asked it to disperse in an orderly way. Palach's family then proceeded alone to the burial grounds at suburban Olsany Cemetery. The marshalling of the silent and restrained public was completely in the hands of students.

The Prague government had expected that Palach's funeral would evoke disturbances and possible violence. The government had warned Jan. 23 that "all legal means" would be taken to prevent demonstrations during the funeral ceremonies. Dubcek Jan. 24 had issued a statement warning citizens "not to permit spontaneous and uncontrollable actions" at Palach's funeral. He added that "attempts at provocation of the present tense situation by extremist forces ... might lead to unpredictable consequences." On Prague TV that night, Jaroslav Havelka, chairman of the Government Committee for Press & Information, said that troops would be brought into Prague to help maintain order during the funeral and that the government would take "all necessary steps" against disturbances. During the day an estimated 70,000 persons filed by the bier at Charles University. At noon, all traffic in Prague halted and the city was shrouded in silence in observance of a student slogan that "Sorrow is Silent."

Disturbances erupted in Prague Jan. 26, as students and workers clashed with police in Wenceslas Square. Defying the ban on demonstrations and posters relating to Palach's death, 1,000 persons attempted to decorate St. Wenceslas' statue with a Czechoslovak national flag and a portrait of Palach. When the crowd began shouting "Russian stooges" and "Gestapo" at the police, the police moved in, using tear gas to disperse the demonstrators. A crowd of 500 youths then attempted to march on the residence of Pres. Svoboda but was halted by the police.

In Slovakia, Interior Min. Egyd Pepich prohibited all public gatherings without authorization and warned that violators would be prosecuted. The police reported Jan. 27 that 199 students had been seized in the Jan. 26 demonstrations.

Students and police again clashed Jan. 27 near the St. Wenceslas statue when youths tried to raise the national colors and a photo of Palach. But no attempt was made to evict the students from the area. In the youth newspaper *Mlada fronta* Jan. 27, Michal Dymacek, described as a student leader, declared that his group had agreed to halt demonstrations but had rejected an order to remove posters and flowers from the statue. In a communique issued Jan. 27, the CPCS Presidium warned of attempts to stir unrest "through antisocial and even antisocialist, directed provocations."

The Czechoslovak trade union newspaper *Prace* Feb. 1 denied a charge by Vilem Novy, a member of the Czechoslovak party Central Committee, that Palach had been tricked into immolating himself by West German agents. Novy allegedly said that Palach's suicide was due to "a machination installed by certain Western powers, especially our nearest Western neighbor [West Germany]."

Police officials had reported Jan. 26 that 9 other Czechoslovak youths had taken or tried to take their lives. Blanka Nachazelova, 18, a student, committed suicide by gas Jan. 22. She left a note saying that her motives "were the same as Jan Palach's." A 24-year old Yugoslav locksmith, Marijan Lombar, attempted to immolate himself in Ljubljana Jan. 23. Jan Zajic, 18, committed suicide by fire in a courtyard near Wenceslas Square Feb 25; his death took place on the 21st anniversary of the Communist takeover of the country. Sources in Prague said that Zajic, a high school student from Sumperk, in northern Moravia, had left a note saying he was "Human Torch Number 2" and was taking his life in support of Palach's protest against Soviet censorship. Zajic was buried in Prague Mar. 2. In contrast to Palach's immolation, Zajic's suicide reportedly aroused little public concern. (Since Palach's death, about 30 Czechoslovaks had attempted such self-sacrifices. Prague authorities had attributed almost all of the attempts to mental disturbances and family problems.)

Shortly before Zajic's death, Dubcek, had said: "We have succeeded in overcoming the most acute stage of the political crisis that occurred in January." Dubcek's statement, in apparent reference to Palach's death, was made in an address to 400 delegates of the people's militia—the party's paramilitary forces—at a ceremony at Prague Castle Feb. 25 commemorating the 1948 Communist coup.

Opposition Continues

In a resolution adopted Feb. 24, the Czechoslovak union of TV and film artists rejected the theory of "limited sovereignty" advanced by the USSR to justify the occupation. The union also stressed the "desire for democratic elections."

Writing in the CPCS newspaper *Rude pravo* Feb. 28, Zdenek Bradac asserted that the world Communist movement could not "return to outdated centralist forms" of unity. In the article, written on the 50th anniversary of the founding of the Communist International (Comintern), he recalled the relative openness of the organization under Lenin. (The Comintern later became an instrument of Moscow and was dissolved by Stalin in 1943.) Bradac questioned whether the forthcoming world Communist meeting scheduled for May in Moscow might not play a role similar to that of the Comintern.

In another reference to the Communist movement under Lenin, the author obliquely condemned the Soviet invasion. "Lenin and some other Comintern functionaries," Bradac said, "were aware that a permanently active concentration of revolutionary forces could not be fruitful through mere military occupation." He warned that because of variations under which Communist countries develop, "principles of democratic centralism corresponding to parties' internal

structures can no longer be applied to their mutual relations....
Mechanical imitation tends to violate ties of international
solidarity rather than strengthening them."

Karel Polacek, chairman of Czechoslovakia's Central
Trades Union Council, declared Mar. 4 that the trade unions
intended to become a force independent of the Communist
Party. Speaking at the opening session of the 7th Czechoslovak
Trade Union Congress held Mar. 4-7 in Prague, Polacek said
that the 5½ million-member union grouping "recognized the
leading role of the party," but this would not impede the unions'
"independent approach, restrict their own attitudes or push
them into a 2d-class position as mere executors of party
decisions." Polacek stressed, however, that the unions would not
become an opposition force; rather, they would refuse to accept
arbitrary decisions by the CPCS. "We shall not allow a return
to the situation before January [1968] either in the trade unions
or in the society," he pledged.

Polacek's address supported the formation of workers'
councils, which in the form currently under study would have a
role in the election of factory managers and would negotiate
work contracts with enterprises. Dubcek, who attended the
meeting, appealed for moderation by the unions but said that it
was not his intention to "limit discussion and the possibilities to
express various demands and points of view."

On the 2d day of the congress, Vlastimil Toman, chairman
of the Metal Workers' Union, rejected the idea that the trade
unions should remain silently obedient to government policy.
Toman warned: "We cannot tolerate at any price that
uncontrolled power be established in our country." While he
agreed that the country needed calm, Toman cautioned on the
adverse effects of "quiet at any price." "Such calm solves
nothing," he said, "but, on the contrary, creates conditons for
the activities of conservative and extremist forces."

A Czechoslovak team's 4-to-3 victory over a Soviet team at
a world championship hockey tournament in Stockholm Mar.
28 touched off widespread anti-Soviet demonstrations in
Prague and in other parts of the country. A torchlight victory
parade held late Mar. 28 in Wenceslas Square began the
demonstrations. Carrying posters marked "4-3," the
demonstrators shouted "Russians go home" and "Today
Tarasov [the Soviet hockey coach] tomorrow Brezhnev."

Riot police finally dispersed the crowd. In the early morning hours of Mar. 29, some people ransacked the Prague offices of Aeroflot, the Soviet airline. After smashing windows and signs, the perpetrators started a bonfire with pictures of Lenin, travel posters and furniture.

The Soviet press charged March 31 that Josef Smrkovsky, chairman of the House of Peoples in the Federal Assembly, had taken part in the demonstrations. An editorialist added to the charge, made by the Soviet Communist Party newspaper *Pravda,* by claiming that it was not the first time that Smrkovsky had participated in an "anti-Soviet outburst." *Pravda* also criticized the Czechoslovak leadership for allowing demonstrations following Czechoslovakia's first hockey victory against the Soviet team in Stockholm Mar. 22. The *Pravda* editorialist said: "The events of recent days have shown that the right-wing anti-Socialist forces once again seek to aggravate the situation in Czechoslovakia."

The Czechoslovak Interior Ministry denied Mar. 31 that Smrkovsky had taken part in the demonstrations. The ministry conceded that the violence had been widespread and had amounted to "anti-Soviet hysteria." Soviet military vehicles were reported to have been burned, troop barracks damaged and Soviet officers insulted; 39 persons were arrested, and 51 Czechoslovak policemen were reported to have been injured. The ministry said that the "most serious situations" had occurred in Prague, Bratisava and Usti and Labem. Other anti-Soviet "hysteria and attacks" were reported in Olomouc and Brno.

The Czechoslovak government continued to tighten censorship following the imposition of new press curbs Apr. 2. The official news agency Ceskoslovenska tiskova kancelar (CTK) reported Apr. 8 that the government had relieved Josef Vohnout "at his own repeated request" from his post as chairman of the Czechoslovak Press & Information Office Apr. 4. Vohnout, a known liberal, was replaced by Josef Havlin, a former deputy minister of education and member of the Communist Party's ideological commission. Havlin, a conservative, reportedly had been responsible for ordering a police attack on a student demonstration in Prague Oct. 31, 1967. (The Yugoslav press agency Tanyug reported Apr. 10 that a committee of the Czechoslovak Artistic & Creative

Unions had supported the Students' Union in a protest against the appointment of Havlin.)

In an article in *Rude pravo* Apr. 11, Jiri Svoboda, the newspaper's commentator, reported that many journalists disagreed with the CPCS Presidium's censorship orders. Svoboda wrote: "I have heard from various directions that if future developments and the possibility of writing are not in keeping with the honor of a journalist, it will be better to give up."

According to a survey of factory workers' opinion throughout Czechoslovakia, published by the trade union newspaper *Prace* Apr. 12, workers had demanded the right "to express their views in the trade union press without fear that the editors might be subjected to punitive measures." Respondents also had expressed opposition to distribution of the Czech-language Soviet occupation newspaper *Zpravy* and had called for non-interference in Czechoslovak internal affairs.

Col. Emil Zatopek, former Olympic runner, was suspended as an army athletics trainer, CTK reported Apr. 21. The report said that Zatopek had been dismissed "on suspicion of spreading untruthful reports" and for misconduct.

A sit-in demonstration by students at Charles University in protest against the ouster of Dubcek from the post of the CPCS first secretary ended Apr. 24 after university officials told the demonstrators that their action might force the closing of the university. The demonstration, which had begun Apr. 21, reportedly had received no support from the workers and unions.

CTK reported May 2 that police in Bohemia and Moravia had arrested 1,225 persons in raids on "criminal and anti-Socialist elements" Apr. 28-30. The police booked 524 persons and detained 141 persons on criminal charges, "mostly violence, theft, etc." Caches of stolen goods reportedly were recovered, including 24 cars, firearms and building materials.

Czech Interior Min. Josef Groesser disclosed Apr. 29 before the Czech National Council that legal action would be taken against an "underground group of conspirators operating in south Moravia." Groesser claimed that the alleged group had a political program and "links with military circles" and was being supplied by arms factories in the area. He also asserted that thefts of weapons and ammunition had increased greatly during the past 6 months.

Groesser had been summoned by the Council to explain his attacks on the characters of ex-Vice Premier Ota Sik, ex-Foreign Min. Jiri Hajek and Prof. Vaclav Cerny of Charles University. The Council directed Groesser to limit himself to verified facts in his future public pronouncements.

Rude pravo May 7 published a statement by the Academy of Sciences demanding an end to press censorship. The statement, which had been adopted by the academy Apr. 3, was accompanied by an apology by the newspaper's editor, Jiri Svoboda, for not having published it immediately after its adoption. (The newspaper instead had published an article by 4 staff members of the academy attacking its leadership.) Svoboda said the academy had demanded publication of its statement and had requested *Rude pravo* in the future to present "the views and statements of legally elected representatives of the employees of the academy and not replace them by statements of self-styled groups."

A large, pro-American demonstration took place in Plzen May 5, the 24th anniversary of the city's liberation by the U.S. Army. A reported 5,000 demonstrators, some chanting "U.S.A., U.S.A.," clashed with the police.

The Czech Journalists' Union June 9 elected a reportedly conservative Presidium and reelected the union's chairman, Vlado Kaspar. Kaspar, who had supported the reform movement in 1968, explained that the charges were necessary to restore a dialogue with the Communist Party leadership. Kaspar also rejected the May 17 manifesto, signed by pro-Soviet journalists, which accused journalists of instigating an anti-Soviet campaign. The union agreed to set up a commission to prepare a self-critical document acknowledging journalists' faults during the 1968 reform period, but it refused to accept responsibility for stirring up anti-Soviet feelings among the Czechoslovak people. (The Czech Affairs Bureau June 26 rebuked the union for its refusal.)

Charter members at the founding congress of the Czech Writers' Union June 10 elected what was described as a progressive 30-member central committee and Jaroslav Seifert as the new union's president. The central committee members included Ludvik Vaculik, author of the "2000 Words" manifesto, Milan Jungmann, ex-editor of *Listy,* Eduard Goldstuecker, ex-president of the old Czechoslovak Writers' Union and then in England. Those voting at the congress adopted a final resolution, which the press in Prague did not publish, on the problem of censorship and the methods used by the Czechoslovak Press & Information Bureau. In the resolution, they appealed to the Federal and Czech Assemblies to investigate the legality of measures taken against the press. They held that these measures were "without parallel in the history of Czechoslovak policy concerning culture, both in extent and scope." The resolution also contained a protest against the banning of *Listy,* the journal of the former Czechoslovak Writers' Union.

The Czechoslovak Union of Film & Television Artists Nov. 7 gave one of its highest awards to a film that had been banned in October, *All Good Fellow Countrymen.* The film, directed by Vojtech Jasny, portrayed life in a small Moravian village during the time of the collectivization of farms in the 1950s. The film earlier had received the Workers' Festival award, and it had been shown throughout the country. Sources in Prague said the award confirmed the refusal of the country's intellectuals to heed the government's political line.

TV officials denounced the union Nov. 10 for giving another of its awards to Vlastimil Vavra for his 4-part serialization on the death of ex-Foreign Min. Jan Masaryk in 1948. The officials said the serial, entitled *To the Assistance of the General Prosecutor's Office,* had "contributed towards the suggestive spreading of fabrications concerning the death of Masaryk" and to anti-Soviet and anti-Communist feelings.

Rude pravo reported Nov. 7 that Czech Culture Min. Miroslav Bruzek had denounced certain stands taken by writers, artists and creative unions in regard "to questions of present political development in the country" as "incorrect and essentially incompatible with state policy."

Hundreds of students jeered Czech Education Min. Jaroslav Hrbek in a question-and-answer session in Prague Nov. 4. This was the first reported encounter between a new pro-Soviet cabinet member and student supporters of the 1968 liberalization program.

Workers Protest Against Government Policies

Growing resentment over the Communist Party's domination in Czechoslovakia's trade unions was expressed in a resolution adopted by union officials of the United Steel Mills National Enterprise (SONP) Kladno steelworks May 27. The resolution, in which they rejected "the differentiation of trade union functionaries according to political affiliations," in effect demanded equal status for Communists and non-Communists. *Rude pravo,* which had been conducting a campaign against activities of so-called "right-wing unionists," denounced the resolution June 16, charging that such a policy "would mean the party's giving up its influence in the trade unions."

Tribuna, a new weekly published by the CPCS Central Committee's Bureau for Party Affairs in the Czech Lands, ran an attack in its June 25 issue on the demands raised by foundry maintenance workers in Ostrava and Kladno. The discontented trade unionists June 6 had sent a resolution from 8 foundry cells in Bohemia and Moravia to the Czech Metal Workers' Union central committee, in which they said:

"In view of the fact that the current political situation is moving toward a sharp conflict with the moral feelings of the overwhelming majority of the workers of our state and that this affects adversely the mission of the trade union organization—to defend the interests of the workers—we turn to you, our democratically elected officials, with the following urgent appeal:

"(1) Of late the independent status of the trade unions has been damaged by statements of some leading personalities in public and political life. The works organizations make it impossible for us to pursue independent trade union policies and to put our own decisions into effect. Our will—our trade union work at the plants—is being frustrated and our opinions are not being taken into consideration.

"The current political situation is moving toward a sharp conflict with the moral feelings of the overwhelming majority of the workers of our state.

"(2) We do not believe that price increases for the necessities of life represent the way out of the current difficult economic situation. On the contrary, we believe that the road to economic recovery is to be found in consistent and undistorted application of the new economic system, in the enactment and implementation of the laws on Socialist enterprises and business methods, and in the law on workers' enterprise councils—legislation which has again and again been deferred.

"(3) We are alarmed by the fact that in this Socialist state the Czechoslovak Society for Human Rights * has been dissolved by administrative action and that to date we have failed to ratify the Declaration of Human Rights, although we have signed it. Fundamental articles in the declaration are not being respected under present conditions, and it is paradoxical that we must continuously struggle for our basic rights.

"(4) We find it difficult to accept the consequences of censorship, which also affects our trade union press and our internal trade union life. We cannot agree to censorship as such. The banning of some periodicals goes beyond the bounds of normalization, and has turned the clock back far beyond Jan. 1968.

"(5) We do not admit anyone's right to exert pressure on us with regard to our relations with students and with creative and artistic associations. We regard this as a flagrant violation of our rights, and are convinced that it is precisely these relations which strengthen the ties between the workers and the intelligentsia.

"(6) We are surprised that the highest trade union bodies have failed to object to the statement made by Comrade Strougal Apr. 21, 1969 regarding the so-called autonomy of various social and interest organizations, and we should like to add that we do not know of any so-called autonomy, but only of some so-called 'leaders.'

"(7) We do not consider it proper for Comrade Polacek to hold 2 important official posts; we regard his presence in the Presidium of the Central Committee of the Communist Party

---

* A society formed by intellectuals after World War II, suppressed by the Communists after 1948 and resurrected in the spring of 1968. The Czechoslovak Interior Ministry banned it May 28, 1969 as an unauthorized political organization lacking representation in the National Front (Rude pravo, May 29).

of Czechoslovakia as representing a conflict of interests which does not contribute to independent trade union work.

"(8) We regard the holding of elections of all representative organs as a primary requirement in solving the economic and political problems in this country. The present provisional state administrations are not competent to ratify important political documents and laws; they are only entitled to ensure the holding of democratic elections.

"(9) We request the Central Committee of KOVO [Metal Workers' Trade Union] to make an analysis of the obstacles that prevent it from carrying out its own decisions, and to inform the basic organizations of the Revolutionary Trade Union Movement of the results of this analysis.

"We wish to point out that we do not intend indefinitely to confine ourselves merely to declaring our stand and that, in accordance with the decisions of our trade union congresses, we are firmly determined to use all trade union means to ensure fulfillment of all justified demands of the workers."

The London *Times* reported June 24 that the works committees of Prague's 20 largest industrial plants had decided to begin July 1 to withhold membership dues from the central trade union organizations. The purpose of the action reportedly was to show disapproval of leaders who had failed to comply with a request to discuss trade union demands. However, it was reported that the committees would continue to pay their union dues to the 900,000-member Czech Metal Workers Union.

(Rude pravo subsequently disclosed June 25 that payment of party dues had declined sharply in Czech areas. In some areas $1/3$ of all party members reportedly were 3 months or more in arrears. *Rude pravo* said 17.48% of the local party organizations had not settled their arrears, as compared with 5.03% in 1967. In areas where party members were paying dues, the local organizations apparently had banked the money locally and collected the interest "as a sign of disagreement with policy." *Rude pravo* reported that the Czech Bureau had issued instructions for disciplinary proceedings against the party committees that had failed to forward their dues. According to party statutes, any member 3 or more months in arrears would be open to epulsion from the party.

Trade unions and workers drew criticism from both the new CPCS First Secy. Husak and Premier Cernik June 26. Husak announced that a concerted ideological effort to unify the party line would be carried down to local and factory organizations. He said "rightist-opportunist" forces had gained key positions in various works committees because of the weakened role of Communists in the trade unions in 1968.

Cernik denounced the "considerable drop in work discipline" among workers and criticized those "who think it is possible to work $4\frac{1}{2}$ days a week and turn out goods of inferior quality and at the same time demand cheap products, low railroad and transit fares and plenty of foreign currency for traveling abroad."

In urging stricter labor legislation, Czech Premier Stanislav Razl July 7 accused the Czech labor force of idleness, slovenly work, lack of discipline and an attitude of laissez-faire.

At a meeting of the Central Council of the Revolutionary Trade Movement July 9, Husak announced a purge of "hostile elements" from trade unions, including the chairmen and members of works committees.

Workers at Czechoslovakia's largest steel mill in Ostrava posted a letter form chess champion Ludek Pachman that "rudely attacked" Husak, *Rude pravo* reported July 12. Pachman, who shortly beforehand had been suspended from the party, apparently had written the letter in response to an invitation to participate in a forum at the plant. The letter reportedly had caused a 2-hour work stoppage while workers read and then voted indorsement of its contents. *Rude pravo* said action would be taken against the factory's union leadership for its "provocative attempt to affect the efforts of the party."

Rude pravo conceded July 24 that unrest among Ostrava workers had reached serious proportions and warned that hostile forces in the Klement Gottwald steelworks would be fought "consistently and more resolutely."

In line with its declared aim of strengthening the power and role of the party, the Central Committee expelled several known liberals from its own ranks. These included Frantisek Kriegel, a former chairman of the National Front and public health minister, and Frantisek Vodslon, a deputy in the Federal Assembly. They were ousted because they had voted against the

Oct. 15, 1968 Moscow Protocol legalizing the presence of Soviet troops in Czechoslovakia.

Kriegel, in a statement before his ouster (reported in full by the *Washington Post* June 5), had explained that he had voted against the protocol because it had been imposed "in the atmosphere of military occupation without the benefit of consultation with constitutional bodies and in contradiction to the feelings of the people of this country." Kriegel declared that exCzechoslovak Premier Jozef Lenart, exChairman Otto Simunek of the defunct State Commission for Economic, Scientific & Technical Cooperation and the former party ideologue Jiri Hendrych were among those responsible for the terror in the 1950s and for the current Czechoslovak economic crisis. Kriegel urged that the entire Czechoslovak question be discussed at the world Communist conference opening in Moscow June 5. His defense statement was regarded as the most outspoken denunciation of the Soviet invasion by a leading Czechoslovak public figure.

The public disclosure of Kriegel's defense statement to the party Central Committee May 29 evoked strong criticism from official sources. In a Czechoslovak radio and TV broadcast June 12, listeners were warned that it was illegal to circulate copies of Kriegel's speech. The broadcast's author charged that Kriegel wished to maintain the "crisis in the party" and that his supporters were "acting at variance with the constitution and valid laws of this country."

Rude pravo reported June 12 that Kriegel's speech had been distributed and discussed June 6 at a workers' meeting in Kladno, 15 miles west of Prague, and had been circulated among members of the foundry workers union at the Klement Gottwald steelworks in Ostrava. The newspaper accused the Ostrava workers of trying to organize "anti-party, anti-government action hostile to the state." The party committee at the Ostrava plant reportedly suspended the leader of a group of union officials and workers who had visited Kriegel.

Rude pravo confirmed June 16 that the Kriegel ouster and the decisions of the May 29-30 Central Committee meeting had brought a wave of critical and anonymous letters to the press. It denounced them as "anti-Socialist poison."

Leaders of the Czech Metal Workers' Union urged members June 14 to dissociate themselves from "seditious" pamphlets circulating in industrial plants.

In a display of worker-student solidarity, workers at the CKD factories in Prague threatened to strike after workers' delegates June 23 informed Vlastimir Toman, head of the Metal Workers' Union, that an Interior Ministry ban on the Bohemian and Moravian student unions had caused widespread discontent. Although the strikes did not materialize, the *N.Y. Times* reported June 25 that locomotive workers at the CKD plant had participated in a 15-minute work stoppage.

The Interior Ministry June 20 had dissolved the Czech Union of Students for violating sections of the law on public order concerning voluntary organizations. A decree by the ministry justified the decision by citing speeches and published statements by union leaders and by citing the group's other activities allegedly contrary to "important foreign policy interests" of the state, to the Socialist economic system and to the (1960) constitution.

Anniversary of Soviet Invasion

The first anniversary of the Soviet occupation was marked by protest demonstrations in Prague and other Czechoslovak cities Aug. 19-22. Disregarding government warnings, demonstrators conducted massive, orderly protests against the Soviet actions and the regime of Communist Party First Secy. Gustav Husak. The demonstrations, which were quelled by police and Czechoslovak army troops, culminated in tighter police controls and new emergency laws issued by the government Aug. 22.

The London *Times* had reported June 28 that a 10-point plan by students and workers, which had been circulating in Prague, had proposed that the anniversary be observed as a "day of shame" and mourning. Citizens were asked, in part: (1) to avoid using municipal transportation; (2) to boycott stores, restaurants, theaters, coffeehouses and movie houses; (3) to buy no newspapers; (4) to halt all work for five minutes at noon; (5) to decorate memorials; (6) to halt all vehicles at noon. Other leaflets circulated in July urged the population not to be tricked by fraudulent appeals for violence or insurrection and not to stage general strikes. Czechoslovaks were warned that Soviet agents would stage "provocations" as pretexts for further curtailment of freedoms or for a coup to bring additional pro-Soviet leaders to power. The Czech Metal Workers' Union appealed to its 900,000 members July 25 to aviod antiSoviet acts on the anniversary.

Acknowledging the wide distribution of the leaflets, the Czechoslovak government had appealed repeatedly for calm on the anniversary. The government instructed courts and prosecutors Aug. 14 "to proceed immediately and with all severity" against persons who threatened public order. It announced that the army and the "people's militia" would help the police maintain "calm, public order and security." The government warned plant managers they would be held responsible for any disturbance or disruption of production.

In a nationally televised address Aug. 17, Pres. Ludvik Svoboda warned against alleged foreign subversion, which, he said, was inciting unrest. Svoboda also denied that the USSR planned to annex Czechoslovakia.

In a speech instructing party officials on how to deal with anti-Soviet disturbances, Husak Aug. 19 rejected the portrayal of Czechoslovakia as a Soviet-occupied country. Czechoslovakia, he said, "is a fully sovereign, independent state, politically, economically and militarily." He pledged that his government would defeat all subversive forces in the country, and he warned that any hostile demonstrations on the anniversary would be repressed.

Only hours after Husak's warning, disorders erupted in Prague's half-mile-long Wenceslas Square Aug. 19. Shouting "Gestapo!" hundreds of students clashed with the police, who reportedly beat demonstrators with clubs. At 8 p.m., armored cars began to chase the demonstrators along the square and dispersed the estimated crowd of 1,000 with tear gas. Scores of demonstrators reportedly were detained.

A 9-hour demonstration Aug. 20 ended with police and army troops battling demonstrators with armored cars, tear gas and water cannons. Some soldiers reportedly fired submachine guns over the heads of the demonstrators. The government announced Aug. 21 that 2 persons had been killed and more than 320 arrested during the demonstrations.

Czechoslovak army reinforcements moved into the center of Prague in the early morning of Aug. 21 and took control of major intersections. Other units waited in readiness in suburban industrial plants, streetcar terminals and other installations. Although none of the Soviet occupation troops joined the Czechoslovak army units, the *N.Y. Times* reported Aug. 24 that Soviet staff officers had been flown into Prague the night of Aug. 20. (A Soviet delegation headed by Gen. Aleksei Yepishev, political chief of the armed forces, returned to Moscow Aug. 21 after a 16-day visit to Czechoslovakia.)

At noon Aug. 21, a crowd estimated at 50,000 converged on Wenceslas Square chanting "Russians go home," "Long live Dubcek" and "Husak is a traitor!" Chanting and car-horn blasting was permitted for 40 minutes before police and army units fired tear gas and moved in to clear the square. Shops and public transportation were boycotted during the day, while thousands of people stopped working for short intervals. At night the Czechoslovak army sent more than 100 tanks to disperse the crowd in Wenceslas Square.

The Czechoslovak press agency CTK reported Aug. 21 that the country was quiet except for "attempts at riots" in Prague, Liberec and Brno. An estimated crowd of 5,000 students clashed with army troops and club-swinging police in Brno Aug. 22 following a wreath-laying ceremony for 3 persons killed in anti-Soviet demonstrations earlier in the week.

CTK reported Aug. 25 that 1,893 people had been detained on political charges in Bohemia and Moravia, 1,239 of them in Prague, during the anniversary demonstrations. CTK said that disturbances had also occurred in Ostrava and Usti nad Labem; "isolated rallies of several hundred demonstrators" were reported in the Slovak capital, Bratislava. The Prague District Committee reported Aug. 22 that 66 foreigners had been arrested during the demonstrations.

In an effort to restore order, the Federal Assembly Aug. 22 adopted emergency laws extending to Dec. 31; they broadened police powers and instituted summary court proceedings for political offenders. The laws, announced in an order signed by Svoboda, Premier Oldrich Cernik and Federal Assembly Chairman Dubcek, included: (1) stiffer prison terms for disorderliness, defamation of other Socialist states and harming Czechoslovakia's interests abroad; (2) antistrike provisions, including fines or arrest, for laxity at work; (3) expulsion of students and the firing of workers involved in protest demonstrations. Legal protections, such as pretrial hearings and access to evidence, were suspended. The new laws also allowed a 3-week detention of suspects "to ascertain if they are organizers of actions which disturb the public order."

Cernik said Aug. 23 that "anti-Socialist and counterrevolutionary elements" had organized protest riots in an attempt to overthrow the government. A Radio Prague broadcast the same day included the demand that those responsible for the rioting "be removed from public life." The 2 statements hinted at more arrests and the removal of some government officials.

The Czech Interior Ministry reported Aug. 25 that of the 3,690 people arrested during the 3 days of rioting, 1,893 were still in custody.

In a report Sept. 1 to the defense and security committee of the House of the People (one of the Federal Assembly's 2 chambers), Deputy Interior Min. Frantisek Vasek disclosed official figures on the 3 days of demonstrations in Prague and Brno. He said that 2,414 people had been detained, including 2,003 under 25 years old. Vasek said that 416 of those arrested had served prior prison terms for criminal offenses.

Vasek estimated that property damage in Prague and Brno had totaled 4.8 million korunas (official rate: 7.20 korunas to $1). He said that 424 soldiers, policemen, members of the militia and firemen had been hurt, 48 of them seriously, but that only 37 demonstrators had been injured. (The London *Times* had reported Aug. 26 that at least 70 civilians had been hospitalized in Prague, with one hospital alone treating 60 victims of police clubbings. Other Western press reports said that inquiries at 3 hospitals in Prague had revealed that 4 civilians had died, while 4 more reportedly were killed in Brno.)

Lt. Col. Jiri Hecko, an army political officer, complained in *Rude pravo* Aug. 25 that hospital medical staffs had neglected injured police and troops. The trade union newspaper *Prace* charged the same day that Prague's Vrsovice Hospital had refused out-patient treatment to injured policemen.

Rude pravo reported Aug. 25 that prior to the demonstrations Interior Ministry units had detained a group of young people in Nove Role, near Karlovy Vary, Western

Bohemia, on charges that they had planned to "drag citizens into a demonstration on 21 August by means of demagogic slogans" and then attack a district police department building. In the same town, *Rude pravo* said, the police also had detained 4 young people possessing "a whole arsenal of weapons."

Svoboda, the daily party newspaper of Central Bohemia, reported Aug. 26 that 80% of the region's population had boycotted public transportation and shops Aug. 21.

POLISH DISSENT & REPRESSION

Intellectuals Sentenced

Jacek Kuron and Karol Modzelewski, former university teaching assistants, were convicted in Warsaw Jan. 15 and given 3½-year prison sentences on charges of participating in, and acting as "spiritual instigators" of the Mar. 1968 student riots. The 2 men, both in their early 30s, were convicted under a 1946 "small penal code" dealing with anti-Communist groups. They were charged with having led an illegal "commando" organization composed mainly of Jewish students, "Zionists," "revisionists" and Stalinists. A 2d charge, connecting the defendants with the Belgian-based Trotskyite Fourth International, was dropped.

Modzelewski, a Jew and stepson of Zygmunt Modzelewski, Polish foreign minister in 1947-51, had been arrested with Kuron Mar. 8, 1968. Both had been jailed in 1965 for issuing a public letter urging the overthrow of the government; they were released in 1967, for good behavior, before completing their sentences.

3 Warsaw University students, Irena Lasota, Irena Grudzinska and Teresa Bogucka, were given 18-month jail terms by a Warsaw court Apr. 22. They were charged with taking part in the Mar. 1968 demonstrations and were sentenced under a section of the penal code that covered "membership in a secret organization." (Miss Grudzinska's father, Jan Grudzinski, had been ousted from his post as state undersecretary in the Forestry Ministry Mar. 12, 1968.)

Since the Warsaw student demonstrations, 7 trials of alleged protest leaders had been held. 15 defendants had received jail terms ranging from 18 months to 3½ years. The April issue of the American monthly *East Europe* reported on the trials and sentencing of other alleged participants in the 1968 demonstrations. In the 6th trial, Antoni Zambrowski, an assistant lecturer at Warsaw University, was sentenced Feb. 21 to 2 years' imprisonment. (2 Warsaw University students, Henryk Szlajfer and Wiktor Gorecki, who were serving sentences imposed down in an earlier trial, were released at about this time, but 2 others convicted with them, Adam Michnik and Barbara Torunczyk, remained in prison.)

Zambrowski, who was of Jewish descent, was the son of ex-Politburo member Roman Zambrowski, who had been ousted from the party after the Mar. 1968 disturbances, had been denounced as a "ringleader of the revisionists" and had been dismissed from his post as vice chairman of the State Control Commission. Antoni Zambrowski was accused of membership since 1963 in an underground "Trotskyite" organization with which Kuron and Modzelewski were allegedly affiliated. He was accused of distributing publications "falsely presenting political and social relations in Poland" and of publicly vilifying the Polish nation.

According to the November-December issue of *East Europe,* 8 students had been sentenced to prison terms of up to 3 years for distributing leaflets attacking Poland's participation in the Aug. 1968 invasion of Czechoslovakia. They were Boguslawa Blajfert (who received a 3-year sentence); Eugeniusz Smolar (18-month sentence); Wiktor Magorski (one year); Ireneusz Szubert (one year); Sylwia Poleska (8 months) and Piotr Zebrun, Tadeusz Markiewicz and Romuald Lubaniec (sentences not disclosed).

In Paris, *Le Monde* reported Oct. 7 that the Polish authorities were readying a new trial of scholars and students accused of a plot to overthrow the government. The main defendant was Maciej Kozlowski, a journalism student at Warsaw University, who had been arrested in Aug. 1968 in Stary Smokovec in Czechoslovakia. Maria Tworkowska, who had lived in Paris in subsequent months, was arrested with him. They were accused of having mimeographed, in

Czechoslovakia, a statement that they tried to distribute in Poland.

Other defendants were Aleksander Smolar, Eugeniusz Smolar (one of 8 people sentenced for distributing leaflets opposing the Czechoslovak invasion), Adam Wlodek, grandson of the chairman of the Polish Writers' Union, Jaroslaw Iwaszkiewicz, Maciej Geller, a biology lecturer at Warsaw University, and Krzysztof Szymborski of the Polish Academy of Sciences.

Defections

Jan Tyrakowski, 40, a Polish opera singer, and a Polish engineer asked for asylum in Denmark Jan. 16. Danish police said they had arrived in Copenhagen on the Polish cruise ship *Batory*.

Zbigniew Byrski, a Polish journalist, announced in New York Apr. 14 that he had decided to seek asylum in the U.S. after the Czechoslovak invasion and years "of doubts about the basic validity of communism." Byrski, 55, had been a consul in Detroit and vice-consul in Chicago.

Mrs. Alicja Lisiecka, a literary critic and historian, asked for asylum in the West, the London *Times* reported Aug. 21. Mrs. Lisiecka, who had been deputy editor of Poland's leading literary weekly, *Nowa Kultura,* until it was closed in 1962, reported in the *Times* Aug. 21 and 22 on the difficulties of intellectuals in Poland. She said: "Polish writers and the intelligentsia in general are today helpless objects of the intraparty struggle for power. They are disorganized, constantly pressed to submit to the demand for loyalty to the ascending new team; they have lost the last remnants of the freedom of expression gained in 1956; they are subjected to administrative chicaneries, blackmailed by threats, and under permanent police surveillance." (Describing the struggle for power in Poland, Mrs. Lisiecka said: "After Mar. 1968, the leading functions in the party apparatus ... were finally consolidated in the hands of some 3,000 relatively young people aged 35 to 45, who are noted for their opportunism and careerism, their intellectual primitiveness and political ruthlessness.")

A Polish (LOT) airliner, en route from Warsaw to Brussels by way of Schoenefeld airport in East Berlin, was hijacked Oct. 19 by 2 East German youths. The youths, 19 and 20, forced the plane to land at Tegel airfield in the French sector of West Berlin. The youths requested and received political asylum. After a 3-hour stop-over, the aircraft, with its remaining 61 passengers and 9 crew members, proceeded to Schoenefeld. This was the first time an airliner had been hijacked from a Communist country.

Jewish Emigration

The Polish government announced June 10 that its relaxed procedures on Jewish emigration to Israel would terminate Sept. 1. After that date—according to the announcement— "passport authorities will examine all applications in accordance with the generally binding procedure." The government gave no reason for its decision, and it did not enforce the Sept. 1 deadline in 1969.

An official policy of "unrestricted emigration" by Poles of Jewish origin had taken effect soon after the June 1967 war between Israel and Syria, the United Arab Republic, Jordan, Iraq, Algeria, Sudan and Kuwait had ended in an armistice. Polish United Workers' Party First Secy. Wladyslaw Gomulka Mar. 19, 1968 had reaffirmed the policy, asserting that Polish Jews would continue to be permitted to emigrate to Israel.

The Polish Press Agency (Polska Agencja Prasowa, or PAP) reported for the first time June 10, 1969 on the number of Jewish emigres. From July 1, 1967 through May 1969, PAP reported, "5,264 Polish citizens of Jewish nationality left Poland declaring their departure for permanent residence in Israel."

Margaret Reynolds, a British journalist, wrote in the American weekly *New Republic* Mar. 21, 1970 that "of the estimated 25,000 Jews who lived in Poland up to 1967 ..., probably far fewer than 10,000 remain ... out of a total Polish population of 32.5 million." She added that Polish Jews had been entraining for Vienna at the rate of 1,000 persons a month from Warsaw and that 2,000 Polish Jews had "made their way to Denmark in the past 18 months." Other reception centers for the exiles were set up in Rome and Stockholm, she wrote.

Despite the official position that these persons were emigrants, Miss Reynolds reported, the Danish government had granted the incoming Polish Jews "political asylum within a few weeks under the 1951 UN Convention on Refugees." All Jews departing from Poland were charged an exit fee corresponding roughly to the degree of their professional training and had to surrender all diplomas and certificates before leaving, she wrote.

The Polish Interior Ministry, which had jurisdiction in the matter, had a Jewish Section in which research was going forward into the ethnic background of all Polish citizens and that classified anyone with a Jewish grandparent as a Jew. Section Organizer Tadeusz Walichnowski was keeping up-to-date a card index he had compiled since 1967 "of 300,000 'half-Jews'," Miss Reynolds reported.

OTHER EVENTS

Albanian Nationalists in Yugoslavia

East Europe reported in its May issue that during March and April, courts in the Kosovo-Metohija (Kosmet) Autonomous Region of southwestern Serbia, bordering on Albania, had handed down at least 21 sentences on citizens of Albanian nationality who had allegedly either taken part in or instigated demonstrations and who were found guilty of fomenting "national hatred and intolerance among Yugoslavia's nationalities and minorities."

The largest group—7 students, a teacher and a journalist—were sentenced to 3 to 5 years in prison by the district court of Pristina Apr. 7 on charges of organizing a "hostile demonstration" there in late Nov. 1968. The Yugoslav press agency Tanyug reported Apr. 7 the court's assertion that the demonstrators had carried only Albanian flags and had urged "citizens to undertake forcible and unconstitutional changes in the state order and to wreck brotherhood and unity."

12 others had been arraigned in Skopje in March, but 5 of them were freed for lack of evidence. The other 7 were sentenced to 3 to 6 years at hard labor for allegedly

participating in "chauvinist demonstrations" in Gostivar, Macedonia in Dec. 1968. The group included 2 professors, 2 teachers, a student, a dentist and a housewife.

The Skopje court Mar. 19 and 25 sentenced Mehmed Ali Hoxha, 45, and Kreyzi Feydi, 43, to 5 and 7 years' "rigorous imprisonment," respectively, for what it termed provocative activities. Hoxha was punished severely on charges of disseminating national hatred and of "being in accord with participants in last year's [Dec. 1968] chauvinistic demonstrations in the town of Tetovo, Macedonia." Feydi, a former teacher, was accused of stirring up students and colleagues at the senior pedagogical school in Skopje.

A 20-year-old pipe fitter was sentenced to 7 years for his role in the Tetovo outbreak, but a 19-year-old student at a teachers college in Gnjilane, Kosovo, received only one year in prison for participating in and helping to organize a demonstration there Nov. 27, 1968. In Bitola, Macedonia, a 31-year-old man was convicted of helping the Albanian embassy in Vienna indoctrinate visiting Yugoslavs; he received a 4-year sentence.

Radio Belgrade Apr. 7 reported the opening of a trial in Urosevac, Kosovo, of a teacher, Ali Mehmetu, and of 2 students, Kismet Ramadani and Hasan Abazi, who were accused of "inciting national and religious intolerance and discord."

The August-September issue of *East Europe* reported that the Kosmet was still undergoing disturbances. It was charged at the plenum of the Kosmet League of Communists that "extremists" had engaged in obstructionist activities during the general elections in April. Radio Belgrade had reported July 3 that the Kosmet League of Communists had expelled 33 of its members, including some public functionaries, "for nationalist and chauvinist activities."

15 alleged organizers of nationalist demonstrations at Tetovo, Macedonia in 1968 went on trial in Skopje June 2. They were indicted on charges of seeking to detach Tetovo and 4 other towns from Macedonia by force and of planning to make them part of the Kosmet. The alleged plan called for the Kosmet then to secede from Yugoslavia and become part of Albania. The defendants were accused of collecting money to

buy arms, of having links with Albanian diplomats in Yugoslavia and of provoking national intolerance and hatred.

Radio Belgrade reported June 30 that 4 of the "main" organizers of the 1968 disturbance had gone on trial in Skopje June 23, had been convicted and had been sentenced to terms of up to 5 years.

Radio Belgrade reported June 24 that the Yugoslav Supreme Court had reduced from 38 to 19 years the prison sentences previously imposed by the Skopje court on 7 defendants. The high court held that most of the defendants were young and misguided, had admitted their guilt and had repented. The court stressed that harsh punishment was unnecessary because the political situation in Yugoslavia was stable.

Yugoslav Dissenting Intellectuals

Dragoljub Golubovic, a writer for the weekly journal *Nin,* was expelled from the League of Yugoslav Communists Mar. 27. The basis for his expulsion reportedly was a 1966 article in which Golubovic, 44, had exposed the allegedly luxurious privileges of party leaders. Warned by the party, Golubovic took his case to the Serbian Journalists Association and to the party congress in March. Golubovic's latest action apparently angered the party unit at the Politika publishing house, which issued *Nin,* and the party leaders voted to expel him.

Zoran Gluscevic, former editor of the literary fortnightly *Knjizevne Novine,* was sentenced to 6 months in jail Oct. 28 for denouncing the occupation of Czechoslovakia. In an article that appeared prior to the visit of Soviet Foreign Min. Andrei A. Gromyko to Belgrade Sept. 2-6, Gluscevic accused the USSR of depriving the Czechoslovak people of their freedom.

According to the July issue of *East Europe,* the anniversary of the June 3, 1968 student protests passed without demonstrations but not without continued disaffection. Students had expressed growing impatience at the "slowness" of the Yugoslav government in implementing the 4-point action program adopted in June 1968, and student "extremists" presented this complaint to the student association of Belgrade University:

"Nothing has changed. The same social differences remain. The highest-paid functionaries earn 40 times as much as the lowest paid. The right to work is guaranteed by the constitution, but it is not carried out in everyday life. Privileges and abuses remain. The plunder of public property continues. No decisive measures have been taken, or are proposed, against corruption, bribes and other immoral acts. All this demoralizes the workers and the youth.

"Nothing has been done to solve unemployment. A systematic solution has not been presented. The authorities are not looking for a solution. The powerful, cumbersome, expensive state administration exists, but it has not solved current social problems. The state does not solve them because it does not want to intervene where self-management is involved.

"There is talk about changes in self-management, but none has been made.

"The [June 1968] Action Program requested a fundamental and rapid democratization of all social organizations, particularly in the League of Communists. But there has been only the rotation of some of the older functionaries.

"In culture, nothing has been done to eliminate commercialism and trash.

"Nationalist tendencies [among the nationalities of Yugoslavia] have reached frightful dimensions.

"Nothing has been done to counter the free play of market forces, which jeopardize the stability of the economy."

The complaints of the student protesters were rejected by the Committee of Students of the University of Belgrade.

Non-Conformist Artists in Bulgaria

At celebrations commemorating the 8th international Theater Day in Sofia Mar. 27, Prof. Vladmir Trendafilov warned artists that they should take a strong stand against "deviations" within the theatre. Trendafilov urged a "united militant front against the reactionary schemes of those who want to stop the progressive historical development by an ideological diversion in the field of art." Trendafilov's warning was part of an official campaign in Bulgaria against Western influences and "revisionist" nationalism in the arts that had begun Jan. 31 at a conference of the Bulgarian writers' union. A number of writers and professors had been denounced for their "deviations." The official theme was that any trend away from "Socialist realism" would lead to "open anti-Sovietism."

Kadar Urges Dialogue with Dissenters

In an interview published in the Italian Communist newspaper *L'Unita* Nov. 30, Hungarian Communist Party

First Secy. Janos Kadar cautiously promised more "Socialist democracy" for Hungary. He said: While the leading role of the party must be maintained, "a Socialist society is not built only for Communists but for all the working people.... Everyone is entitled to equal rights and respect, regardless of his party position, world outlook, background and occupation, if he participates in the work of building socialism." Kadar also urged meaningful discussion with dissident intellectuals, rather than censorship or restrictive cultural policies.

East Germany Clamps Down on Universities

In a move to establish greater control over the universities, especially to cope with student demands for democratization and student power, East Germany was reported in the *N.Y. Times* Jan. 8 to have begun a program to link the schools with industry. At the University of Jena, research facilities in physics and chemistry were turned over to the Zeisswerke optical instruments factory. Under the agreement, professors and students were to conduct their research in the plant's laboratories or in special projects at the university.

The purported goal of the program was to turn universities and colleges into training schools for specific professions. Fred M. Hechinger, the *Times* educational editor, wrote that the move appeared to be designed to end the "traditional dominance of German universities by the humanities and the social sciences." He viewed the plan as similar to one attempted, unsuccessfully, in the Soviet Union in the 1950s. By the end of the year, 900 units and institutions at East Germany's 41 universities and colleges were to be united into 190 "sections." 92 sections had already been started. Opposition to the plan reportedly had crumbled under political and economic pressures.

1970

Dissent by minority groups in the Soviet Union continued unabated despite increased repression. Jews in the Soviet Union became particularly vocal in their demands for the safeguarding of their religious and ethnic identity and for permission to emigrate to Israel. Efforts in this direction culminated in June in what was alleged to be an attempt by a group of Jews to hijack a Soviet airliner. All the alleged participants were arrested, and the incident aroused worldwide sympathy for those apprehended.

Outspoken Soviet intellectuals suffered continued harassment by the authorities. Some were sent to prison, others confined to mental asylums—a form of punishment based on the state's presumption that in a society where the undesirability of nonconformism is self-evident, dissent equals insanity. The most prominent among the victims were geneticist Zhores A. Medvedev, writer Andrei A. Amalrik and novelist Aleksandr I. Solzhenitsyn—the latter a target of official attacks especially after the Swedish Academy of Literature had awarded him the Nobel Prize. Unrest among the scientific and intellectual elite was indicative of growing strain between the Soviet Union's conservative political structure and the forces of modernization.

2 years after the disruptive events in Czechoslovakia, another outbreak of popular dissatisfaction occurred in Poland. Price increases decreed on the eve of the Christmas holidays touched off workers' demonstrations that spread despite forceful intervention by the police and the armed forces. Unlike the 1968 ferment in Czechoslovakia, however, the Polish disturbances were predominantly economic in origin; they did not aim at the ideological substance of the regime. Limited in goals, they were ultimately successful when the Polish party expelled a leadership, under Wladyslaw Gomulka, identified

*with economic inefficiency and repression. The new party First
Secy. Edward Gierek was acclaimed as an advocate of greater
responsiveness to the needs of the people, particularly to their
material plight.*

*The situation in Czechoslovakia was marked by further
repression, particularly of the Communists implicated in the
reform movement of 1968. The majority of them were expelled
from the party and suffered discrimination in their jobs. Many
of them escaped to the West. A few who did not recant were
taken into custody. Others accommodated themselves to the
new regime. Open manifestations of dissent were less and less
frequent as demoralization spread—more among the reform-
minded Communists than among the population as a whole.*

*Centrifugal tendencies in eastern Europe did not grow in
the course of the year. Rumania, weakened by domestic
difficulties after disastrous floods, was less assertive in its
independent line and consented to the long-delayed renewal of
an alliance with the Soviet Union. Yugoslavia and Albania,
alarmed by the Soviet penetration into the Mediterranean,
moved closer together, but Belgrade moderated the anti-Soviet
stand it had adopted in the wake of the invasion of
Czechoslovakia.*

OPPOSITION IN THE USSR

Jews Seek to Leave

The state of Israel Jan. 5 forwarded to UN Secy. Gen. U
Thant a copy of a letter in which 2 Soviet Jews had appealed to
Israeli Premier Golda Meir for help in emigrating to Israel. In
the letter, dated Dec. 9, 1969 and signed by Yosif Y. Kazakov
and his wife, the couple said that they wanted to join their son
in Israel but that appeals to Soviet leaders had proven fruitless.
Kazakov reported Mar. 2 that he had been dismissed from his
job.

The Kazakovs' son, Yasha, 23, fasted outside UN
headquarters in New York for 9 consecutive days in late March
and early April in protest against the Soviet refusal to let his
parents emigrate to Israel. He ended his fast Apr. 3 and

returned to Israel Apr. 6 after his parents, still in the USSR, had appealed to him Mar. 31 to discontinue the fast. The Israeli government had made a similar appeal Mar. 29. During the fast, Yosif Kazakov and 3 members of his family had sent a letter Mar. 27 appealing to Soviet Premier Aleksei N. Kosygin, Pres. Nikolai V. Podgorny and Communist Party Gen. Secy. Leonid I. Brezhnev for permission to leave the Soviet Union.

A new letter from Moscow Jews June 10 appealed to U Thant for help in winning Soviet permission to emigrate to Israel. Copies of the letter were sent to the Soviet Foreign Ministry. All signers listed their addresses and occupations. Yosif Kazakov, who was one of the signers, said in a separate letter that at the time of his son's fast outside UN headquarters, Thant had promised to try to help the Kazakov family.

The London *Times* had reported Jan. 9 that still another appeal by 10 Jews for permission to emigrate to Israel, made in Sept. 1969, had reached the West.

Izvestia Mar. 9 printed a statement signed by Moscow's chief rabbi and other religious leaders declaring that "the real motherland of Soviet Jews is our Native Soviet Union." Bernard Gwertzman of the *N.Y. Times* reported Mar. 9 that the statement and a Mar. 4 press conference was assumed to have been organized by the government. In a letter Mar. 8 to Leonid M. Zamyatin, who had chaired the Moscow press conference, 39 Soviet Jews protested that "the emotional heat of anti-Israeli propaganda is now very great." The letter's writers, criticizing the press conference, emphasized that "it is the very preservation of the national identity of Jews that is the problem in the Soviet Union." (Yuli Telesin, one of the signers of the letter, emigrated to Israel May 6.)

An alleged attempt to hijack an airliner in Leningrad June 15 resulted in the arrest that day of 12 persons and the detention of 8 others. After a trial in December, a Leningrad court Dec. 28 ordered death sentences for 2 of the defendents and prison terms for 9. But the Russian Republic's Supreme Court commuted the death sentences Dec. 31 and reduced 3 of the prison terms.

The official account of the arrests in the Leningrad Communist Party newspaper *Leningradskaya Pravda* June 16 said only that "On June 15, in Smolny Airport, a group of criminals, trying to seize a scheduled airplane, was apprehended. An investigation is being carried out."

Apparently the group was arrested while walking from the terminal to board a small Aeroflot AN-2 plane for a flight from Leningrad to Petrozavodsk, in the Soviet Republic of Karelia on the Finnish border. Police said those arrested were carrying 2 pistols and several knives. Only the following 5 were initially identified: Eduard S. Kuznetsov and his wife, Silva Y. Zalmanson, both of Riga, Yuri Tarakandov of Leningrad, Yuri P. Fyodorov of Moscow, and Aleksandr Murzhenko, from a town near Kharkov. Kuznetsov and his wife were Jewish, and had reportedly signed in 1969 a letter to Premier Kosygin asking for permission to emigrate to Israel.

After the airport arrests, police June 15 searched the homes of at least 50 Jews in Leningrad, Riga, Moscow and Kharkov. Those detained as a result of the searches: David Chernoglaz, Lev Kornblit, Lev Yagman, Lassal Kaminsky, Vladimir Mogilever, Anatoly Goldfeld, Solomon Dreiser and Grigory Butman. Kaminsky, Mogilever and Chernoglaz were said to have been among the signers Feb. 1 of an open letter asking the UN Human Rights Commission for help in emigrating to Israel.

In a letter to the Soviet prosecutor general, reported June 27, David Boguslavsky, a Leningrad Jew, protested that those detained had no connection with the alleged hijacking attempt. One of them, Boguslavsky said, had been on vacation in Odessa when the incident took place. He said that security police had confiscated as "implements of crime" letters and postcards from Israel and Yiddish and Hebrew historical texts.

The alleged hijackers went on trial in a Leningrad court Dec. 15. During the trial, Mark Y. Dymshits, a former air force pilot, reportedly admitted helping organize the hijacking plot because of his opposition to the anti-Semitism prevalent in the Soviet Union. The prosecutor Dec. 21 asked for death sentences for Kuznetsov and Dymshits and for prison terms of 5 to 15 years for the other 9 defendants. The *N.Y. Times* reported Dec. 27 that in their final statements Dec. 24 all defendants had admitted taking part in the plot but had expressed surprise, in view of the attempt's failure, at the harsh sentences demanded by the prosecutor. Many of the accused said they had considered the hijacking only after the failure of repeated attempts to obtain permission from Soviet authorities to emigrate to Israel.

Leningradskaya Pravda declared Dec. 25: "It was established during the court proceedings that the preparation for the commission of this crime was carried out not without the knowledge of Zionist circles in the state of Israel." Tass said Dec. 28 that the 2 capital and 9 harsh prison sentences meted out by the Leningrad court were "in the spirit" of the antihijacking convention passed Dec. 16 by the International Civil Aviation Organization. The Israeli Knesset (parliament) Dec. 25 asked the Soviet Union to lift "the shadow of death from the condemned men" and to liberate "these Jews who—as no one knows better than you—are completely innocent." The Knesset, in its resolution added: "Let not world opinion allow this atrocity to be perpetrated. In order not to acquiesce in the oppression of the spirit of man, lift up your voices."

Among those protesting Dec. 26 were the French and British Communist parties and the International Commission of Jurists. The Italian Communist Party, the Belgian government and the Danish, Norwegian and Australian premiers appealed for clemency Dec. 27.

U.S. State Secy. William P. Rogers was reported Dec. 31 to have written a letter on the matter the previous day to Soviet Foreign Min. Andrei A. Gromyko.

Andrei D. Sakharov, the prominent Soviet physicist active in civil rights causes, was reported Dec. 28 to have sent an appeal to Soviet Pres. Podgorny not to "allow the execution of Dymshits and Kuznetsov." "This would be unjustified brutality," he declared. "Lighten the punishment of the other accused." Among those signing the appeal with Sakharov were 4 other scientists, including Valery N. Chalidze and Andrei N. Tverdokhlebov, and 52 Soviet Jews, including Leonid G. Rigerman, who was himself seeking permission to leave the USSR on the claim that he was a U.S. citizen. Sakharov was present in court during appeal deliberations in Moscow Dec. 30-31.

The Supreme Court of the Russian Republic Dec. 31 commuted to 15 years in prison the death sentences imposed on 2 of the defendants. The court reduced the sentence of Kuznetsov from death to 15 years in a special labor camp, the severest type of Soviet camp, and that of Dymshits from death to 15 years in a strict camp, a less severe form of detention. The court also reduced the sentences of 3 other defendants. Yosif M. Mendelevich received 12 instead of 15 years; Leib G. Khnokh was given 10 instead of 13 years, and Anatoly Altman received 10 instead of 12 years. All were sentenced to strict camps. The sentences of the 6 other alleged plotters were upheld Dec. 31. Those assigned to strict camps and their terms of imprisonment were: Silva Y. Zalmanson, the wife of Kuznetsov, 10 years; Izrail Y. Zalmanson, Silva's brother, 8 years, and Boris Penson, 10 years. Yuri P. Fyodorov and Alexander Murzhenko, the only non-Jewish members of the group, received sentences of 15 years in a special camp. Mendel Bodnya, an invalid, was sentenced to 4 years in an enforced labor camp, less severe than the strict category. (Volf Zalmanson, a brother of 2 of the accused and the 12th person arrested at the airport in June, was to be tried separately by courtmartial because he held active status in the Soviet army.)

The Tass report on the Supreme Court ruling Dec. 31 said that the court had "proceeded from the fact that the hijacking attempt was averted in time and that under Soviet law the death penalty is an exceptional measure of punishment." The prosecution had invoked an article of Soviet law that makes an intended crime as serious as one that is carried out.

Leonid G. Rigerman, 31, a graduate physicist and Soviet Jew who claimed U.S. citizenship, was sentenced Nov. 12 in Moscow to 7 days in jail for disobeying a police order. The charge grew out of 2 attempts Nov. 9 by Rigerman to enter the U.S. embassy to discuss his citizenship claims with officials there. Both times he was intercepted by Soviet policemen. The U.S. embassy accused the Soviet Foreign Ministry Nov. 9 of a violation of the Soviet-American consular convention. Rigerman was asking to be declared a U.S. citizen on the grounds that his mother, born in New York, had married his Soviet-born father in the U.S. and his paternal grandfather had been a naturalized U.S. citizen. (Rigerman finally received a U.S. passport Feb. 16, 1971, and he and his mother later were allowed to leave for the U.S.)

Tatars & Lithuanians

Sources in Moscow reported Jan. 19 that 2 dissenters protesting against the treatment of Crimean Tatars had been sentenced to 3 years in a labor camp on charges of defaming the Soviet state and social system. The dissenters were Ilya Gabai, a poet and teacher, and Mustafa Zhemilyev, a leader of a Crimean Tatar group. They had been among the 55 signers of the May 1969 appeal to the UN against alleged repression of human rights in the USSR.

Western newspapers reported Apr. 27 that security police had intercepted more than 100 Crimean Tatars who had planned to demonstrate at the Moscow Lenin centenary for permission to return to their homeland. (The Tatars had been expelled from Crimea by Stalin for alleged collaboration with the Nazis.)

A Soviet Aeroflot AN-24 airliner, on a domestic flight between the Black Sea ports of Batumi and Sukhumi in the Georgian Republic, was hijacked by 2 Lithuanians Oct. 15 and forced to land in Trebizond, Turkey. The hijackers, identified as Pranas S. Brazinskas, 46, and his son Algirdas, 18, took control of the plane shortly after takeoff and ordered the pilot to fly to Turkey. According to the elder Brazinskas, he and his son accidentally fired their weapons when the pilot "started flipping the plane" in order to throw the hijackers off balance by aerial maneuvers. Nadezhda Kurchenko, the stewardess, was killed, and the pilot and navigator were injured. Passengers later reported that Miss Kurchenko had been shot while trying to block entrance to the pilots' cabin. Both hijackers surrendered to police officials in Turkey and asked for political asylum.

Soviet Amb.-to-Turkey Vasily F. Grubvakov Oct. 16 submitted to Turkish Foreign Min. Ihsan Caglayangil a formal request for the extradition of the hijackers. But a Trebizond court Oct. 17 ordered the hijackers released on the grounds that their offense had been political. This ruling was apparently influenced by Brazinskas' assertion that he had carried out the hijacking in order to have his son educated "in a free country." A Turkish Justice Ministry official said Oct. 18 that the 2 would remain in custody until their case had been reviewed by the ministry in Ankara.

The Soviet government newspaper *Izvestia* warned Oct. 20 that "continued procrastination" in returning the hijackers might "cast a shadow" over Soviet-Turkish relations. Tass took note of the lower court decision Oct. 19, calling it a "more than strange verdict contrary to generally known facts." The Soviet Communist Party newspaper *Pravda* Oct. 18 had portrayed Brazinskas as a former convict, thief and embezzler who had deserted 2 wives and had abused his mother before taking to air piracy. Brazinskas was a resident of Uzbekistan.

Scientists

In a letter reportedly sent to Soviet Communist Party First Secy. Brezhnev and Premier Kosygin, 3 Soviet intellectuals Mar. 19 offered wide-ranging proposals for the reform of Soviet life. The letter was made available to Western correspondents in Moscow by Russian sources. Extracts were published by leading Western newspapers Apr. 3.

The letter reportedly was the work of Andrei D. Sakharov and Valentin F. Turchin, both physicists, and R. A. Medvedyev, an historian. (Sakharov had written a similar critique, published in the *N.Y. Times* in 1968, entitled "Progress, Co-existence & Intellectual Freedom." Another letter published under Sakharov's name in the West earlier in 1970 was expressly declared a forgery in a footnote to the Mar. 19 letter.) The document's basic arugment was that the Soviet Union was falling behind the West, economically and technologically, because of a lack of democracy and "limitations on the exchange of information and on intellectual freedom."

"The source of our difficulties is not the Socialist system," the letter writers asserted, "but, on the contrary, it lies in those peculiarities and conditions of our life that run contrary to socialism and are hostile to it. This source is the antidemocratic traditions and norms of public life that appeared during Stalin's period and have not yet been completely eliminated." "One can really see the distrust toward those who think critically, creatively and actively," the letter asserted. "Under these conditions only those who, in their own words, display staunchness toward the cause of the party, but who, in reality, are concerned with their personal interest, and not those who really have professional qualities, can move upward." "One can neither understand nor justify such absurd, extremely harmful acts as the expulsion from the Union of Writers of the greatest and most popular Soviet writer [Alexandr Solzhenitsyn], who is a deeply patriotic and humane man in all his activity, or the destruction of the editorial section of *Novy Mir,* which gathered round it the most progressive forces of the Marxist-Leninist Socialist movement."

The letter writers also criticized Soviet foreign policy, particularly in the Middle East, West Berlin and Communist China. In response to these and other problems, the authors proposed a 14-point program of "democratization," which, they said, ought to be acceptable to the Communist Party and could be expanded by further studies. Otherwise, they predicted, hostility would grow between the intelligentsia and political rulers, and the non-Russian peoples of the USSR would become increasingly nationalistic. Their recommendations included: measures to increase democratization; dissemination, at first restricted, of information on the state of the country; an end to the jamming of foreign broadcasts; free sale of foreign books and periodicals; unrestricted international mails; direct, multiple-choice elections to party and government posts; broader powers for local and national legislatures, and restoration of the rights of all nationalities forcibly resettled by Stalin.

Sakharov, the physicist Mikhail A. Leontovich and 2 other scientists protested June 1 against the continued detention of ex-Maj. Gen. Pyotr G. Grigorenko. The 2 others were Turchin and Valery Chelidze, both physicists.

In a report whose release was timed to coincide with the Lenin centenary, Amnesty International had said Apr. 19 that while "Lenin's purpose was to set men free" there were "undoubtedly thousands of prisoners of conscience in Soviet prisons and camps." (Amnesty International was a British organization working for the release of political prisoners.) "A great many prisoners of conscience in the Soviet Union are confined, with or without trial, to the so-called special psychiatric hospitals," the report charged. "Often it seems that a decision to confine a patient is taken merely to avoid the publicity a trial would attract among protest circles in the Soviet intelligentsia." The report asserted that prisoners who did not renounce their convictions "are subjected to physical torture, on the pretext of treatment, to injections of large doses of 'animazin' and 'sulfazin,' which cause depressive shock reaction and serious physical disorders. Sometimes odium animate, a strong narcotic, is administered by injection to weaken the patient, and after the injection he is interrogated."

Zhores A. Medvedev, a geneticist and brother of R. A. Medvedev, an author of the Mar. 19 letter to Brezhnev and Kosygin, was arrested May 29 and taken to a mental hospital at Kaluga, 100 miles southwest of Moscow. No reason was given for the arrest. Medvedev received a medical examination May 31 following protests by prominent scientific and literary figures May 30. Although found normal, he was told he would be freed after a week of observation. A 2d team of psychiatrists examined Medvedev June 4 and ruled he should be detained for a month. The 7-man team reportedly included Grigory Morozov, director, and D. R. Lunts, of the staff of the Serbsky Institute for the Criminally Insane in Moscow. (Lunts had reportedly been one of the examiners of Grigorenko.)

Medvedev was the author of *The Rise and Fall of T. D. Lysenko,* a book dealing with genetic theories imposed under Stalin. In an unpublished work entitled *International Cooperation of Scientists and Foreign Borders,* Medvedev had written of the difficulties faced by Soviet scientists in trying to correspond with colleagues abroad. Until 1969, he had been attached to the Institute of Medical Radiology at Obninsk, about 45 miles southwest of Moscow, a job from which he was reportedly dismissed for failure to confine his writing to pure science.

Signing telegrams May 30 protesting Medvedev's arrest were fellow geneticist Boris L. Astaurov, physicists Sakharov and Pyotr L. Kapitsa and biochemist Vladimir E. Engelhardt. All were members of the Soviet Academy of Sciences. Also signing the telegram was Aleksandr T. Tvardovsky, former editor of *Novy Mir.*

Sakharov joined the physicists Leontovich and Igor Y. Tamm, a 1958 Nobel Prize winner, in a letter sent June 4 to the ministers of health and public order and to the procurator general. Asserting that Medvedev was sane and that his public activity had been pursued on "strictly legal grounds," the 3 observed: "Not one honest and principled scientist will be sure of his own security if similar grounds can bring about his own repression in the form of confinement to a psychiatric hospital for an indeterminate period with the deprivation of all human rights except the right to be an object of examination for doctors."

Medvedev was provisionally released June 17 and allowed to return home. The decision to release him reportedly was taken at a meeting June 11 chaired by Public Health Min. Boris V. Petrovsky and attended by Sakharov and other scientists who had protested against Medvedev's detention. In view of the examining psychiatrist's testimony that Medvedev appeared to be suffering from an unspecified mental illness, the authorities made Medvedev's release provisional.

Sakharov had written June 6 to Brezhnev in protest against Medvedev's detention, which Sakharov described as "a potential threat to the freedom of science." He asked Brezhnev "to become involved in the affair in the interests of Soviet law and democracy."

Aleksandr I. Solzhenitsyn June 16 released a statement in which he described "the incarceration of free-thinking healthy people in madhouses" as "spiritual murder." He said of Medvedev that it was "precisely for the diversity of his gifts that he has been charged with abnormality: a split personality. It is precisely his sensitivity to injustice, to stupidity, that are made to seem a sick deviation: poor adaptation to the social milieu."

Sakharov also protested against the arrest in July, on charges of "anti-Soviet slander," of Revolt I. Pimenov, a Leningrad mathematician specializing in general relativity. In a letter made public Oct. 11 and sent the previous week to the Kaluga regional court, Sakharov said his concern was increased by the "well-known severity of sentences which has been the practice in recent years in such cases." Sakharov and 4 other scientists gave notice of their intention to appear for Pimenov's trial, scheduled to begin Oct. 14, in order "to see and hear how justice is carried out on such important questions as freedom of expression and exchange of information." Also signing the letter were physicists Turchin, Chalidze and N. N. Belooserov and a biological sciences student, S. A. Kovalev.

Copies of the unpublished works of Sakharov and Solzhenitsyn had been taken from Pimenov's apartment following a police search in April. Pimenov was summoned Apr. 20 to the office of V. A. Medvedev, the Leningrad party official in charge of ideology, and a copy of the ensuing conversation was reported Oct. 7 to be circulating in Moscow.

During the conversation, Pimenov reportedly declared that Soviet scientists were unable to work effectively because of fears for their personal security and lack of faith in the future. Medvedev was said to have replied: "If you think that we ever will allow somebody to speak and write anything that comes into his head, then this will never be.... Of course, we don't have enough power to force all people to think the same, but we still have enough power not to let people do things that will be harmful to us."

3 Soviet physicists Nov. 15 released to Western newsmen in Moscow copies of a declaration establishing a Committee for Human Rights to help guarantee personal freedom in the Soviet Union. The statement of principles was signed by Sakharov, whose local Communist Party organization at the Lebedev Physics Institute was criticized in October, Chalidze and Andrei N. Tverdokhlebov. In the document the 3 declared: "The problem of the maintenance of human rights is important for the creation of favorable conditions for people's lives, the consolidation of peace and the development of mutual understanding." They stated that the goals of the organization would be "to cooperate on a consultative basis with the further efforts of the state in the creation of guarantees for the defense of rights, taking into account the specific character of the problem in the conditions of the Socialist system and the specific character of the Soviet traditions in this field."

Excluded from joining the committee were "members of a political party.... or other organizations claiming participation in governmental management," as well as members of groups "whose principles allow participation in orthodox or opposition political activity." Observers noted that the last phrase in this section could be applied to known political dissidents. (Some members of an organization called the Initiative Group for the Defense of Civil Rights, formed in 1969, were in jail.)

The signers pledged "constructive criticism of the contemporary conditions of the system of the legal rights of personal freedom in Soviet law" and welcomed contact with nonofficial foreign organizations that "proceed from the principles of the United Nations and do not pursue the goal of bringing harm to the Soviet Union."

The 3 signers were joined Nov. 15 by 6 other scientists, including Mikhail A. Leontovich, in publishing a letter of protest against the sentencing to Siberian exile in October of Pimenov. In the letter, addressed to the Supreme Court of the Russian Federation, the 9 declared that Pimenov and his codefendant Boris B. Vail had merely exchanged information in their possession.

Dr. Viktor P. Silin, chairman of the party unit at the Lebedev Institute of Physics, a research body with which Sakharov was associated, took note in a *Pravda* interview Dec. 2 of criticism of the institute by the party Central Committee. Silin asserted that "the [Central Committee] resolution, in my opinion, does not affect only us.... In a word, this document is yet another sign of the party's concern for the development of science." Silin delivered an indirect reproach to Sakharov's Human Rights Committee when he said: "Anyone who trumpets his nonparty attitude plainly and simply makes himself useful to the enemy." (Solzhenitsyn and Aleksandr Galich, a singer, were reported by the *N.Y. Times* Dec. 10 to have joined Sakharov's Human Rights Committee.)

Writers

In an open letter published in the London *Times* Jan. 17, Aleksandr Daniel, son of the jailed writer Yuli M. Daniel, appealed to Graham Greene, the British novelist, to help his father and another political prisoner, Valery Ronkin. Young Daniel, 18, protested against the transfer of the 2 men to Vladimir Prison in July 1969. He added that he had written to Greene as "our last hope."

Aleksandr Ginsburg, who had protested in Dec. 1969 against the transfer of Yuli Daniel from the Potma labor camp, was reported Aug. 23 to have been moved from Potma to Vladimir Prison.

Daniel was released from the prison Sept. 12 and exiled to the city of Kaluga, 90 miles southwest of Moscow.

Andrei Voznesensky's play *Watch Your Faces* was closed Feb. 10 on the grounds of "ideological shortcomings" after one performance at the Taganka Theater in Moscow.

The party newspaper *Pravda* Nov. 13 criticized Moscow's Taganka Theater for "substantial shortcomings" in ideological work. The criticism, contained in a Nov. 11 report to the city's party central committee by First Secy. Viktor Grishin, was directed at the theater's party organization for "not having a proper influence on the choice of the repertoire and the creative life of the company."

Pravda said that Grishin had also rebuked the party organization at the Institute of Philosophy of the Academy of Sciences for not having "shown the necessary concern for the creation of a businesslike, creative atmosphere at the institute" and for not "instilling in the employes the [notion of] responsibility for the ideological content of scientific works, and the strengthening of the principle of party spirit in the sciences."

It was reported in Moscow Feb. 14 that Aleksandr T. Tvardovsky, editor-in-chief of *Novy Mir,* had resigned in protest over changes in the journal's editorial board. He had been under attack by conservatives for failing to understand alleged ideological threats from the West and for wanting to publish quality works even when they pointed to shortcomings in the Soviet society. He reportedly was replaced by Vasily A. Kosolapov, a moderate, who had been a former chief editor of the weekly journal of the Union of Soviet Writers, *Literaturnaya Gazeta.* Kosolapov had been named to *Novy Mir's* editorial board Feb. 11 along with 3 others after the Secretariat of the Union of Soviet Writers had dismissed 4 members of the board, including the deputy editor, A. I. Kondratovich. Tvardovsky reportedly had argued that the changes in the board's membership made it useless for him to continue in his post.

Tvardovsky was reported Feb. 18 to have resigned as vice president of the European Community of Writers. Soviet news analysts indicated that this move was forced on him. His resignation followed a special meeting of the Union of Soviet Writers Feb. 11 at which it was decided to withdraw from the European union because of opposition by its secretary general, Giancarlo Vigorelli, to Soviet treatment of Solzhenitsyn.

The Manchester *Guardian* Mar. 21 published the smuggled text of a letter from Tvardovsky to Konstantin A. Fedin, first secretary of the board of the Soviet Writers Union. (As a member, under Tvardovsky, of the editorial board of *Novy Mir,* Fedin's favorable evaluation of the manuscript of *One Day in the Life of Ivan Denisovich,* Solzhenitsyn's first novel, had been partially responsible for its publication in that journal.) The burden of Tvardovsky's letter was that Fedin should use his influence to get the union to drop its demand that Solzhenitsyn "give a rebuff" to the anti-Soviet campaign in the Western press and abjure his letter of Nov. 10, 1969. "Otherwise," Tvardovsky told Fedin, "you will not publish his book *[Cancer Ward]."*

"Just think that the solution of this whole 'Solzhenitsyn complex' could depend on a single secret 'piece of paper'!" Tvardovsky said. "That is the level to which we have been reduced: a piece of paper—one or 2 pages long—for us writers is more important than a novel of 600 pages already prepared for publication which might become, according to the majority of those who have read the manuscript, the treasure and pride of our literature today—this piece of paper is more important than the fate of a writer whose remarkable talent is not disputed even by his fiercest antagonists."

Soviet authorities arrested Andrei A. Amalrik at his country home in Ryazan Province, southeast of Moscow, May 21. Amalrik, whose book, *Will the Soviet Union Survive Until 1984?* was published by Harper & Row in March, was reportedly arrested under article 190 of the Criminal Code of the Russian Republic for spreading "falsehoods derogatory to the Soviet state and social system." Under Soviet law he was not entitled to a lawyer until an investigation was completed.

Amalrik's analysis of Soviet society as likely to disintegrate by 1984 from internal dissension and war with China had been challenged in an open letter Mar. 28 by Pyotr I. Yakir, historian and civil rights activist. Yakir argued that Amalrik's essay had successfully captured the psychology and ideology of contemporary Soviet society but said its predictions were less convincing. His own view was that the democratic movement, though narrowly based, was "the beginning of an irreversible process of self-liberation."

Amalrik was convicted Nov. 12 after a 2-day trial in Sverdlovsk and sentenced to 3 years in a labor camp. Amalrik's co-defendant, Lev G. Ubozhko, accused of bringing 2 documents from Moscow to Sverdlovsk, was also sentenced to 3 years but in a less severe type of camp. Ubozhko, who testified that he had never met Amalrik, was convicted of transporting an open letter from Amalrik to Anatoly V. Kuznetsov, the Soviet writer who had defected to Great Britain in 1969, and of possessing a leaflet distributed by 2 Italian students at a Moscow department store in January.

Amalrik reportedly refused to enter a plea of guilty or not guilty or to answer any of the questions put to him during the trial. In his hour-long defense Nov. 12, Amalrik denounced "the cowardice of a regime that regards as a danger the spreading of any thought, any idea alien to its top bureaucrats." He said: "In particular, the fear of my thoughts, of the facts expressed in my books, forces these people to put me in the dock as a criminal. This fear led them also to be afraid of trying me in Moscow. They brought me here, thinking that here the trial would attract less attention."

The prosecutor's case was based on Amalrik's books, his open letter to Kuznetsov and 2 interviews given to William Cole, a CBS correspondent expelled from Moscow after the interviews were broadcast on TV in the U.S. in July.

A Moscow court July 7 ruled that Natalya Gorbanevskaya, a young poetess prominent in the movement of dissent, was not responsible for her actions. It confined her to an insane asylum for an undetermined period. The young woman, active in the movement since 1968, had protested against illegal trials, the intervention in Czechoslovakia and the expulsion of Solzhenitsyn from the Writers' Union. She was a signatory to 2 appeals to the UN.

The London *Times* and *Daily Telegraph & Morning Post* Aug. 26 published excerpts from a letter addressed to Solzhenitsyn July 20 in protest against the imprisonment of ex-Maj. Gen. Pyotr G. Grigorenko. The letter was written by Aleksandr Sergeevich Yesenin-Volpin, 46, the son of the prominent Russian poet Sergei Yesenin, who had committed suicide in 1925 because of his disillusionment with the Soviet regime. Yesenin-Volpin, himself a poet and mathematician, had been prominent in the Soviet protest movement.

Solzhenitsyn Wins Nobel Prize

Aleksandr I. Solzhenitsyn, the Soviet novelist whose works were banned in his country, was awarded the 1970 Nobel Prize for Literature Oct. 8. The Swedish Academy of Literature said Solzhenitsyn had been chosen winner because of "the ethical force with which he has pursued the indispensable traditions of Russian literature."

In a phone conversation Oct. 8 with Per Egil Hegge, correspondent for the Swedish newspaper *Svenska Dagbladet,* Solzhenitsyn said: "I am grateful for the decision. I accept the prize. I intend to go and receive it personally on the traditional day [Dec. 10] insofar as this depends on me. I am well. The journey will not hurt my health." Karl-Ragnar Gierow, secretary of the Swedish Academy, received a telegram Oct. 11 in which Solzhenitsyn called the award "a tribute to Russian literature and to our arduous history."

A declaration by 37 Soviet political dissidents, published by the *N.Y. Times* Oct. 11, welcomed the award and said: "The civic inspiration, philosophical depth and high artistic craftsmanship of the works of Solzhenitsyn are recognized by the whole world.... [He is] a powerful contemporary writer, the humanitarianism of the positions he has adopted and which he consistently and courageously defends, all this fully deserves an award of such high distinction.... We are proud of our literature ... which, no matter what the barriers, produces such first-rank masters. In addition, we are prepared for the awarding of the prize to become another of those regular occasions for continuing the badgering which consistently takes place here against him and which we consider a national shame." Among those signing the declaration were Pyotr I. Yakir, an historian, and Zinaida Grigorenko, wife of ex-Maj. Gen. Grigorenko, who had been confined to a mental institution for his political views.

(The Nobel Prize had twice before been awarded to Soviet writers. Boris Pasternak was compelled to refuse the prize in 1958. Mikhail A. Sholokhov received the Nobel Prize in 1965.)

Although there was no official government reaction to the award, the Soviet Writers Union, from which Solzhenitsyn had been expelled in 1969, said Oct. 9 that the choice of Solzhenitsyn was "deplorable." The statement, issued by the union's secretariat, criticized the Nobel committee for allowing itself "to be drawn into an unseemly game that was not started in the interests of the development of the spiritual values and traditions of literature but was prompted by speculative political considerations." The secretariat also claimed that Solzhenitsyn's expulsion from the union had been "actively supported by the entire public of the country."

Sergei V. Mikhalkov, chairman of the Russian Republican Writers Union, said Oct. 14 that the prize had been given Solzhenitsyn for "purely political aims" that were "dictated in no way by concern about Russian literature." *Literaturnaya Gazeta,* journal of the Soviet Writers Union, declared that "members of the [Nobel] committee, under the expression 'ethical force' had an anti-Soviet direction in mind." The journal also said Oct. 14 that *Sentry,* a Russian emigre publication in Brussels, and Arts & Progress, a French intellectual organization, had taken credit for promoting Solzhenitsyn's candidacy. In the first personal attack on Solzhenitsyn since the award was announced, the Novosti press agency Oct. 16 called him a man of "morbid self-importance" who had "made of his loneliness not a tragedy but a business." The agency also claimed that Solzhenitsyn's work lacked "positive content, and that he simply does not believe and trust the people among whom he lives." The Communist Youth League newspaper *Komosomolskaya Pravda* said Oct. 17 that Solzhenitsyn was "a man of great vanity" and that comparison of his works with those of the great Russian novelists was "blasphemy."

In a letter sent to 4 major Soviet newspapers Nov. 12, cellist Mstislav Rostropovich intervened on behalf of Solzhenitsyn. Explaining his action, Rostropovich said "it is no longer a secret that A. I. Solzhenitsyn lives a great part of the time in my house near Moscow" and there was "no reason to hide my attitude toward him at a time when a campaign is being waged against him." Rostropovich commented on past Nobel awards to Soviet writers by pointing out: "It now happens that we selectively sometimes accept Nobel prizes with gratitude, and sometimes we curse them.... What if the next time the prize is awarded to Comrade Kochetov? Of course, it will have to be accepted." (Vsevelod A. Kochetov, a conservative novelist and editor of the literary journal *Oktyabr,* was a known opponent of Solzhenitsyn.)

Referring to the "nonsense" that appeared when the press attacked Soviet musicians in 1948, Rostropovich asked: "Has that time really not taught us to tread cautiously before destroying talented people? In 1948 there were lists of forbidden works. Now oral prohibitions are preferred, based on the contention that 'opinions exist' that a work is not recommended. It is impossible to establish where that opinion exists and whose it is.... I don't speak about political or economic questions in our country. There are people who know that better than I, but explain to me please why, just in our literature and art, people absolutely incompetent in this field so often have the final word? Why they receive the right to discredit our art in the eyes of our people?... I know that after my letter there will undoubtedly be an opinion about me, but I am not afraid and I openly say what I think. Talents of which we are proud must not be subjected to the assaults of the past."

Solzhenitsyn informed the Swedish embassy in Moscow Nov. 27 that he would not go to Stockholm to accept the Nobel Prize in December as he originally planned. In a letter forwarded to the Swedish Academy of Literature by Swedish Amb.-to-USSR Gunnar V. Jarring and made public Nov. 30, Solzhenitsyn explained that "in recent weeks, the hostile attitude toward my prize, as expressed in the press of my country, and the fact that my books are still suppressed ... compel me to assume that my trip to Stockholm would be used to cut me off from my native land, simply to prevent me from returning home." Solzhenitsyn added that "in the Nobel celebrations there are many ceremonies and festivities that are tiring and not in keeping with my character and way of life."

Solzhenitsyn suggested in his letter that because "personal presence at the ceremony is not an obligatory condition to receiving the prize.... I could receive the Nobel diploma and medal ... in Moscow from your representatives, at a mutually convenient time." Solzhenitsyn expressed his "gratitude for the honor bestowed upon me" and remarked: "Inwardly I share it with those of my predecessors in Russian literature who because of the difficult conditions of the past decades did not live to receive such a prize or who were little known in their lifetime to the reading world in translation or to their countrymen even in the original."

7 Nobel Prize winners gathered in Stockholm Dec. 10 to take part in the Nobel ceremonies, and all received gold medals from Sweden's King Gustaf VI Adolf. Solzhenitsyn did not attend.

The address for Solzhenitsyn was read by Dr. Karl-Ragner Gierow, permanent secretary of the Swedish Academy, who said that the absent writer was "of the incomparable Russian tradition.... The same background underlies the gigantic predecessors who have derived from Russia's suffering the compelling strength and inextinguishable love that permeates their work.... The words of Aleksandr Solzhenitsyn speak to us of matters that we need to hear more than ever before, of the individual's indestructible dignity." At the end of his address, Gierow said: "The Swedish Academy regrets the reason that Aleksandr Solzhenitsyn has deemed it impossible to be with us today.... In accordance with his own wish, the prize will be awarded at a place and time to be agreed upon."

At a banquet following the award-presentation ceremonies, Gierow read a letter from Solzhenitsyn in which the novelist said he hoped his "involuntary absence" would not "darken the fullness of today's ceremony." Solzhenitsyn noted that Dec. 10 was Human Rights Day, and urged those listening in Stockholm to "see in this a symbol." The Dec. 21 edition of *Time* reported that the letter contained the following passage, which Gierow did not read: "May the people at this rich table not forget the political prisoners now on hunger strikes in protest against the total destruction of their rights."

Pravda declared Dec. 17 that Solzhenitsyn was being used to aid an anti-Soviet campaign in the Western press. The article, bearing the pen-name I. Aleksandrov, used for major policy statements, also contained a denunciation of Andrei Amalrik and Anatoly V. Kuznetsov as "the riff-raff who hang around foreign press centers begging for whisky and cigarettes in exchange for dirty fabrications." But "having failed with such rascals," Aleksandrov said, "the heralds of anti-Communism resolved to use provocations in a bigger scale and to raise a clamor around the name of Solzhenitsyn." The Nobel Prize laureate was described as an "internal emigre who is alien and hostile to all of Soviet life." Solzhenitsyn's major works were said to be "lampoons on the Soviet Union ... which blacken the achievements of the heroic victories of our motherland and the dignity of the Soviet people."

A 5-minute statement was broadcast on Moscow TV Dec. 17 by author Arkady Perventsev, who said the case of Solzhenitsyn had to be publicized "because he is being used as armament by our ideological enemies."

Other Protesters

Viktor van Brantegem, a Belgian student identified as a member of 2 Flemish activist groups, startled the audience during an intermission of a performance of *My Fair Lady* at Moscow's Operetta Theater Jan. 18 by shouting support for Soviet intellectual and political dissidents, chaining himself in the balcony and showering the audience with leaflets. The leaflets urged Soviet composer Dmitri D. Shostakovich to support the release of ex-Maj. Gen. Pyotr Grigoryevich Grigorenko. Van Brantegem was arrested.

Teresa Marinuzzi, 22, and Valentino Tacchi, 23, members of a civil rights group called Europa Civilta, chained themselves to stair railings in the GUM department store in Moscow Jan. 17 after dropping leaflets demanding the release of 4 Soviet political prisoners. The leaflets called on Premier Kosygin to free Grigorenko, Anatoly Y. Levitin, Yuri Galanskov and Natalia Gorbanev, who had been arrested in late Dec. 1969 and reportedly had been sent to a mental institution. The 2 Italians were arrested.

The 3 foreign students were sentenced Feb. 11 to a year in a labor camp. Marinuzzi, Tacchi and van Brantegem were convicted of "malicious hooliganism." Diplomatic sources in Moscow said that the 2 Italians were released Feb. 15 as a result of an exchange of letters between the Soviet and Italian governments. The Belgian, van Brantegem, was released Feb. 22, as was Gunnar Gjenseth, a Norwegian involved in another incident.

Using *samizdat* (underground publication) sources, Western newspapers Apr. 27 reported that the sentence of Grigorenko, the advocate of Tatar rights who had been ruled insane in Dec. 1969, had been confirmed by the Supreme Court of Uzbekistan. Grigorenko was being held in a mental hospital in Kazan.

Ivan Yakhimovich, the former chairman of a collective farm in Soviet Latvia, who had joined Grigorenko in an appeal against the Soviet invasion of Czechoslovakia and had been convicted of distributing anti-Soviet materials, was reported to have been sentenced to a mental hospital after a 2d trial Apr. 17. Arkady Z. Levin was sentenced to 3 years in a labor camp after a trial in Kharkov Apr. 24 for distributing an appeal to the UN and a letter defending Grigorenko.

The *N.Y. Times* reported May 20 that Valerian Novodvorsky, 19, had been sent to a mental institution Mar. 16 for distributing leaflets charging lack of freedom in the Soviet Union. Vladimir Ponomarev and Vladislav Nedobora were sentenced to 3 years in a labor camp Mar. 10—11 for possessing anti-Soviet literature.

The London *Times* said May 20 that Georgi Vins, a Russian Baptist leader, had been arrested in Kiev and sentenced to a year at forced labor. Other Baptists were reportedly imprisoned for alleged violations of laws governing religious activity.

Irina Kaplun and Vyacheslav Bakhmin, arrested in Nov. 1969 for preparing civil rights leaflets to be distributed on the late Joseph Stalin's birthday, were reportedly released Sept. 23. Olga Ioffe, arrested in the same case, was committed to a psychiatric institution Aug. 20.

UNREST TOPPLES POLISH REGIME

Dissent continued to manifest itself in Polish life in 1970 but remained confined to the fringes of Poland's society of more than 32.5 million people—for the first 11 months of the year. Then, in December, the Gomulka-Cyrankiewicz regime fell, following disorders caused by serious economic dissatisfaction.

Dissenters & Defectors

A Warsaw court Feb. 24 convicted 5 Polish intellectuals for alleged subversive activities in collaboration with an emigre group in Paris. The defendants had been charged with smuggling to and from Poland materials considered inimical to the Polish government and people. These materials reportedly included copies of the Czechoslovak novelist Ludvik Vaculik's June 1968 manifesto *2000 Words,* printed in Prague, and *Kultura,* a Polish magazine published in Paris. A Warsaw radio broadcast Feb. 18 had said that the 5 had planned to recruit others and to establish a clandestine radio station. Maciej Kozlowski was sentenced to 4½ years in prison, Maria Tworkowska and Krzysztof Szymborski to 3½ years, Jacub Karpinski to 4 years, and Maria Szpakowska to 3 years. The period of detention before trial in each case was included and accordingly reduced the sentences.

A 29-year-old Polish butcher armed with hand grenades hijacked a Polish Airlines jet from Warsaw June 5, forcing the pilot to land in Copenhagen. On arrival in Copenhagen, the hijacker allowed the 23 passengers to leave, then asked for political asylum. The Polish embassy in Denmark requested June 8 that he be extradited to Poland, but the Danish government Sept. 7 decided against extraditing the butcher.

The Danish island of Bornholm was the terminal point of additional hijackings Aug. 19, 25 and 31. 3 men and 2 women sought asylum Aug. 19 after using hand grenades to commandeer a Polish airliner. Asylum was sought Aug. 25 by 5 young Poles who hijacked a trawler from Darlowo. Another 10 Poles, including 2 children, arrived in Bornholm Aug. 31 in a hijacked trawler and asked for asylum.

The Polish news agency PAP reported Aug. 27 that Rudolf Olma was injured when he accidentally detonated an explosive device with which he had threatened the captain of a Polish airliner in a hijacking attempt. The plane, with 10 of its passengers injured by the blast, returned to Katowice.

Price Increases Provoke Disturbances

A series of major price increases caused the groundswell of popular dissatisfaction that ultimately overthrew the Gomulka-Cyrankiewicz regime.

The government announced the rises effective Dec. 13. They included increases of 11%-33% in prices of meat and meat products, 8%-25% for cheese, flour, fish and milk, 92% for wheaten *(ersatz)* coffee and 10%-20% for coal. Sharp price cuts were announced at the same time for electrical appliances, including TV sets, and medicines. The Polish press explained Dec. 13 that the increased costs would be offset further by greater family assistance payments, lower TV taxes and installment-buying costs and greater subsidies to farmers. Increased meat prices were understood to have been decided on to counter the effects on domestic meat supplies of the poor 1969 and 1970 grain harvests and to avoid losing foreign exchange by diverting meat production intended for export to domestic consumption. Polish United Workers' Party First Secy. Gomulka told the party Central Committee at a meeting Dec. 14 that despite "unprofitable prices for bread, cereals, macaroni and flour, per capita consumption of these articles has not increased but has slightly diminished in past years as a result of the increased consumption of meat." (A Radio Free Europe research report Dec. 3 said the supply of meat had declined 2.4% between January and August 1970.)

The price increases touched off disorders in Gdansk (formerly Danzig) on the Baltic coast. The disturbances spread Dec. 15 to the nearby cities of Sopot and Gdynia. The riots were reportedly accompanied by looting and burning of shops.

According to one account, workers at the Lenin Shipyards in Gdansk had been visited Dec. 13 by Deputy Premier Stanislaw Kociolek, who came to deal with their objections to a wage incentive plan scheduled to replace the existing bonus system. Kociolek reportedly informed the workers of the price changes to be announced to the nation later that day. The Lenin Shipyard workers left their jobs Monday Dec. 15 and marched to the local Communist Party headquarters, demanding that someone hear their grievances. Violence erupted when police tried to prevent the demonstrators from reaching the building. According to Kurt Karlsson, a reporter for the Stockholm newspaper *Expressen:* "Riot police brought in from all over northern Poland fired on the demonstrators, but all eyewitnesses agree that only a few soldiers used their weapons." Karlsson estimated that 300 persons lost their lives Dec. 15 and in the days following.

A government communique Dec. 16 said that 6 people had been killed and scores injured when "hooligans and adventurers having nothing in common with the working class" clashed with police the previous day.

A letter attributed to workers of the Paris Commune Shipyard in Gdynia criticized police units trained by Gen. Mieczyslaw Moczar, the former interior minister, for their role in the mid-December riots. In the document, (published in the *N.Y. Times* and London *Times* Jan. 27, 1971), it was asserted that workers returning to the job Dec. 16 in response to an appeal that day by Deputy Premier Stanley Kociolek had been fired on by police units while crossing a railroad bridge. When the group marched on the town hall to obtain an explanation for the shooting, they were again fired on by police, according to the letter, and an estimated 210 people were killed. (The official account, cited by the *N.Y. Times* Jan. 27, 1971, reported the events as occuring Dec. 17, did not mention Kociolek's appeal and justified as self-defense the police actions at the Gdynia town hall.)

Premier Jozef Cyrankiewicz confirmed in a nationwide radio-TV address Dec. 17 that "Gdansk and the coast" had been "the scene of street disturbances and violations of authority and public order" for "the last 3 days." Cyrankiewicz said that during "these events militiamen and soldiers ... have been attacked and shot at. Tragic clashes followed in which the forces of order were compelled to use arms. There were casualties, a number of dead in the teens, several hundred wounded—militiamen and civilians." He said that the situation had been exploited by "anarchists" and "enemies of socialism," and he appealed for calm. Cyrankiewicz read a government order empowering militiamen "to take up all legal means of enforcement, including the use of weapons." His order amounted to a declaration of a state of emergency.

Dockworkers in the Baltic port of Szczecin were met at Communist Party headquarters Dec. 17 by government tanks. According to Anders Thunberg, a Swedish radio reporter: "Tanks moved against the population to give them a shock. The people fled to avoid being run over, but a mother and her child were unable to make it. An oncoming tank struck both of them. A young soldier, standing nearby and watching, broke into tears."

Demonstrations were reported Dec. 18 in the Silesian mining town of Katowice, and phone communications with the area were restricted.

The widespread unrest appeared to have ended Dec. 19. Stores were being repaired and work resumed in Gdansk, Sopot and Gdynia. Warsaw, which had experienced no disturbances, was reported normal, with shops in the downtown area well-stocked with meat for the holidays.

The state of emergency imposed Dec. 17 was lifted by a decree of the Council of Ministers (cabinet) Dec. 22. The decree said that "order has returned to the coastal towns and life has returned to normal where public order was seriously disturbed."

Gomulka Replaced by Gierek

A news broadcast Dec. 20 carried the first announcement of the resignation of Gomulka. The broadcaster said that the party leader had been hospitalized the previous day because of circulatory ailments. Later Dec. 20, Edward Gierek, former party leader in Katowice province, succeeded Gomulka as party first secretary.

Gierek told the country in a TV address Dec. 20 that the disturbances had resulted from "hasty concepts of economic policy," which "we will remove." He said: The Politburo had been instructed by the party Central Committee to find ways of "improving the material situation of families of the lowest incomes and with many children, who, as a result of the recent changes of prices, have felt the cut most in their budgets .... We will have to reconsider carefully the problem of the national economic plan for the next year and for the whole new 5-year period." "Although we understand that the motives behind" the disturbances were "mostly honest," soldiers and militiamen "fulfilled the duty imposed on them" by giving a "firm rebuff" to the "asocial and criminal elements" associated with the protests.

The news broadcast disclosing Gierek's promotion also carried word of the appointment of 5 new members of the Politburo. They were Gen. Moczar, the former interior minister; Edward Babiuch, former head of the Central Committee's organizational department; Pyotr Jaroszewicz, former vice premier in charge of Comecon activities; Stefan Olszowski and Jan Szydlak. Gierek and Moczar had taken opposing positions on the 1968 student demonstrations. The new members replaced 4 prominent Polish leaders: Zenon

Kliszko, considered the party's ideologist; Boleslaw Jaszczuk, largely responsible for the planned economic reforms; Ryszard Strzelecki, and Marian Spychalski, president of Poland.

The Soviet news agency Tass reported the Polish government changes Dec. 20. Soviet Communist Party Gen. Secy. Leonid I. Brezhnev Dec. 21 sent Gierek a congratulatory telegram, describing Gierek as "a prominent party leader and statesman of people's Poland, a sincere friend of the Soviet Union, a staunch Communist-internationalist." Brezhnev said he was "firmly convinced" that Gierek would be able to "overcome successfully" the recent difficulties.

Jaroszewicz Becomes Premier

The Polish Sejm (parliament) Dec. 23 accepted the resignation of Premier Cyrankiewicz and ordered food prices frozen for 2 years, except for seasonal fluctuations. Cyrankiewicz, who declared he was resigning because of "recent events in our country which I was unable to prevent," was elevated to the post of president, replacing Marshal Spychalski. Pyotr Jaroszewicz was named premier.

(Gierek, who already had announced the price-freeze on food, had also revealed the establishment of a $300 million fund to aid large families, retired persons and low-income groups most affected by the price increases. Gierek had said that 100 factories had been chosen to discuss apportionment of the new fund.)

Jaroszewicz told the Sejm Dec. 23 that he would "strive for a full normalization of relations with the church" and that he hoped this would "meet with understanding" from the Catholic hierarchy. (In what some observers considered a response to Jaroszewicz, Stefan Cardinal Wyszynski declared in his Christmas message Dec. 25: "We are capable of, and we can afford, true democracy in Poland, because it lies in the traditions of the Polish people since the times of the kings. We can afford from our Christian spirit to obtain more active cooperation with the Lord's children of this whole land.")

The Dec. 23 parliamentary session ratified the appointments of Deputy Premiers Franciszek Kaim and Jan Mitrega. Kaim was replaced as minister of heavy industry by his deputy, Woldzimierz Lejczak. Mitrega retained the portfolio of minister of mining and power. Tadeusz Wrzaszcyk was named minister of engineering, replacing Janusz Hrynkiewicz, whose appointment as deputy chairman of the Committee for Science & Technology was regarded as a demotion.

Commenting on the situation in Poland Dec. 24, the Soviet Communist Party newspaper *Pravda* declared: "It will take great exertions by party organizations, a strong sense of purpose and constant efforts to improve the style and methods of work to resolve the difficulties that have arisen." The Warsaw weekly *Polityka* said Dec. 30: "Although there are various degrees of responsibility, the party is responsible for the causes that gave rise to the tragic events. Elements of stagnation were growing in the economy. The picture presented by propaganda was far from reality."

OTHER DEVELOPMENTS

Rumania Reaffirms Independence

An article in *Lupta de Clasa (Class Struggle),* the theoretical journal of the Rumanian Communist Party Central Committee, served to indorse the value and importance of national views in the international Communist movement. In the article, reprinted by the Rumanian press agency Agerpres Feb. 2 and entitled "The Dialectics of National and International in the Development of the Socialist Society," the authors defined the world Socialist system as "a community of 14 free, independent, sovereign and equal states that organized relations between themselves, cooperate and reciprocally help each other" and that recognized the need for the development and prosperity of each member.

The authors rejected arguments that a Communist party should "follow the correct road"; rather, they said that opinions that "negate the diversity of conditions, forms and methods in which the new society is achieved" were unfounded. They declared: "Socialism does not abolish the national particularities of different peoples but creates, for the first time in history, objective premises for the full assertion of their national identity, for the multilateral flourishing of their material and spiritual life in the conditions of unity, collaboration and cooperation with the other Socialist states, with other peoples."

The authors, M. Nedelea and D. Csiki, also rejected the argument of one party imposing its will or "standard" on others. "The theory of 'standard' in the revolutionary struggle for socialism," they said, "ignores the fact there does not exist and cannot exist on an international scale an infallible guardian of the Marxist-Leninist theory and of the correct Marxist-Leninst   political orientation, that there does not exist and cannot exist a 'leading center,' that the idea of a 'leading party,' of a 'leading center,' has long ago been abandoned by the international Communist movement." Equally, the authors asserted, "there is no national communism and international communism: any delimitation in this domain is artificial, lacking a scientific basis. The national and international character of communism is an organic, dialectical whole."

Rejecting attempts to contrast "proletarian internationalism with the other principles that must govern reciprocal relations" between Socialist states, they declared: "The principles of Socialist internationalism, equal rights, independence and sovereignty, noninterference in internal affairs [and] commradely mutual assistance are a single whole, and one cannot speak of establishing some grades, some criteria of observing them in a differentiated manner. The essential premise for the application of Socialist internationalism is the strengthening of national independence and sovereignty, primordial attributes and fundamental coordinates of the prosperity of each nation." The authors also called for increased cooperation with the West and claimed that it was out of date to regard Western moves toward cooperation as attempts to undermine Socialist unity.

At a meeting of armed forces leaders in Bucharest Feb. 5, Pres. Nicolae Ceausescu, the Communist Party general secretary, affirmed the independence of Rumania's military forces. He asserted: "The only chiefs of the Rumanian armed forces are the party, the government and the supreme military command of the country. They alone are qualified to give orders to our army, and only their orders can be executed in [Rumania]." While calling for close military cooperation with other Warsaw Pact and Socialist countries "without any exception," Ceausescu emphasized that treaties between

Communist nations "exclude any interference in the internal affairs of the countries and armies involved." "The Rumanian army has all it needs to fulfill always its obligations to our people, our allies and friends in the fraternal Socialist countries," he declared.

According to a *N.Y. Times* report Feb. 9, the Soviet Union once again was applying pressure on Rumania. It was thought that the USSR was insisting that Bucharest participate in Warsaw Pact military activities.

Rumania celebrated the 22d anniversary of its 20-year friendship treaty with the Soviet Union Feb. 4, but there was no mention of a renewal of the document. The treaty had lapsed in early Aug. 1968 but continued to be in force under an automatic 5-year renewal. Rumania's failure to renew the treaty before its lapse was a demarche unique in the annals of the postwar Soviet bloc. Soviet pressure grew for its renewal.

Finally, a new 20-year Soviet-Rumanian friendship treaty, to come into effect when instruments of ratification had been exchanged, was concluded July 7 in Bucharest. The document was signed by Premier Ion Gheorghe Maurer for Rumania and Premier Aleksei N. Kosygin for the USSR. The signing of the treaty, initialed in 1968, had been delayed by the Soviet invasion of Czechoslovakia in August of that year. The draft was left virtually unchanged, according to the *N.Y. Times* July 7. This surprised some observers, since the Soviet Union had in the meantime—May 6—forced an unequal treaty on Czechoslovakia.

Among the highlights of the treaty was a statement in the preamble in which both sides pledged support for the Warsaw Pact "during the period of the action of the treaty concluded in response to the threat of NATO." Observers noted that this could be read in light of Rumania's repeated proposals for the abolition of military blocs in Europe. The preamble contained no mention of the "Brezhnev doctrine" of limited sovereignty for Socialist countries as had the Soviet-Czechoslovak friendship treaty concluded in May.

Article 5 of the Soviet-Rumanian treaty emphasized the need to solve disputes among states by peaceful means. Article 6 bound the 2 states to the "ensuring of peace in Europe," with particular mention of "the Balkan peninsula and the Black Sea region." Article 7 stressed cooperation with the Warsaw Pact "to ensure the inviolability of the frontiers of the member states."

Article 8 read: "In case one of the high contracting parties is subjected to an armed attack by any state or group of states, the other party, implementing the inalienable right to individual or collective self-defense in accordance with Article 51 of the UN Charter, will immediately render it all-round assistance with all the means at its disposal, including military, essential to repulse armed attack." Although this passage resembled Article 10 of the Soviet-Czechoslovak treaty, Rumanian officials were said to have declared July 8 that the article was to be interpreted along with the treaty's preamble and with Articles 5-7. It was further pointed out that the articles of the 2 treaties did not exactly correspond and that Rumania was entitled, according to the wording of Article 8, to decide which armed attacks required "individual" and which "collective" defense.

Party General Secy. Ceausescu was reported by the newspaper *Scinteia* July 10 to have emphasized that the friendship treaty with the USSR was based on respect for national sovereignty and noninterference in internal affairs. He also said at a party Central Committee meeting held July 8-9 that Communist unity could be achieved "only on a new basis that assures the full autonomy and independence of each Communist party." Echoing his previous calls for an international Communist conference, Ceausescu said that "the advancement of the ideas of communism presupposes a large and free debate, a scientific analysis and interpretation of the changes [that have] come about in the world and ... creative development of the Marxist-Leninist teaching in concordance with the new economic and social conditions."

(Ceausescu and a high-level Rumanian delegation had been in Moscow May 18-19 for talks with Brezhnev and other Soviet leaders. A Tass communique May 19 said the meeting had been "frank and comradely," a phrase normally used to mask disagreement. [At the Comecon meeting May 12-14, Rumania had been the only member refusing to indorse plans for a joint International Investments Bank.] Western diplomats expressed surprise that Ceausescu would leave Rumania at a time when major floods had kept the cabinet in almost daily session.)

A new 20-year Rumanian-Polish friendship treaty was signed Nov. 12 in Bucharest. The document, patterned after the Soviet-Rumanian treaty, was signed for Rumania by Ceausescu and Premier Gheorghe Maurer and for Poland by the then-Party First Secy. Wladyslaw Gomulka and then-Premier Jozef Cyrankiewicz.

A 2d Rumanian-Bulgarian friendship treaty was signed Nov. 19 in Sofia by Ceausescu and Maurer and by Bulgarian Party First secy. Todor Zhivkov and Georgi Traykov, president of the National Assembly.

Yugoslav-Albanian Rapprochement Defies USSR

Enver Hoxha, Albanian Labor (Communist) Party first secretary, said May 30 that although "between us and the Yugoslav leadership there is a deep and irreconcilable ideological conflict," the Albanian people, "in case of danger, will be on the side of the Yugoslav peoples against any aggressor who menaces [our] freedom, sovereignty and national independence." This was the first time since the Tito-Stalin split of 1948 that an Albanian leader had publicly alluded to an identity of interest between the 2 countries.

Speaking at a Tropoje District rally in Bajram Curri, Hoxha noted that "there have been periods" when Albanians living in Yugoslavia had been "subjected to various chauvinistic injustices," but said he was glad that members of the "youth and intelligentsia of Kosovo [Yugoslavia] attend Albanian schools and are making great efforts to strengthen and develop the Albanian ... culture."

Ana Kovacevic, a spokesman for the Yugoslav Foreign Secretariat, said in Belgrade June 4 that "first impression suggests the increased readiness of Albania for normalizing relations with Yugoslavia." (Albania and Yugoslavia had severed their formerly close diplomatic relations as a result of the 1948 break.)

A similar exchange had occurred after an article appeared Apr. 5 in *Zeri i Popullit,* the Albanian Labor Party's daily newspaper. The article, on Yugoslavia's struggle for independence, was welcomed by Belgrade radio as "an effort to portray certain historic facts realistically." Milika Sundic, a Zagreb radio commentator, said Apr. 7 that while "one article alone, no matter how well written, does not provide ground for grand conclusions.... Yugoslavia wishes to have good relations with Albania on the same principles for which it is fighting on the broader international level." "We are also aware," Sundic remarked, "of the appetite of the great powers for the geographical area in which Albania and Yugoslavia are situated, and in this we see room for cooperation in the form of resistance to such aspirations." The League of Yugoslav Communists' newspaper *Borba* responded Apr. 8 with favorable mention of George Kastrioti Skanderbeg, the 15th century Albanian hero.

In a related development, the Soviet foreign affairs weekly *Novoe Vremya (New Times)* charged Apr. 3 that China had been trying to turn Albania into its "arsenal in the Balkans." In a Zagreb radio commentary Apr. 4, Sundic cited *Novoe Vremya's* assertion that there were 500 Chinese specialists in Albania supervising the building of rocket installations, and commented: "The question here is the meaning of Moscow's anxiety in this connection and of Moscow's right to worry about Albania's fate and about the passage of ships through the Adriatic. Why is or why should the Chinese presence in Albania be dangerous to the interests of the Soviet Union and not to the interests of Albania's neighbors also? And, finally, what are these Soviet interests in Albania and the Adriatic, when we know that the Soviet Union is neither a Balkan nor a Mediterranean state?"

(The Yugoslav party newspaper *Borba* reported Apr. 3 that the Federal Chamber of Economy had established a Mixed Trade Commission to discuss further expansion of trade between Yugoslavia and Albania. A Radio Free Europe research report Apr. 16 carried the estimate that trade between the 2 countries in 1970 was projected at $8 million, an increase of 25% over 1969.)

A delegation headed by the deputy rector of the State University of Tirana arrived July 29 in Pristina, capital of the Kosovo-Metohija Autonomous Region of the Serbian Republic, to discuss cooperation with Pristina University. A report from the Yugoslav news agency Tanyug said the delegates were expected to discuss such subjects as an exchange of scientific teaching staff and the engagement of teachers from the Albanian university by primary schools in Kosovo.

Pres. Tito responded favorably Aug. 7 to the May 30 speech by Enver Hoxha suggesting better relations between the 2 countries. Speaking at Zabljak in Montenegro to a group of wartime partisans, Tito noted that during World War II Albania and Yugoslavia had "fought shoulder to shoulder against the common enemy" and that afterwards "we started well, but we did not succeed." Tito continued: "Today, however, the international situation is such that we have much in common, so that we should strive as much as possible to understand each other.... I think that we have the possibilities to cooperate successfully on the questions of preserving our independence, our integrity and noninterference in our internal affairs.... Apart from that, there are possibilities for expanding our relations in the economic field.... Therefore I think that in these relations we should not remain, as it were, in a state of sleep and dozing, but that we should in full measure cooperate on all problems in which Albanians and Yugoslavs are equally interested."

Czechoslovak Purges, Protests & Defections

Purges of the Czechoslovak Communist Party(CPCS) and Slovak Communist Party (CPS) apparatuses continued into 1970 and intensified with the CPCS-directed loyalty checkup of the party's 1.5 million members, begun Feb. 3. Before the year was out, most of the leading figures in the liberalization movement of 1968 had been ousted or disciplined.

Those punished included ex-Party First Secy. Alexander Dubcek, ex-Federal People's Chamber Chairman Josef Smrkovsky, ex-Federal Premier Odrich Cernik (who resigned from the government July 8), ex-Foreign Min. Jiri Hajek, ex-Czech National Council Chairman Cestmir Cisar, the former party ideologists Josef Spacek and Zdenek Mlynar (author of the Action Program of Apr. 5, 1968), ex-Planning Min. Frantisek Vlasak, ex-Science Academy Pres. Frantisek Sorm, ex-Charles University Rector Oldrich Stary and the Prague city party members Bohumil Simon, Vanek Silhan and Martin Vaculik, believed responsible for having summoned the clandestine 14th Party Congress of Aug. 22, 1968. Thousands of other members also were purged, including all dissenting liberal labor union leaders and reform-minded enterprise managers.

The wave of apathetic dejection that swept the country after the onset of the purges deepened with the imposition of the 3d—and least palatable—20-year bilateral friendship treaty with the Soviet Union closed all avenues of hope for change but flight. There were no anti-Soviet demonstrations of any moment on the 2d anniversary of the Aug. 21, 1968 invasion.

The 3d 20-year Czechoslovak-Soviet friendship treaty, to enter into force when instruments of ratification had been exchanged, was signed May 6 in Prague. Signing for the Soviet Union were Communist Party Gen. Secy. Leonid I. Brezhnev and Premier Aleksei N. Kosygin; for Czechoslovakia, Communist Party First Secy. Gustav Husak and Premier Lubomir Strougal.

After reaffirming the obligations of the 2 countries under the 1955 Warsaw Treaty, the UN Charter and within the framework of the Council for Mutual Economic Assistance (Comecon), the USSR and Czechoslovakia, in the preamble of the 14-article agreement, declared that the "support, the strengthening and the protection of Socialist acquisitions, which were achieved through heroic efforts and sacrifice-filled toil by the people of the 2 countries, are the joint international duty of the Socialist countries."

Article 10, which committed Czechoslovakia to possible military support of the Soviet Union outside Europe, contained the statement that "each signatory party pledges ·to consider any armed attack against the other party, by any state or group of states, as an attack directed against itself and to supply it without delay all necessary aid, including military aid."

Article 6 contained an observation of the invalidity of the 1938 Munich agreement. Article 9 expressed the 2 countries' belief that one of the principal conditions for European security was the "immutability of state borders in Europe formed after the 2d World War," and it pledged both powers to ensure "the inviolability of the borders of the member states" of the Warsaw Treaty.

The Soviet delegation returned to Moscow May 7 after participating in ceremonies marking the 25th anniversary of the liberation of Czechoslovakia by the Soviet army.

Heavy police patrols and other security measures helped insure the failure Aug. 21 of a passive resistance campaign planned to mark the 2d anniversary of the invasion of Czechoslovakia by Soviet and Warsaw Pact forces.

The resistance appeal, reported Aug. 4 to have been circulated by hand in Prague, had called for a boycott of shops, theaters and newspapers, together with a voluntary 7 p.m. curfew. The appeal had read in part: "They can forbid us to do something, but they cannot prevent us from not doing something. They can forbid us to go into the streets, but they cannot prevent us from not going into the streets." The only incident known to have occurred Aug. 21 was the detention by police of 3 young East Germans and 2 Italians who arranged flowers and candles at the grave of Jan Palach. Shortly after midnight Aug. 20, the East Germans had been prevented by police from laying flowers at the statue of St. (Prince) Wenceslas in a main Prague square.

Soviet and Czechoslovak military units conducted joint exercises Aug. 10-17. Entry into the country was temporarily denied Aug. 14 to "all persons born but not domiciled in Czechoslovakia" as well as to foreign journalists, students, lawyers and clergymen. By Aug. 16, Czechoslovak border officials had turned back more than 400 prospective visitors, and the ban was extended Aug. 20 to include vacationing members of the West German armed forces.

The official news agency CTK revealed Aug. 24 that 6,217 persons had been detained and a number of rifles seized during the days preceding the invasion anniversary. The agency referred to those detained as "hidden manipulators ... who wanted to disrupt the quiet lives of our citizens."

Some unmistakable manifestations of dissent did occur in Czechoslovakia in 1970, but these were generally isolated and the work either of individuals or of small groups.

Religious disturbances occurred Mar. 4 in the village of Zazriva, Slovakia following the arrest of Albin Senaj, a Roman Catholic priest. The villagers injured one policeman. A Prague broadcast Mar. 16 criticized the way Western news agencies had covered the incident and said Senaj had been anti-Semitic and pro-Nazi.

Pavel Verner, 32, an official of a Czechoslovak uranium plant, hijacked a company airplane May 5, forcing the pilot to land in Horching, Austria. The pilot, Pavel Bidermann, 30, was taken to the hospital after being stabbed with a penknife by Verner. Another passenger, Miroslav Rocnak, 47, whom Verner had knocked unconscious with a shoe, said he wanted to return to Czechoslovakia. Verner was sentenced Sept. 3 by a court in Linz, Austria, to a year in prison for hijacking the airplane.

The prosecuting attorney in Nuremberg, West Germany announced June 23 that charges of deprivation of liberty and duress would be brought against 5 Czechoslovaks who forced a Czechoslovak National Airlines plane to land there June 8.

3 men hijacked a Czechoslovak airliner on a domestic flight from Prague to Bratislava and forced it to land in Vienna Aug. 8. The men, all Czechoslovaks, requested political asylum.

Kristina Hanzalova, Miss Czechoslovakia of 1969, sought political asylum Aug. 2 in Nuremberg, West Germany.

Defections of Czechoslovaks stationed abroad continued in 1970. Jiri Mladek, Czechoslovakia's 3d ranking diplomat at the UN, was reported Feb. 18 to have sought asylum in the U.S. Mladek, who also asked for asylum for his wife and son, was said to have been reprimanded by the Czechoslovak Mission at the UN for his failure to show enthusiasm for government policies. It was reported Feb. 20 that Mladek had been granted permanent residence status.

Czechoslovak Amb.-to-Denmark Anton Vasek asked for asylum for himself and his family June 26 in Copenhagen following orders from the Czechoslovak Foreign Ministry to return home.

A spokesman for the U.S. State Department said in Washington June 30 that Antonin Nenko, scientific affairs officer at the Czechoslovak embassy, had requested political asylum for himself and his family. The spokesman added that Nenko's request, reportedly made after orders to return home, was "under consideration."

Karel Sachar, head of the Czechoslovak commercial mission in Ecuador, disappeared with his wife and 2 sons July 7 and was reported to have sought political asylum in the U.S. Sachar had terminated all his functions at the mission June 30.

First Secy. Vaclav Albert of the Czechoslovak embassy in Kenya was said Aug. 24 to be in London, after resigning his post Aug. 21. A British spokesman declined to reveal whether Albert had sought political asylum.

2d Secy Vaclav Cihac of the Czechoslovak embassy in The Hague was provisionally granted political asylum in the Netherlands Aug. 26.

Ladislav Bartos, a Czechoslovak consular official in Sydney, was granted resident status in Australia Sept. 2. Bartos, due to return to Czechoslovakia on leave Sept. 1, had represented Koospol, the Czechoslovak foreign trade corporation.

(Stanislav K. Neumann, who had received a Klement Gottwald Prize for poetry in the 1950s, committed suicide Sept. 18 because of disillusionment with government policies. Neumann left a note that read: "I decided to kill myself because I see more and more that the ideals for which I entered the party and for which my closest friends were executed May 2, 1945 [at the Terezin concentration camp] are not being realized but have been trampled upon in political practice.")

Other Defections

ADN, the East German press agency, reported Mar. 10 that a young East German couple had killed themselves after an unsuccessful attempt to hijack a plane en route from Berlin to Leipzig.

A Hungarian air force lieutenant flew his MiG-15 fighter to Italy Apr. 7, landing at an abandoned airport near Udine. The pilot, Sandor Zaboki, 26, was granted political asylum.

3 Hungarians accompanied by a woman and 2 small children hijacked a Tarom Airlines (Rumanian) plane Sept. 14 and forced it to land in Munich, West Germany. The 89 passengers and crew had been bound from Bucharest for Prague. West German police arrested the hijackers, who asked for political asylum.

Victor Dimitriu, former Rumanian ambassador to France, requested political asylum for himself and his wife Nov. 10 in Paris.

An acrobat with the Moscow Circus, Mikhail Suponitsky, went into hiding at Vaesteraas Nov. 24 after a 3-month tour of Sweden.

INDEX

U